D1436841

INTERNATIONALIZATION

THE ACADEMY OF INTERNATIONAL BUSINESS SERIES

Published in association with the UK Chapter of the Academy of International Business

THE STRATEGY AND ORGANIZATION OF INTERNATIONAL BUSINESS
Edited by Peter J. Buckley, Fred Burton and Hafiz Mirza

INTERNATIONAL BUSINESS AND EUROPE IN TRANSITION
Edited by Fred Burton, Mo Yamin and Stephen Young

INTERNATIONALISATION STRATEGIES
Edited by George Chyrssochoidis, Carla Millar and Jeremy Clegg

INTERNATIONALIZATION: PROCESS, CONTEXT AND MARKETS
Edited by Graham Hooley, Ray Loveridge and David Wilson

Internationalization

Process, Context and Markets

Edited by

Graham Hooley

Ray Loveridge

and

David Wilson

First published in Great Britain 1998 by
MACMILLAN PRESS LTD
Houndmills, Basingstoke, Hampshire RG21 6XS and London
Companies and representatives throughout the world

A catalogue record for this book is available from the British Library.

ISBN 0–333–69943–2

First published in the United States of America 1998 by
ST. MARTIN'S PRESS, INC.,
Scholarly and Reference Division,
175 Fifth Avenue, New York, N.Y. 10010

ISBN 0–312–21329–8

Library of Congress Cataloging-in-Publication Data
Internationalization : process, context, and markets / edited by
Graham Hooley, Ray Loveridge, and David Wilson.
p. cm.
Includes bibliographical references and index.
ISBN 0–312–21329–8 (cloth)
1. International business enterprises.   I. Hooley, Graham J.
II. Loveridge, Ray.   III. Wilson, David.
HD2755.5.I5876 1998
658'.049—dc21   97–42409
                                                              CIP

This book is printed on paper suitable for recycling and made from fully managed and
sustained forest sources.

10   9   8   7   6   5   4   3   2   1
07 06 05 04 03 02 01 00 99 . 98

Printed and bound in Great Britain by
Antony Rowe Ltd, Chippenham, Wiltshire

Contents

List of Figures

List of Tables

Preface

The 23rd Annual Conference of the UK Chapter of the Academy of International Business took place at Aston Business School, Birmingham, in March 1996. Its theme was 'taking stock and moving forward' and had the twin objectives of assessing the current state-of-the-art research into international business phenomena and looking forward to emerging research themes for the new millennium.

Categorizing the work of academics is never straightforward, however, and attempts to identify themes in the work submitted are necessarily arbitrary. Nevertheless some clear themes did emerge and are reflected in this collection of papers selected from the conference.

A first, dominant theme, concerned the *internationalization process*. Over one-third of the papers submitted to the conference fell into this broad category, addressing issues such as entry mode choice, foreign direct investment, international joint ventures, and the internationalization of the firm. This theme also attracted the largest number of doctoral papers indicating that it will continue as a dominant theme for the next few years at least. The first four chapters of this collection reflect the breadth of conceptual and empirical work under way.

A second major theme to emerge was *competitive advantage in an international context*. The four papers included on that theme demonstrate the integration of the resource-based view of the firm into international business research, together with the significant opportunities for advantage created through strategic alliances and networking.

The third theme was *international business in emerging markets*. While definitions of 'emerging' may well vary, it was noticeable that a major focus of much work at present is on the transition economies of Central and Eastern Europe. Four of the five papers in the final section deal with developments, opportunities and strategies in the region, while the fifth considers IJV formation in sub-Saharan Africa. It is to be expected that future 'emerging market' studies will focus more specifically on countries further afield such as China and India.

All competitive papers at the conference were double-blind refereed, and the papers selected for this collection subjected to a further two rounds of review and revision. We would like to extend our thanks to the many reviewers involved.

FRED BURTON
(*Chair, UK AIB*)

GRAHAM HOOLEY
(*Conference Chair 1996*)

Notes on the Contributors

Shaukat Ali is Lecturer in International Business and Marketing, Graduate School of Business, Assumption University, Thailand, and formerly worked for BICC for eight years. Apart from his interest in Eastern Europe, he is researching the Thai Mobile Phone and Airways Industries.

Jim Bell is Associate Professor of Marketing at the University of Otago, Duneain, New Zealand. He obtained his PhD from the University of Strathclyde in Scotland. His main research interests are in the areas of export development and small-firm internationalization. Prior to joining the University of Ulster, he held a number of international marketing positions in industry. He has been a visiting Professor in the USA and has undertaken export development programmes in a number of Eastern European countries.

Jozsef Beracs is Professor of Marketing and Chair of the Marketing Department at the Budapest University of Economic Sciences, Hungary. He is founder director of the International Studies Centre at BUES and president of the general Marketing Subcommittee of the Hungarian Academy of Sciences. He has co-authored over 40 articles and presented papers in conferences across the world.

Julian Birkinshaw is Assistant professor at the Institute of International Business, Stockholm School of Economics. He obtained his PhD from the Richard Ivey School of Business, University of Western Ontario in Canada. Dr Birkinshaw's research is focused on management processes in multinational corporations, including entrepreneurship in subsidiary units, the development of centres of excellence, post-acquisition integration processes, and the internal transfer of best-practises. His work has been published in *Strategic Management Journal, Journal of International Business Studies*, and other journals.

Keith D. Brouthers is Reader in Strategic and International Management, East London Business School, University of East London. He obtained his DBA from US International University. Dr. Brouthers' work has been published in leading academic journals including *Journal of International Business Studies, Management International Review*, and *International Business Review*.

Lance E. Brouthers is Member of the Faculty of the Division of Management and Marketing at the University of Texas at San Antonio. He obtained his PhDs from the University of Florida, and Florida State University. His work has appeared in many journals including *Journal of International Business Studies*, *Long Range Planning*, *Columbia Journal of World Business*, *Policy Studies Journal*, *American Political Science Review*, and *International Business Review*.

Godfrey R. Carr is Senior Lecturer in German and Business Studies, Warwick Business School, University of Warwick, Director of the joint degree programme in German and Business Studies. Educated at Manchester (BA Modern Languages) and Birmingham (PhD German Studies) Universities. Taught for two years at the University of Erlangen-Nürnberg, and for one year at the University of Saskatschewan, Regina, in Canada before being appointed lecturer in the German Department, Warwick in 1970. Publications on modern German literature and society.

Mark Casson is Professor of Economics at the University of Reading, UK. His recent publications include *Entrepreneurship and Business Culture* (1995), *The Organization of International Business* (1995), *Information and Organization: A New Perspective on the Theory of the Firm* (1996) and an edited volume on *The Theory of the Firm* (1996).

Tony Cox is Senior Lecturer in Marketing at Aston Business School, UK. His research interests include marketing and strategic management in Central and Eastern Europe and the cultural influences on strategic planning in SMEs in the UK, Greece and Singapore.

John Fahy is Lecturer in Strategic Marketing at the University of Dublin, Trinity College. His teaching and research interests are in the areas of business strategy, global competition and international marketing. He has published over forty articles on those topics in Europe, the United States and Japan. He was Visiting Professor of International Management at Senshu University, Tokyo, in 1993 and at Texas A&M University in 1997.

Krzysztof Fonfara is Professor of International Marketing at the University of Economics in Poznan, Poland. He is also President of the Wielkopolska Business School and international executive training centre affiliated to the Poznan University of Economics. His research interests span issues of market orientation, the internationalization process and relationship marketing.

Roy W. Hill was formerly Professor of Marketing and Product Management at Silsoe College, Cranfield University. His experience includes working for multinational companies and twenty-eight years in management education, initially at Bradford University's Management Centre, and then at Silsoe College, Cranfield University. He maintains contact with international public and private sector organizations by undertaking consultancy, training and research supervision for Cranfield University.

Neil Hood is Professor of Business Policy and Director, Strathclyde International Business Unit at Strathclyde Business School, University of Strathclyde, Glasgow. He was formerly Dean of the Business School and a Deputy Principal of the University. Among his previous responsibilities was Director, Locate in Scotland, the inward investment agency for that country. He combines academic life with directorships and advisory roles with several major public and private companies. He has published widely on international business strategy and industrial development.

Graham Hooley is Professor of Marketing and Head of the Marketing and Law Group at Aston Business School, Aston University, UK. He has held academic positions at the Universities of Bradford and Warwick in the UK, and Otago in New Zealand. His research interests centre around marketing strategy, competitive positioning and the transition of Central and Eastern Europe. He is the author of over 100 papers and four books on marketing-related topics.

Ray Loveridge is Professor of Strategic Management and Director of Research at Aston Business School, Aston University, Birmingham; Visiting Fellow, Science Policy Unit, University of Sussex; and Visiting Professor Ecole Superieure des Sciences Economiques et Commercials, Paris. He has published extensively on business strategy, technological innovation and occupational labour markets.

Hafiz Mirza is Professor of International Business at the University of Bradford Management Centre. His principle research interests include the political economy of Japanese internationalization, transnational corporate strategy in East Asia, transnational corporations and the transfer of business culture, the international transfer of technology by SME transnationals and regionalization and zones of growth. He is currently involved in a number of projects with the European Commission, UNCTAD (including the report *Sharing in Asia's Dynamism*), the UN Economic Commission for Africa (Japanese investment in Africa), the UN Staff College and the ASEAN secretariat (foreign direct investment into and within ASEAN).

George Nakos is Assistant Professor of Marketing at Clayton College and State University, Georgia. He obtained his DBA from US International University. Dr Nakos has extensive consulting experience in both the US. and several foreign countries. His main consulting expertise is in international marketing. Dr Nakos has authored, co-authored, and presented many papers at national and international conferences. His main research interests are export management and international market entry.

Habte G. Selassie is Senior Lecturer at Luton Business School, University of Luton. He lectures in International Business, International Marketing, and Marketing Research. His research interests include international business collaboration strategies, and small business promotion. Over the past 20 years, Dr Selassie has accumulated a considerable research and practical experience in international marketing, agribusiness management, and regional development planning and evaluation, with frequent travels to European, African, and Middle Eastern countries.

Diana Rosemary Sharpe is Lecturer in Organizational Management at Birmingham University Business School, and Docterol Researcher, Manchester Business School, UK. The work presented in her chapter draws on research carried out as part of a Phd programme at Manchester Business School. The research involved a period of fifteen months' work on the shop floor across the two sites studied. She is interested in cross-cultural management issues and ethnographic approach to understanding shop-floor practices. Other publications from her research have focused on studies of shop-floor cultures and changes in work practices in Japanese organizations operating in the UK.

Vivienne Shaw is Lecturer in Marketing and Strategic Management at Warwick Business School. She has a first degree in German and has several years' experience of industrial marketing management in engineering consultancy and manufacturing organisations. Her research interests focus on the international marketing strategies and headquarter–subsidiary relationships of international competitors in the UK and the relationship between engineers and marketers.

Peter Sher is Lecturer at the Graduate Institute of International Business Studies at the National Chinan University, Taiwan. He is finishing his PhD at Warwick Business School. His research interests include technology policy and the assimilation of externally sourced technologies within NIC companies.

Satwinder Singh is Lecturer at Gyosei College, Reading, and was formerly Senior Research Fellow, Economics Department, University of Reading. His research has focussed on multinational technology transfer and he has co-authored (with Robert Pearce) *Globalising R&D* (1992).

Boris Snoj holds a PhD in Marketing from the School of Economics and Business, University of Maribor, Slovenia, where he teaches marketing. He has extensive international experience including holding visiting positions at universities in the UK, USA, Austria and Croatia. He has published over 70 papers and three books in the field of marketing.

James Taggart is a member of the Strathclyde International Business Unit and teaches international business at the Strathclyde Business School. His research focusses on corporate and subsidiary strategy within multinational corporations: he has also published on aspects of the international management of technology.

David Wilson is Professor of Strategic Management at Warwick Business School. Prior to that appointment he was Professor and Director of Research at Aston Business School, and has also held appointments at Bradford Management Centre. David's research interests are in the areas of organizational behaviour and strategic change.

Veronica Wong is Reader in Marketing and Strategic Management at Warwick Business School. Her research interests include international competitiveness, global product development and innovation management. She has published in the *Journal of International Business Studies*, the *Journal of Product Innovation Management, Industrial Marketing Management* and the *Journal of Global Marketing*.

Stephen Young is Professor with the Strathclyde International Business Unit at the University of Strathclyde. He has spent his whole career in the fields of marketing, exporting and international business. He entered academic life after a period as an economist with the government of Tanzania and then with a food organization, and he has maintained strong industrial links. He has been a visiting professor at schools in the USA and Europe, and has undertaken research and teaching assignments in numerous countries in Africa and Asia. His publications relate to exporting, international business and economic development.

Part One

The Internationalization Process

Introduction to Part One

Ray Loveridge

A major element in so-called new international trade theory is the role of the multinational enterprise (MNE) as an active participant in the construction of markets in societies outside of their country of origin. In the past the development of cross-national trading has tended to be explained in a demand-led sequence of staged developmental forms leading from exporting to local distributors to eventual foreign direct investment (FDI). In the first chapter in this section Bell and Young examine the recent evolution of the theoretical explanation of internationalization from such linear models of 'establishment chains' (Johanson and Wiedersheim-Paul, 1975) to the emergence and development of Dunning's (1988) three-pronged explanation requiring examination of the advantages to the MNE of exploiting its internal capabilities through internationalization, as well as the locational specific advantages and proprietorial advantages. The authors go on to review the more dynamic approaches to interactions between these and other situationally specific contingencies (Reid, 1981) and experiential or learning models (Mitchell and Bradley, 1986). They conclude with their own typology of the range of theoretical explanations available to the analyst.

One of the reasons for the re-examination of internationalization theory has been the historical experience of the rise of local demands for 'voice' in the control of regional markets. This has come from the governments of newly developing countries and from within the subsidiary business units or affiliates of MNEs. Bell and Young touch upon this theme in the opening chapter, and it is further developed by Birkinshaw and Hood in Chapter 2 concerning the determinants of subsidiary mandates within MNEs. In this chapter the authors build on a range of recent studies which have taken particular dimensions of subsidiary autonomy as their focus and attempt to construct a comprehensive range of empirical measures. These are tested in a survey of manufacturing subsidiaries located in Canada, Scotland and Sweden, countries selected for a high living standard, small size and peripherality with respect to dominant neighbouring markets. The model of subsidiary autonomy constructed by the authors is itself a conceptually significant advance on previous definitional attempts. The findings that upstream capabilities, most specifically those of R&D, are critical to the performance of the parent enterprise is, perhaps, not surprising. They tend to confirm the importance of the proximity of significant value-chains to the influence of strategic business units within the internal hierarchy of the MNE.

This theme continues to drive Chapter 3 authored by James Taggart. This is an exploration of the role of governments and regional development agencies in attempting to establish connections in the transfer of ideas through the agency of science parks. The author provides an empirical examination of the effectiveness of science parks in Cambridge, Cardiff, Edinburgh and Glasgow in attracting and facilitating the performances of plants from within the pharmaceutical industry. The explanatory contingencies are seen to lie in five groups of factors: proximity to appropriate markets, the regulatory regime within the region, the availability of appropriate resources and sectorally specific factors including local image, and finally a range of life-style factors. The overwhelming strong position of Cambridge along all of these five dimensions is affirmed, but in the following discussion of a previous cross-national comparative survey carried out by the author this position is evaluated against a more sophisticated model.

Part One concludes with an ethnographic study of FDI across two British-based business units, one newly established by a Japanese–Italian joint venture parent, the other acquired as part of the alliance. The study by Diana Sharpe explores the long and emotionally, as well as economically, costly process of tri-national learning. In particular it focuses on the adjustment of British nationals to the expectations and aspirations of expatriate Japanese managers *and vice-versa*. This learning is traced back to the evolving strategies of the Japanese and Italian parents and to the socio-economic environments in which the two plants are situated. The cases provide rich evidence of mutual adjustment between market and hierarchical forces that takes place within the process of internationalization.

1 Towards an Integrative Framework of the Internationalization of the Firm

Jim Bell and Stephen Young

INTRODUCTION

'Stage' theories and their accompanying models proliferate in the internationalization and broader international business literature (Vernon, 1966; Wells, 1968; Johanson and Wiedersheim-Paul, 1975; Pavord and Bogart, 1975; Bilkey and Tesar, 1977; Khan, 1978; Cavusgil, 1980; Czinkota, 1982). These suggest that the process of 'going abroad' involves a (logical) sequence of international development steps. The problem with these conceptualizations is, first, that attempts to simplify complexity have resulted in oversimplified perspectives that have subsequently been accepted – almost, without question – as irrefutable fact; secondly, that such blind obeisance has obfuscated the truth regarding the actual processes involved. Indeed, most models – notably, those involving life-cycle theories – suffer from limitations concerning time-scales (Giddy, 1978). Moreover, their ability to delineate boundaries between stages or adequately explain the processes which lead to movement between stages is rather limited (Andersen, 1993).

This chapter explores the underlying assumptions inherent in many of the best-known internationalization 'stage' theories and models. It contends that such approaches can no longer be accepted, as many of their fundamental tenets are fatally flawed. Thereafter, it examines alternative conceptualizations of the internationalization process, such as contingency theory (Reid 1986), network/interaction perspectives (Turnbull and Valla, 1986; Johanson and Mattsson, 1988) and internalization/transaction cost approaches (Buckley and Casson, 1976). Finally, it seeks to incorporate elements of these diverse – and often contradictory – approaches into a more cohesive framework on the internationalization of the firm.

THE INTERNATIONAL EXPANSION OF THE ENTERPRISE

The topic of the internationalization of the firm (incorporating the export development process, and the emergence of the multinational enterprise (MNE)) is principally concerned with smaller and medium-sized enterprises (SMEs). Nevertheless, multinational production and service activity (the 'final stage' in some models) is mainly the domain of larger firms, and exporting too is dominated by large companies. Despite the fairly extensive interest in internationalization, it is important to recognize that only a segment of international business activity is included within the topic. For example, the Uppsala internationalization model (Johanson and Wiedersheim-Paul, 1975) is chiefly applicable to *market seeking* international activity, as opposed to operations motivated by natural resource seeking, efficiency seeking (including investments designed to take advantage of differences in the availability and cost of labour and other factors of production) and strategic asset seeking (Dunning, 1993).

Secondly, there is an implicit assumption of organic evolution in the literature on the internationalization of the firm, rather than expansion through mergers, acquisitions and alliances (MAAs). According to UNCTAD (1994), worldwide cross-border acquisitions and mergers accounted for 70 per cent of the foreign direct investment (FDI) inflows to developed countries in the years 1986–90. As in domestic business strategy, mergers and acquisitions may provide a faster route into internationalization; while international strategic alliances may not only have a variety of motivations but may also utilize different (non-equity) modes of operating and involve a variety of elements in the value chain.

Third, the internationalization concepts have less relevance to the established multinational firm, either as investor or as exporter. It is true that new MNEs are emerging all the time – perhaps at a rate of 4000 to 5000 a year (Dunning, 1994) – but this initial investment is relatively small in comparison with sequential investment undertaken by established MNEs. The latter probably accounts for 70–90 per cent of worldwide FDI. There has been relatively little systematic study of the motivations or patterns of this sequential investment. For many MNEs, strategies of integrated international production at regional or global levels have been associated with production rationalization and increased cross-border product or process specialization (an exception may relate to the behaviour of acquisitive MNEs where affiliates have tended to be less integrated; see Ivarsson, 1996).

There is also emerging evidence of subsidiaries developing somewhat independently of parent strategies. A variety of subsidiary strategy/role typologies has been postulated by different authors (White and Poynter, 1984; Bartlett and Ghoshal, 1986; Birkinshaw and Morrison, 1995); and structurally, the classic hierarchical model has been challenged by alternative conceptualizations such as Bartlett and Ghoshal's (1989) 'transnational' or Hedlund's (1986) 'heterarchy'. Even if quasi-autonomous subsidiaries, possessing world product mandates, and heterarchical structures are relatively little in evidence, development patterns of MNEs are more complex than hitherto.

The importance of the subsidiary's capabilities or resources as the driver of its product or process mandates has been confirmed in the literature (Birkinshaw, 1996). And there have been suggestions of a life-cycle in subsidiary strategies as mandates are gained and lost over time consequent on changing ownership and locational advantages. It is still the case, nevertheless, that much work remains to be undertaken on the evolutionary processes of multinational firms.

Despite the fact that the topic of the internationalization of the firm applies to only a small constituent of international business activities, its importance lies in the fact that it deals with the new and developing international firm, which is commonly a smaller or medium-sized enterprise. Policy interest in and involvement with such firms is high, as efforts are made to provide guidance and training to support companies' entry and development into international markets (see Crick, 1995, on the targeting of UK export assistance). The requirement for and receptiveness of companies to such assistance is also higher than among larger and multinational enterprises. Until satisfactory models, which reflect the environment of the approaching millennium, have been devised and validated empirically, however, policy advice may be severely distorted if not simply wrong.

INTERNATIONALIZATION 'STAGE' THEORIES

Although preceded by the seminal works of Hymer (1960), Kindleberger (1962) and Aharoni (1966) into the growth of multinational enterprise and international production and product life-cycle theories developed by Vernon (1966) and Wells (1968), much of the research into the internationalization of the firm has been influenced by the conceptualizations which emanated from the 'Uppsala School' in the mid- to late 1970s. Of particular significance was the 'establishment chain' theory proposed by Johanson and Wiedersheim-Paul (1975).

Based on their study of four Swedish firms, this postulated that two patterns relating to internationalization could be discerned. Firstly, that

> a firm's engagement in a specific foreign market develops according to an establishment chain, i.e. at the start no export activities are performed in the market, then export takes place via independent representatives, later through a sales subsidiary, and, eventually manufacturing may follow.

According to Johanson and Vahlne (1977, 1978, 1990), this sequence of 'stages' indicates increased commitment to the market due to greater knowledge and experience.

The second postulated pattern was that firms initially target nearby countries and subsequently enter foreign markets with successively greater 'psychic distance' in terms of cultural, economic and political differences and also in relation to their geographic proximity (Vahlne and Wiedersheim-Paul, 1973; Carlson, 1975).

Other behavioural models also emerged from North America in the late 1970s and early 1980s. Some viewed the development of export activities as an innovation-adaption cycle, based on Roger's (1962) diffusion theory (Lee and Brasch, 1978). Others suggested an export development 'learning curve', influenced by external 'attention-evoking' stimuli – for example, unsolicited orders or enquiries – and/or internal factors, such as managerial ambitions or excess capacity (Bilkey and Tesar, 1977; Cavusgil, 1980; Czinkota, 1982). All of these models propose an incremental 'stages' approach – although the precise number of stages is contested – and generally support the notion of psychic distance. However, less emphasis is placed on the development of alternative market entry modes. Rather, these behavioural models highlight firms' increased dependence on exports and greater commitment to a growing number of foreign markets. Thus, from being unwilling to export, firms proceed through various stages to become experienced, highly committed exporters (see Figure 1.1). Indeed, as Andersen (1993, p. 212) observes:[1]

> Except for the initiating mechanism, the differences between the models seem to reflect semantic differences rather than real differences about the nature of the internationalization process.

As evidenced in the literature, these internationalization 'stage' theories have gained considerable support. However, they have also attracted significant criticism and a number of empirical studies have challenged their basic proposition (Turnbull, 1987). Thus, for example, Buckley *et al.* (1979) contend that firms do not necessarily adopt consistent organizational approaches to internationalization. Cannon and Willis (1981) also challenge the underlying assumptions of step-wise progression and forward motion, arguing that many passive exporters were, at one time, active, and that firms may omit stages to accelerate the process. Turnbull (1987) provides evidence of British firms, selling to overseas markets for many years, which had not progressed beyond the stages of agency relationships and direct selling. He also identifies instances of 'reversal' of stages, with sales offices being closed in favour of direct selling or the use of agents and distributors. Rosson's (1984) longitudinal investigation of 21 manufacturer–overseas distributor relationships over a seven-year period offers examples of pro-

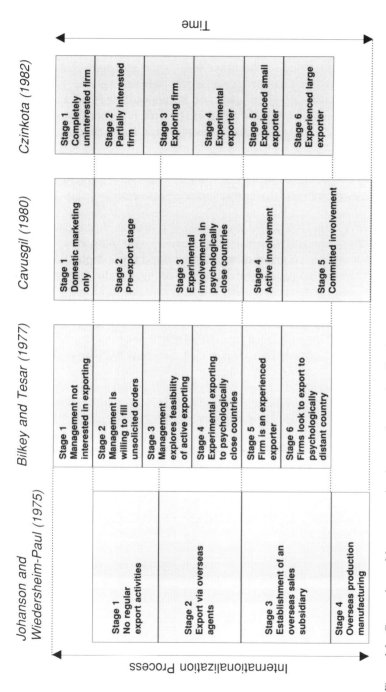

Figure 1.1 Comparison of four export development/internationalization 'stage' models

Source: Adapted from Ford and Leonidou (1991).

gression, but also of regression and termination. All these findings support Reid's (1983) contention that existing models are 'much too deterministic'.

Young (1987) contends that alternative strategies – such as licensing and joint-ventures – are being adopted more widely by smaller firms as initial foreign market entry modes, and other researchers conclude that existing theories of internationalization are inappropriate for service industries (Sharma and Johanson, 1987; Engwall and Wallenstal, 1988; Buckley *et al.*, 1992). Hedlund and Kverneland (1985) also provide evidence of a speeding up of the whole process of internationalization and assert that:

> the establishment and growth strategies on foreign markets are changing towards more direct and rapid entry modes than those implied by theories of gradual and slow internationalization processes.

According to Young (1987), this is most likely to be manifest among high-technology firms where high research and development costs, shorter product-life-cycles and a concentration of the market for high-technology products accelerate the pace of internationalization. Finally, Czinkota and Ursic (1987) and Nordstrom (1990) contend that the notion of 'psychic distance' – which is implicit or explicit in most of the 'stage' models – is much less relevant as global communications and transportation infrastructures improve and markets become increasingly homogeneous.

A fundamental difficulty of all the models concerns their weak theoretical underpinning. It is true that their roots lie in the behavioural theory of the firm, but the linkages and core assumptions are generally not made at all clear. The Johanson and Vahlne (1977, 1990) approach is rather different in that there is a clearcut distinction between the theoretical/explanatory component of the model and the outcomes – what Andersen (1993) calls the 'theory level' and the 'operational level'. The former concerns the interrelationships between knowledge and commitment (Johanson and Vahlne, 1990, p.12):

> experiential market knowledge generates business opportunities and is consequently a driving force in the internationalization process. But experiential knowledge is also assumed to be the primary way of reducing uncertainty. Thus, in a specific country, the firm can be expected to make stronger resource commitments incrementally, as it gains experience from current activities in the market.

The outcomes are the stages of development within a country and the development across countries according to psychic distance. Despite the weaknesses of the Johanson and Vahlne theoretical model (the relationships between the concepts are quite vague, for example – Andersen, 1993), there is at least an explanatory component; this is not the case for most of the alternative frameworks which additionally deal with export market servicing only.[2] The progression in stages in the latter models is represented by greater experience/involvement which is in fact tautological. There is a lack of explanation as to how the development process takes place or how movement between stages can be predicted.

In view of these criticisms (see also Luostarinen, 1994), further deliberation on the internationalization process is highly desirable. This is especially pertinent in the light of the emergence of alternative paradigms – such as contingency theories and the interaction/network perspectives which, together with extant internalization/transaction cost approaches, are discussed hereafter. However, in order to broaden the debate, underlying assumptions of 'stage' theories are first critically evaluated.

UNDERLYING ASSUMPTIONS OF INTERNATIONALIZATION 'STAGE' THEORIES

An examination of the alternative models presented in Figure 1.1 reveals a number of common assumptions: firstly, that firms develop in their domestic market before initiating exports; secondly – with the exception of the Johanson and Wiedersheim-Paul (1975) 'establishment chain' model – that there is some initial resistance to become involved in export activities; thirdly, that firms begin by exporting to psychologically 'close' countries and thereafter move to more 'distant' markets; fourthly, that there is a logical, linear sequence whereby firms begin by exporting before considering alternative market entry modes – in the Uppsala School at least the ultimate stage (indeed goal) is overseas production/manufacturing; finally, that the whole process is uni-directional and – to some extent – inevitable once the first tentative steps have been taken. Each of these assumptions is now explored in more detail.

Domestic Market Development Precedes Exporting

The notion that firms are firmly established in their home markets before venturing abroad is widely accepted in the literature. Indeed, Luostarinen (1979) observes that internationalization may be triggered by an inward technology transfer or a firm's dealings with overseas suppliers, local subsidiaries of foreign multinationals, etc. (see also Welch and Luostarinen, 1993). It also stands to reason that firms will have established the necessary facilities and workforce to supply the home market before seeking to export, especially in the case of manufacturing firms operating in large economies.

However, this is not necessarily so for firms based in smaller countries, or, indeed, for those located in emerging nations. Nor is it always true for small-scale, high-technology firms or service providers. In such cases, a small domestic market is likely to influence firms to internationalize from the outset, especially if their technologies or service offerings are too advanced for the home market or if local demand is limited. Bell (1994) reports cases of Irish and Scandinavian computer software firms established specifically with export markets in mind. Some subsequently obtained domestic sales, others did not. Moreover, even those which had initially obtained domestic sales internationalized very rapidly due to a small home market for specialist software. As most of the software houses surveyed were small and recently established, neither their size nor age were critical internationalization variables.

Thus, it may be argued that an established domestic market is not a precondition for export initiation. Indeed, as will be discussed hereafter, it may in fact inhibit internationalization. As much of the research into exporting has emanated from the advanced industrial economies – notably, the USA – it is not surprising that this assumption persists; however, its validity can no longer be fully accepted.

Although the interrelationships between home and export market development have been discussed in the literature, it is arguable that more consideration should be given to internationalization as a constituent of the overall business strategy of the firm. Certainly there are numerous stages models of small firm growth (O'Farrell and Hitchens, 1988), of which Greiner (1972) is one of the best known; and, not surprisingly, they have been subject to many of the same criticisms as the internationalization stages models. Moreover, Buckley (1995, p.34) has argued that 'Internationalization is not a single unilineal process. It interacts with the development of the organisational structure, with organisational commitment, and with management development.' Other authors have suggested that internationalization itself is a holistic process, with decisions concerning international market selection being interrelated with market servicing methods and choice of products. Similarly, Andersen and Strandsov (1996) argue that the sub-elements in the decision process are not compartmentalized in the minds of executives.

Firms are Reluctant to Initiate Exports

Much of the evidence on this count emerges from US-based research, wherein firms are described as export adverse and reactive rather than proactive (Bilkey, 1977; Cavusgil, 1984). Given the vast size of the US market, these findings are not altogether surprising.

In contrast, European and Scandinavian contributions (Luostarinen, 1970; Dichtl *et al.*, 1983; Bannock, 1987; Verhoeven, 1988), and other studies conducted in the newly-industrialised countries (Cheong and Chong, 1988; Wong and Kwan, 1988; Sharkey *et al.*, 1989; Weaver and Pak, 1990), are much less fixated with the notion that indigenous firms are reluctant exporters. While recognizing that exporters – and small firms in particular – face additional human and financial resource constraints, exporting is accepted as a viable alternative strategy for survival when the scope for domestic expansion is limited.

Clearly, not all small firms have products or services with export potential. However, those that do are more likely to accept the challenge if they are located in small economies. Thus, although their export behaviour may be 'reactive, unplanned and opportunistic' (Mitchell and Bradley, 1986), they are not especially reluctant to export (Leonidou, 1995).

In this context, the observation by Bodur (1986) and others that the findings of many enquiries conducted among US firms cannot be considered to represent the export behaviour of firms primarily based in countries outside the USA must be reiterated. As with the first assumption, the size of the domestic market and the economic conditions therein are critical variables in firms' positive or negative attitudes towards exporting.

Firms Begin by Exporting to Psychologically 'Close' Countries

Although there is ample evidence in the literature that firms began exporting to 'psychically close' countries (for example US firms exporting to Canada, or Swedish firms expanding within Scandinavia) such behaviour is no longer necessarily the case (see Benito and Gripstud's 1992 Norwegian evidence). In addition to the general globalization of markets since the mid-1970s, a number of pertinent influences on choice of initial export market must be considered.

Firstly, firms are likely to gravitate towards markets which present the greatest opportunities for their products. For example, firms producing equipment used in oil exploration and extraction will inevitably target oil-producing countries, irrespective of whether they are psychologically 'close' or not. Sometimes, the geographic proximity of these markets – such as that between Norway and the UK – suggests 'psychic' patterns, which on closer scrutiny are, in fact, industry-related. In the computer software sector, Bell (1994) reports the case of a Finnish developer of hotel reservation systems whose international expansion patterns closely mirrored those of the development of European tourist destinations. This firm began by exporting to Spain and subsequently entered Portugal and Turkey, none of which can be regarded as 'psychically close' markets. In the case of high-technology firms – regardless of country of origin – target markets are most likely to be within the Triad regions (Young, 1987).

Secondly, receipt of an unsolicited order or enquiry can lead to export initiation (Bilkey, 1978; Miesenbock, 1988; Barker and Kaynak, 1992). Just as the source of these enquiries is outside the control of the recipient firm, so – in the event of a positive response – are the eventual export destinations. However, it may be argued that firms might respond negatively to these approaches if perceptions of risk are too great. In a similar vein, firms may follow domestic clients into international markets (Sharma and Johanson, 1987; Johanson and Mattsson, 1988; Bell, 1994). This may result in them developing 'close' export markets after they have entered more 'distant' countries.

Finally, in a European context, there is some evidence that EU programmes – such as SPRINT and Europartenariat – are starting to break down 'psychic distance' barriers because they encourage collaboration between small firms from member states, notably those located at the periphery of the community.

Thus, while 'psychic distance' might have had a bearing on the internationalization patterns of some firms in the past – and may still influence the behaviour of others – it can no longer be accepted as a core assumption pertaining to the internationalization process.[3] The level of foreign market demand, industry-specific factors, relationships with current or potential clients – and even policy-intervention – all exert much stronger influences on initial and subsequent market selection and entry decisions. Andersen and Strandsov (1996), moreover, propose a cognitive mapping approach to international market selection, arguing for the need to uncover the subtle and tacit assumptions of decision-makers. In this way both the highly rational and less rational procedures for selecting markets may be identified.

Internationalization as a Logical, Linear and Sequential Process

The view that internationalization is a logical and sequential process can be challenged on several counts. These include the assumption of linear progression in internationalization and of a step-wise and uni-directional progress of firms through various 'stages' (as well as the implicit belief in the inevitability that they will do so).

First, the 'establishment chain' theory suggests that firms begin by exporting before proceeding to other forms of foreign market involvement. As has already been noted, this is not always the case as certain firms begin the internationalization process with an inward technology transfer – indeed, some recent definitions of 'internationalization' include these inward movements (Luostarinen and Welch, 1990) – or via licensing agreements with parties in export markets. Examples of the latter can be found in the designer clothing, electronics and pharmaceutical sectors. Similarly, franchising has had a major influence in the internationalization of retail operations and on consumer and business services. For other firms, the initial market entry may take place via an acquisition, a joint-venture or a green-field investment. Thus, exporting is not always the preferred entry mode.

As Root (1987) observes, the choice of market entry strategy will be influenced by a number of external and internal factors. Barriers to entry to particular export markets – such as high tariffs – may preclude exporting and encourage licensing or other more direct methods. Foreign ownership regulations may result in a joint-venture, rather than the establishment of a wholly-owned subsidiary. Again, the nature of product or service offerings may render certain strategies unsuitable. Exporters of high-value, low-volume products are unlikely to regard overseas production as either necessary or desirable. Similarly, entry mode decisions of service-intensive firms are likely to be based on the relative ease of information or technology transfer – often via electronic means – and by their ability to provide adequate levels of client support. The lack of internal resources may also restrict the firm's scope to pursue an optimum strategy. Root (1987) therefore contends that:

> the 'right' entry mode is that which maximises the profit contribution over the strategic planning period within the constraints imposed by the availability of company resources, risk and profit objectives.

Secondly, although many firms begin by exporting and then proceed to establish sales offices or production operations in the market, this process is not inevitable (Wheeler *et al.*, 1996). In some cases, firms will continue in the export mode indefinitely. Other firms will continue to use alternative strategies which are 'right' for them in light of the aforementioned external and internal constraints.

Similarly, there is evidence that many firms will try to use their 'preferred' entry strategy for all export markets if they are not prevented from doing so by government regulations in these countries. However, as this is not always possible, it is not unusual for firms to concurrently adopt alternative market entry strategies for different countries. In doing so, they may omit certain 'stages' of the internationalization process.

Thirdly, inherent in all of the internationalization 'stage' models is the notion of continuous forward momentum. This is patently not always the case, as Luostarinen and Welch (1990) contend that firms may also 'de-internationalize'. Such strategies are particularly evident in mature industries such as auto manufacturing (e.g. Chrysler in Europe and VW in the USA) and demonstrate that backward, as well as forward, movement can take place. They also suggest that the internationalization process may be cyclical rather than linear. On a lesser scale, small firms may abandon export markets due to changes in political or economic circumstances in those countries, or because of internal resource constraints. Similarly, uncommitted exporters may revert to selling in the home market due to an improvement in domestic conditions.

Thus, logical step-wise and uni-directional progression from exporting to establishing foreign market operations although an occurring phenomenon is not certain. On the contrary, all the evidence suggests that the process is

highly situation-specific and that internationalization decisions are influenced by an array of factors which include domestic and/or export market
conditions, industry and product or service factors, resource considerations
and, in many cases, relationships with existing clients or fortuitous approaches from potential customers. In fact, as Buckley, Pass and Prescott
(1995) have noted, the choice of foreign market servicing mode may be
highly constrained and indeed there may be few alternatives open to the
company.

It is not simply linear progression in terms of stages of internationalization which has been questioned. The basic theoretical assumption of the
Uppsala model of a linear relationship between market knowledge and
market commitment has also been queried in research by Erramilli (1991).
This work on US service companies identified a U-shaped relationship
between market commitment and market experience.[4]

Therefore, it can be argued that 'stage' models are of limited value
insofar as they merely identify internationalization patterns of certain firms,
but not of others, and they fail to adequately explain the processes involved.
Indeed, even the proponents of such theories (Czinkota and Johnston,
1983; Cavusgil, 1984) concede that, although useful in classifying homogenous groups of firms with broadly comparable export support needs, their
predictive value is weak.

ALTERNATIVE CONCEPTUALIZATIONS

Theoretical contributions on explanations for the emergence and growth of
the multinational enterprise not only pre-date the internationalization stage
models, but have developed quite separately from the latter. Based on
Coase's (1937) work, Buckley and Casson (1976) presented an internalization theory to explain why cross-border transactions were organized by
hierarchies rather than by the market. Much of the subsequent orthodox
economics literature on explanations for international production has followed this internalization/transaction cost tradition and its assumptions of
rational, profit maximizing behaviour. Dunning's (1988) eclectic paradigm
has tended to be sidelined in recent theoretical debates. In fact, its inclusion
of ownership- and location-specific factors (alongside internalization incentive advantages) recognizes the importance of a range of internal and
external environmental variables in foreign market service decisions (see
the discussion on contingency theories below). And other theorists, such as
Hennart (Hennart and Park, 1994) have accepted that there is a location
decision as well as a governance decision in, for example, choosing to
establish foreign production facilities. A criticism of the eclectic paradigm
and other mainstream internalization contributions concerns their static
nature (Young *et al.*, 1989). However, Kogut and Zander (1993) have

attempted to develop an evolutionary theory of the multinational corporation. In any event, there have been a number of recent applications of the eclectic paradigm to the topic of entry modes, including Hill, Hwang and Kim (1990), Agarwal and Ramaswami (1992) and Kim and Hwang (1992), although the emphasis has been mode choice in the multinational enterprise.

A further major stream of work on the subject of internationalization has developed from international industrial marketing, focusing upon interactions, relationships and networks. These approaches postulate that interconnected exchange relationships evolve in a dynamic, less structured manner and that increased mutual knowledge and trust lead to greater commitment between international market actors (Turnbull and Valla, 1986; Johanson and Mattsson, 1988; Nordstrom, 1990; Blankenberg and Johanson, 1992). Thus, the process is not solely dependent on the behaviour of the focal firm.

These network theories do not necessarily negate the notion of psychic distance or challenge existing views concerning the incremental nature of internationalization. Indeed, Johanson and Vahlne (1990) incorporate some elements thereof in their restatement of earlier theories, although more recently (1992) they argue that many new firms enter foreign markets almost blindly. In these circumstances, market entry results from the interplay between actors in the foreign market and the local firm, including social exchange processes. The stress in decision-making is upon interaction rather than strategic choice. Interestingly, in their 1992 work Johanson and Vahlne regard the network approach as presenting a more holistic approach to international corporate development: the foreign market entry process is regarded as an integral part of a more extensive internationalization process.

In the recent past, there has been growing interest in strategic management explanations for the international development of, particularly, the multinational enterprise. For example, Chi and McGuire (1996) developed a strategic option model, incorporating transaction cost variables, to assist the evaluation of market entry modes. And Madhok's (1996) work on multinational decision-making highlighted competitive forces and the capabilities of the firm as increasingly dominant factors in MNEs' entry decisions. In this case the efficiency-driven (transaction) cost-minimizing approach was downplayed in favour of value-related issues. Meyer (1996) has applied a variety of strategic management models to the sales internationalization of the firm, namely, investing perspective (from business portfolio theory) and positioning perspective (from competitive rivalry models) as well as networking and capabilities perspectives. These approaches come closer to the reality of decision-making in organizations where a wide variety of influences may come into play.[5] They fall into the category of partial frameworks or models rather than theories, but they do suggest a need to reflect a range of determining factors in internationalization, hence the revival of interest in contingency models.

Reid (1983), a consistent critic of 'stage' theories, proposes a 'contingency' view of internationalization, wherein a firm's initial reaction to foreign market opportunities – and subsequent strategies – reflects prevailing circumstances and its existing resource capabilities. This behaviouralist view shares some common elements with the rationalist perspectives of the internalization/transaction cost approach. Indeed, Reid (1986) offers a conceptual model which synthesizes and integrates both approaches. The recent resurgence of interest in 'contingency' models among researchers is noteworthy, both those investigating the export behaviour of small enterprise (Yeoh and Jeong, 1995) and the MNE (Calof and Beamish, 1995).

The predictions of the various concepts and paradigms are significantly different. Johanson and Mattsson (1988) have argued that the explanatory power of the internalization model is greater in a situation in which the environment is not internationalized; and that the internationalization 'stages' approach is less valid when both the market and firm are highly internationalized. According to these authors, network theory is especially important in the case of global competition and cooperation in industrial systems. Undoubtedly, each approach has some contribution to make, and as such, the present authors have considerable sympathy for Reid's (1983) contingency view.

'Contingency' and 'interaction' approaches have considerable merit insofar as they suggest that the whole process is much more complex and less structured than earlier theories and models imply. Unlike 'stage' models where internationalization tends to be driven by decisions taken within the firm, they recognize that environmental factors – including relationships with other firms – play a major part in the process. In consequence, both offer more dynamic perspectives of internationalization in which:

> structural or contextual characteristics define the boundaries within which managerial responses are made . . . [and where] commitment decisions [are] primarily dependent on firm idiosyncratic factors. (Reid, 1981)

Nevertheless, it can also be argued that neither approach, on its own, offers a full explanation of the process. This is especially the case with interaction/network perspectives, which fail to explain how certain firms begin to internationalize in the absence of any network connections.

DISCUSSION AND A WAY AHEAD

Given the increasing criticism of internationalization 'stage' theories, it is rather surprising that they continue to be so widely accepted in some quarters. The focus of the subsequent discussion is twofold. Firstly, why and how did they gain such currency in the first place? Secondly, if their underlying assumptions are erroneous how can greater understanding of the process be achieved?

An insight as to why these theories gained such credibility is offered by Kamath *et al.* (1987) who contend that 'the dominant use of logical-empiricist methodology' has 'bedevilled' export research. Many empirical studies, notably the large number emanating from the United States, are almost exclusively based on quantitative approaches. Data collected via mail questionnaires were analyzed, using a variety of statistical techniques, and hypotheses were tested.

Thus, although the Uppsala 'establishment chain' model was generated via case studies, most subsequent 'stage' models were based on positivist methodologies. However, it is generally accepted that this method involves four stages: 'observation, generalisation (i.e. development of a theory and/or model), experimentation and validation' (Rivett, 1972). Its essence is 'its exposure to falsification in every conceivable way the system to be tested' (Popper, 1972), whereby if a hypothesis is not rejected it 'remains on probation as before' (Medawar, 1964). Nevertheless, Andersen (1993) questions the extent to which 'stage' models have been rigorously tested. Thus, it may be argued that the fourth step has not been addressed properly.

Such dominant positivist and ethnocentric influences have also led researchers to ignore other paradigms. Indeed, according to Cavusgil and Nevin (1981), 'a tradition of building upon previous research is not well established in international marketing'. As previously noted, the interaction/transaction cost approaches and stage theories developed independently from each other and Reid's (1983) contingency view did not find much favour until recently. Even now, network/interaction perspectives are perceived to be incompatible with earlier theories and conceptualizations. Thus, Aaby and Slater (1989) contend that 'current export research is balkanised . . . present export inquiry consists of a mosaic of autonomous endeavors'. Unfortunately, these myopic approaches, in terms of method, focus and location, have failed to broaden our understanding of the complex nature of internationalization. On the contrary, they have probably hindered its development. Therefore, the need for methodological and focal pluralism is manifest.

The view of the present authors is that over-great attention has been given to the merits of competing theories and models and too little attention has been paid to their potential complementarities. Moreover, the small firm/export/marketing literature has largely developed in isolation from that on large, multinational firms, alternative modes of foreign market servicing and economics and international business paradigms. In presenting an integrative firm-internationalization framework in Figure 1.2, there are three basic assumptions:

- Both behavioural and transaction cost theories may be appropriate in different circumstances. Despite its weaknesses, the establishment chain model of Johanson and Vahlne is the preferred behaviouralist approach. Thus internationalization proceeds as a consequence of an interplay between increasing commitments to and evolving knowledge about foreign markets. There is no question that network relationships may be significant in particular (but uncertain) instances. Perhaps the appropriate way to incorporate networks is as a contingency to the basic Uppsala model. Johanson and Vahlne (1992) exaggerate the importance of networks in their observation that 'knowledge can *mainly* be gained through experience from current interaction with other actors in the foreign markets' (emphasis added); but on occasions there will be an influence.
- As the evidence cited earlier revealed, the nature and pace of internationalization is conditioned by product, industry and other external environmental variables, as well as by firm-specific factors. These contingencies derive from the resource-based view of the firm (Wernerfelt, 1984; Grant, 1991). Thus the identification of the firm's resources (derived from the internal environment) and the appraisal of its capabilities lead on to strategy choice – in this case in the area of international marketing – subject to external environmental variables.
- The firm's international marketing decisions are made in a holistic way, incorporating products, markets and entry modes. The entry mode issue *per se* has probably been exaggerated in importance in the literature, at least as far as exporting is concerned, and is, in any case, interrelated with markets (countries and customers), products, etc.

In the conceptualization presented in Figure 1.2, the present authors acknowledge that internationalization is an evolutionary process. They posit that the nature and patterns of this process are contingent upon external and internal environmental factors, including the potential networks of the decision-maker and the focal firm. They also contend that firms typically, although not inevitably, initiate export activity in an *ad hoc* intuitive manner, because of key decision-makers' attitudes, attributes and behaviour. Thereafter, although not invariably, firms may become more structured in their approaches to international marketing decision-making.

However, the authors reject the notion of 'stages' of internationalization and linear, logical, uni-directional movement, either in terms of expansion into more psychologically 'distant' markets or changes in market entry mode. Instead they argue that these decisions are also contingent upon firms' prevailing circumstances, industry or sectoral considerations and other external environment factors.

Thus, for example, the initial export decision is often 'unplanned, reactive and opportunistic' (Mitchell and Bradley, 1986). However, some firms may plan export initiation in a proactive and systematic manner; others may

Internationalization Process and Patterns[d]

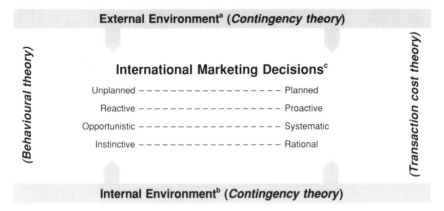

Figure 1.2   An integrative firm-internationalization framework

Notes:
[a] Includes market size and economies of scale; networking requirements and opportunities; transaction specificity of product; technological change; home country variables; host country variables.
[b] Includes entrepreneurial characteristics and networks; demographics (age, education, etc.); firm's resources; firm's knowledge, commitment and performance.
[c] Such as whether to internationalize; which markets; which entry mode; marketing management decisions (product, promotion, price, etc.).
[d] Italics refers to the relevant theory.

have planned to export, but react opportunistically to new foreign prospects. Moreover, some firms may begin by exporting to psychologically and/or geographically 'distant' markets, or continue to operate in an export 'mode' indefinitely. Others may revert from direct to indirect forms of market entry due to changes in the export market environment or the firms' own circumstances.

Clearly, more experienced, better-resourced (and larger) firms will possess the capacity to make more systematic and economically rational decisions in these respects. In their work on the internationalization of UK quoted companies in the EU, Millington and Bayliss (1990, p.159) comment that:

> In the early stages of international development, the firm relies on market experience and incremental adjustment. As the degree of international experience increases, this process is superseded by formal planning and systematic search.

The above does not preclude the fact that, on occasion, firms may adopt opportunistic and reactive strategies due to contingencies or developments within their networks. In these circumstances, firms do not necessarily adopt consistent approaches to internationalization. Nor do they inevitably 'progress' through 'stages'. Rather, firms may reach a 'state' of internationalization which will not necessarily remain unaltered, due to backward or forward momentum.

From the preceding discussion, it is evident that each of the different conceptualizations provides some understanding of the internationalization process, but that their explanatory power is more pertinent in certain situations. Thus, for example, the internalization/transaction cost perspectives are useful in understanding the internationalization strategies of large internationally established companies, while elements of behavioural, contingency and network theories are more appropriate for smaller firms with less export experience. However, these competing theories are not mutually exclusive.

Consequently, the authors believe that the proposed internationalization process framework in Figure 1.2 has a number of potentially important contributions. Firstly, in attempting to draw together disparate theories, it seeks to reduce the schism between proponents of the various alternative conceptualizations. Secondly, it seeks to provide a logical linkage between research conducted primarily among small- and medium-sized firms and other investigations which have focused on multinational enterprise. Thus, the intention is to develop a holistic perspective of the internationalization process rather than a managerially-orientated decision-making framework. Nevertheless, the pursuit of this objective also has policy implications insofar as a better grasp of the issues may help to narrow the manifest gap between theory and practice.

It also has important implications for future research in the area – specifically, that a better understanding of the internationalization process is dependent upon building upon *all* previous research in the area. This involves the acceptance and use of mixed methodologies to explore what is a multiplex issue. It also demands that international marketing researchers recognize the important contributions that have emerged from diverse research traditions. Thus, there is a clear research message, namely, that methodological pluralism will need to replace the over-reliance on positivist paradigms of the past.

The framework presented in Figure 1.2 has important implications for empirical research. Given the new issues which are raised, there is a requirement for broadly based, in-depth exploratory research to consider the international marketing process as a whole and the interrelationships between the various decision areas (of which internationalization in terms of stages of development is only one). In the field of small firm research, the linkages between the development and decision processes of the enterprise in both domestic and international markets should also be investigated. Because of the strong influences of industry factors in internationalization, sector-specific research studies and research which is specifically designed to explore industry differences are called for. Finally, the effect of size of home market needs to be investigated since so many studies have either been based in the USA (with its very large home market) or Scandinavia (with small home markets).

Notes

1. Leonidou and Katsikeas (1996) review eleven export development models, but Andersen's observation is still appropriate.
2. In relation to the Leonidou and Katsikeas (1996) listing of models, a number should more accurately be described as 'categorizations' or 'classifications' rather than 'models' or 'conceptualizations'. And the classification criteria, lacking a theoretical underpinning, predetermine to some extent the findings.
3. Questions have also been asked recently about the definition of psychic distance. See O'Grady and Love (1996).
4. We are indebted to Bent Petersen and Torben Pedersen whose presentation and Workshop paper ('Twenty Years After – Support and Critique of the Uppsala Internationalization Model', 22nd European International Business Academy Conference, Stockholm, 15–17 December 1996) drew attention to this point.
5. In the text by Young *et al.* (1989), a 'business strategy approach' was presented as an alternative to the rational choice transaction cost model and the behavioural stages-of-development models.

References

Aaby, N.-E. and S.F. Slater (1989) 'Managerial influences on export performance: a review of the empirical literature 1978–88', *International Marketing Review*, 6(4), pp. 53–68.
Agarwal, S. and S.N. Ramaswami (1992) 'Choice of foreign market entry mode: impact of ownership, location and internalisation factors', *Journal of International Business Studies*, 23(1), pp. 1–27.
Aharoni, Y. (1966) *The Foreign Investment Decision Process* (Boston, Mass.: Harvard University Press).
Andersen, O. (1993) 'On the internationalization process of firms: a critical analysis', *Journal of International Business Studies*, Second Quarter, pp. 209–31.
Andersen, P.H. and J. Strandsov (1996) 'International market selection: a cognitive perspective', in *Innovation and International Business*, Proceedings of the 22nd European International Business Academy Annual Conference, Institute of International Business, Stockholm School of Economics, 15–17 December.
Bannock, G. and Partners (1987) 'Into active exporting', *BOTB Occasional Papers* (HMSO, Dd 8934782 J0229NJ, London).
Barker, A.T. and E. Kaynak (1992) 'An empirical investigation of the differences between initiating and continuing exporters' *European Journal of Marketing*, 26(3), pp. 27–36.
Bartlett, C.A. and S. Ghoshal (1986) 'Tap your subsidiaries for global reach', *Harvard Business Review*, 64(6), pp. 87–94.

Bartlett, C.A. and S. Ghoshal (1989) *Managing Across Borders: The Transnational Solution* (Boston, Mass.: Harvard Business School Press).

Bell, J.D. (1994) 'The role of government in small-firm internationalization: a comparative study of export promotion in Finland, Ireland and Norway, with specific reference to the computer software industry', Unpublished Ph.D Thesis, University of Strathclyde.

Benito, G.R. and G. Gripstud (1992) 'The expansion of foreign direct investments: discrete rational location choices or a cultural learning process', *Journal of International Business Studies*, 23(3), pp. 461–76.

Bilkey, W.J. (1978) 'An attempted integration of the literature on the export behavior of firms', *Journal of International Business Studies*, 9, pp. 33–46.

Bilkey, W.J. and G. Tesar (1977) 'The export behavior of smaller-sized Wisconsin manufacturing firms', *Journal of International Business Studies*, 8, pp. 93–8.

Birkinshaw, J.M. (1996) 'How multinational subsidiary mandates are gained and lost', *Journal of International Business Studies*, 27(3), pp. 467–95.

Birkinshaw, J.M. and A.J. Morrison (1995) 'Configurations of strategy and structure in subsidiaries of multinational corporations', *Journal of International Business Studies*, 26(4), pp. 729–53.

Blankenberg, D. and J. Johanson (1992) 'Managing network connections in international business', *Scandinavian International Review*, 1(1), pp. 5–19.

Bodur, M. (1986) 'A study in the nature and intensity of problems experienced by Turkish exporting firms', in S.T. Cavusgil (ed.), *Advances in International Marketing* (Greenwich, Conn.: Jai Press Inc.) pp. 205–32.

Buckley, P.J. (1995) 'Barriers to internationalization', in P.J. Buckley (ed.), *Foreign Direct Investment and Multinational Enterprises* (Basingstoke, Hants: Macmillan) pp. 17–37.

Buckley, P.J. and M. Casson (1976) *The Future of Multinational Enterprise* (London: Macmillan).

Buckley, P.J., D. Newbould and J. Thurwell (1979) 'Going international – the foreign direct investment decisions of smaller UK firms', *EIBA Proceedings*, Uppsala, pp. 72–87.

Buckley, P.J., C.L. Pass and K. Prescott (1992) 'Internationalization of service firms: a comparison with the manufacturing sector', *Scandinavian International Business Review*, 1(1), pp. 39–56.

Buckley, P.J., C.L. Pass and K. Prescott (1995) 'Foreign market servicing strategies and competitiveness', in P.J. Buckley (ed.), *Foreign Direct Investment and Multinational Enterprises* (Basingstoke, Hants: Macmillan) pp. 115–36.

Calof, Jonathan L. and Paul W. Beamish (1995) 'Adapting to foreign markets: explaining internationalization', *International Business Review*, 4(2), pp. 115–31.

Cannon, T. and M. Willis (1981) 'The smaller firm in international trade', *European Small Business Journal*, 1(3), pp. 45–55.

Carlson, S. (1975) 'How foreign is foreign trade?', *Acta Universitatis Upsaliensis, Studia Oeconomaie Negotiorum, No 11*, Uppsala.

Cavusgil, S.T. (1980) 'On the internationalization process of the firm', *European Research*, 8(6), pp. 273–81.

Cavusgil, S.T. (1984) 'Differences among exporting firms based on their degree of internationalization', *Journal of Business Research*, 12, pp. 195–208.

Cavusgil, S.T. and J.R. Nevin (1981) 'State-of-the-art in international marketing: an assessment', in B. Evis and K.J. Roering (eds), *Review of Marketing 1981* (Chicago: American marketing Association).

Cheong, W.K. and K.W. Chong (1988) 'Export behaviour of small firms in Singapore', *International Small Business Journal*, 6(2), pp. 34–41.

Chi, T. and D.J. McGuire (1996) 'Collaborative ventures and value of learning: integrating the transaction cost and strategic option perspectives on the choice of market entry modes', *Journal of International Business Studies*, 27(2), pp. 285–307.

Coase, R.H. (1937) 'The nature of the firm', *Economica*, 4(November), pp. 386–405.

Crick, D. (1995) 'An investigation into the targeting of UK export assistance', *European Journal of Marketing*, 29(8), pp. 76–94.

Czinkota, M.R. (1982) *Export Development Strategies: U.S. Promotion Policy* (New York: Praeger).

Czinkota, M.R. and W.J. Johnston (1983) 'Exporting: does sales volume make a difference?' *Journal of International Business Studies*, 14(1), pp. 147–53.

Czinkota, M.R. and M.L. Ursic (1987) 'A refutation of the psychic distance effect on export development', *Developments in Marketing Science*, X, pp. 157–60.

Dichtl, E., M. Leibold, H-G. Koglmayr and S. Muller (1983) 'The foreign orientation of management as a central construct in export-centred decision-making processes', *Research for Marketing*, 10, pp. 7–14.

Dunning, J.H. (1988) 'The eclectic paradigm of international production: an update and some possible extensions', *Journal of International Studies*, 19, pp. 1–31.

Dunning, J.H. (1993) *Multinational Enterprises and the Global Economy* (Wokingham, Berks: Addison-Wesley).

Dunning, J.H. (1994) 'Re-evaluating the benefits of foreign direct investment', *Transnational Corporations*, 3(1), pp. 23–51.

Engwall, L. and M. Wallenstal (1988) 'Tit for tat in small steps. The internationalization of Swedish banks', *Scandinavian Journal of Management*, 4(3/4), pp. 147–55.

Eramilli, K. (1991) 'The experience factor in foreign market entry behavior of service firms', *Journal of International Business Studies*, 22(3), pp. 479–501.

Ford, D. and L. Leonidou (1991) 'Research, developments in international marketing: a European perspective', in Paliwoda (ed.), *New Perspectives on International Marketing* (London: Routledge).

Giddy, I.H. (1978) 'The demise of the product cycle model in international business theory', *Columbia Journal of World Business*, 13(Spring), pp. 90–7.

Grant, R.M. (1991) 'The resource-based theory of competitive advantage: implications for strategy formulation', *California Management Review*, Spring, pp. 114–35.

Greiner, L.E. (1972) 'Evolution and revolution as organisations grow', *Harvard Business Review*, July–August, pp. 37–46.

Hakansson, H. (1982) *International Marketing and Purchasing of Industrial Goods: An Interaction Approach* (Chichester: John Wiley).

Hedlund, G. (1986) 'The hypermodern MNC: a heterarchy?', *Human Resource Management*, 25, pp. 9–36.

Hedlund, G. and A. Kverneland (1985) 'Are strategies for foreign markets changing? The case of Swedish investment in Japan', *International Studies of Management and Organisation*, XV(2), pp. 41–59.

Hennart, J.-F. and Y.-R. Park (1994) 'Location, governance, and strategic determinants of Japanese manufacturing investment in the United States', *Strategic Management Journal*, 15, pp. 419–36.

Hill, C.W.L., P. Hwang and W.C. Kim (1990) 'An eclectic theory of the choice of international entry mode', *Strategic Management Journal*, 11, pp. 117–28.

Hymer, S. (1960) *The International Operations of National Firms*, Doctoral Dissertation, MIT, (Cambridge, Mass. MIT Press) (published 1976).

Ivarsson, I. (1996) *Integrated International Production. A Study of Foreign Transnational Corporations in Sweden*, Series B. No. 90, School of Economics and Commercial Law, University of Gösteborg, Sweden.

Johanson, J. and L. Mattsson (1988) 'Internationalisation in industrial systems – a network approach', in N. Hood and J.-E. Vahlne (eds), *Strategies in Global Competition* (Beckenham, Kent: Croom Helm).

Johanson, J. and J-E. Vahlne (1977) 'The internationalization process of the firm – a model of knowledge development and increasing foreign commitments', *Journal of International Business Studies*, (8)(1), pp. 23–32.

Johanson, J. and J-E. Vahlne (1978) 'A model for the decision making process affecting the pattern and pace of the internationalization of the firm', in M. Ghertman and J. Leontiades (eds), *European Research in International Business* (New York: Croom Helm), pp. 283–305.

Johanson, J. and J-E. Vahlne (1990) 'The mechanism of internationalization', *International Marketing Review*, 7(4), pp. 11–24.

Johanson, J. and J-E. Vahlne (1992) 'Management of foreign market entry', *Scandinavian International Business Review*, 1(3), pp. 11–24.

Johanson, J. and F. Wiedersheim-Paul (1975) 'The internationalization of the firm – four Swedish case studies', *Journal of Management Studies*, (12), pp. 305–22.

Kamath, S., P.J. Rosson, D. Patton and M. Brooks (1987) 'Research on success in exporting: past, present and future', in P.J. Rosson and S.D. Reid (eds), *Managing Export Entry and Expansion* (New York: Praeger), pp. 398–421.

Khan, S.M. (1978) *A Study of Success and Failure in Exports* (Stockholm, Sweden: Academilitteratur).

Kim, W.C. and P. Hwang (1992) 'Global strategy and multinational entry mode choice', *Journal of International Business Studies*, 23(1), pp. 29–53.

Kindleberger, C. (1962) *Foreign Trade and the National Economy* (New Haven, Conn.: Yale University Press).

Kogut, B. (1990) 'Internal sequential advantages and network flexibility', in Bartlett *et al.* (eds), *Managing the Global Firm* (London: Routledge).

Kogut, B. and U. Zander (1993) 'Knowledge of the firm and the evolutionary theory of the multinational corporation', *Journal of International Business Studies*, (24)4, pp. 625–45.

Lee, W.Y. and J.J. Brasch (1978) 'The adoption of export as an innovation strategy', *Journal of International Business Studies*, 9(1), pp. 85–93.

Leonidou, L.C. (1995) 'Export stimulation: a non-exporter's perspective', *European Journal of Marketing*, 29(8), pp. 17–36.

Leonidou, L.C. and C.S. Katsikeas (1996) 'The export development process: an integrative review of empirical models', *Journal of International Business Studies*, 27(3), pp. 517–51.

Luostarinen, R. (1970) *Foreign Operations of the Firm* (Helsinki School of Economics, Helsinki).

Luostarinen, R. (1979) *Internationalization of the Firm* (Helsinki School of Economics, Helsinki: Acta Academiae Oeconomicae Helsingiensis).

Luostarinen, R. (1994) *Internationalization of Finnish Firms and their Response to the Global Challenge* (World Institute for Development Economics Research, United Nation University, Helsinki).

Luostarinen, R. and L. Welch (1990) *International Business Operations* (Helsinki School of Economics, Helsinki).

Madhok, A. (1996) 'Know-how, experience and competition-related considerations in foreign market entry: an exploratory investigation', *International Business Review*, 5(4), pp. 339–66.

Medawar, P.B. (1964) *Is the Scientific Paper a Fraud?* (London: BBC Publications).

Meyer, R. (1996) *The Internationalisation Process of the Firm Revisited: Explaining Patterns of Geographic Sales Expansion*, Management Report No. 300 (Erasmus University, Rotterdam).

Miesenbock, K.J. (1988) 'Small business and exporting: a literature review', *International Small Business Journal*, 6(2), pp. 42–61.

Millington, A.I. and B.T. Bayliss (1990) 'The process of internationalization: UK companies in the EC', *Management International Review*, 30(2), pp. 151–61.

Mitchell, O. and M.F. Bradley (1986) 'Export commitment in the firm – strategic or opportunistic behaviour', *IBAR – Journal of Irish Business and Administrative Research*, 8(2), pp. 12–19.

Nordstrom, K.A. (1990) *The Internationalization Process of the Firm – Searching for New Patterns and Explanations* (Stockholm School of Economics, Sweden).

O'Farrell, P.N. and D.M.W.N. Hitchens (1988) 'Alternative theories of small-firm growth: a critical review', *Environment and Planning A*, 20, pp. 1365–83.

O'Grady, S. and H.W. Love (1996) 'The psychic distance paradox', *Journal of International Business Studies*, 27(2), pp. 309–33.

Pavord, W.C. and R.G. Bogart (1975) 'The dynamics of the decision to export', *Akron Business and Economic Review*, Spring, pp. 6–11.

Popper, K.R. (1972) *The Logic of Scientific Discovery* (London: Hutchinson).

Reid, S.D. (1981) 'The decision-maker and export entry and expansion', *Journal of International Business Studies*, 12(2), pp. 101–12.

Reid, S.D. (1983) 'Firm internationalization transaction costs and strategic choice', *International Marketing Review*, 1(2), pp. 45–55.

Reid, S.D. (1984) 'Market expansion and firm internationalization', in E. Kaynak (ed.), *International Marketing Management* (New York: Praeger) pp. 197–206.

Reid, S.D. (1986) 'Export channel choice and export performance: a contingency approach', in C. Tan, W. Lazer and V. Kirpalani, V. (eds), *Emerging International Strategic Frontiers* (American Marketing Association, Singapore) pp. 260–4.

Rivett, P. (1972) *Principles of Model Building* (Chichester: John Wiley).

Rogers, E.M. (1962) *Diffusion of Innovations* (New York: Free Press).

Root, F.R. (1987) *Entry Strategies for International Markets* (Lexington, Mass.: Lexington Books, D.C. Heath and Co.).

Rosson, P.J. (1984) 'Success factors in manufacturer-overseas distributor relationships in international marketing', in E. Kaynak (ed.), *International Marketing Management* (New York: Praeger), pp. 91–107.

Sharkey, T.W., J.S. Lim and K.I. Kim (1989) 'Export development and perceived export barriers: an empirical analysis of small firms', *Management International Review*, 29(2), pp. 33–40.

Sharma, D. and J. Johanson (1987) 'Technical consultancy in internationalization', *International Marketing Review*, 4(4), pp. 20–9.

Turnbull, P.W. (1987) 'A challenge to the stages theory of the internationalization process', in P.J. Rosson and S.D. Reid (eds), *Managing Export Entry and Expansion* (New York: Praeger), pp. 21–40.

Turnbull, P.W. and J-P. Valla (1986) *Strategies for International Industrial Marketing: The Management of Customer Relationships in European Industrial Markets* (London: Croom Helm).

United Nations Conference on Trade and Development (UNCTAD) (1994) *World Investment Report 1994. Transnational Corporations, Employment and the Workplace* (New York and Geneva: United Nations).

Vahlne, J-E. and F. Wiedersheim-Paul (1973) 'Psychic distance – an inhibiting factor in international trade', Working Paper, University of Uppsala.

Verhoeven, W. (1988) 'The export performance of small and medium-sized enterprises in the Netherlands', *International Small Business Journal*, 6(2), pp. 20–33.

Vernon, R. (1966) 'International investment and international trade in the product cycle', *Quarterly Journal of Economics*, 80, pp. 190–207.

Weaver, K. and J. Pak (1990) 'Export behaviour and attitudes of small and medium-sized Korean manufacturing firms', *International Small Business Journal*, 8(4), pp. 59–70.

Welch, L.S. and R. Luostarinen (1988) 'Internationalization: evolution of a concept', *Journal of General Management*, 14(2), pp. 34–55.

Welch, L.S. and R. Luostarinen (1993) 'Inward–outward connections in internationalization', *Journal of International Marketing*, 9(1), pp. 44–56.

Wells, L.T. (1968) 'A product life-cycle for international trade', *Journal of Marketing*, 32, pp. 1–6.

Wernerfelt, B. (1984) 'A resource-based view of the firm', *Strategic Management Journal*, 5, pp. 171–80.

Wheeler, C., M. Jones and S. Young (1996) 'Market entry modes and channels of distribution in the machine tool industry in the UK', *European Journal of Marketing*, 30(4), pp. 40–57.

White, R.E. and T.A. Poynter (1984) 'Strategies for foreign-owned subsidiaries in Canada', *Business Quarterly*, Summer, pp. 59–69.

Wong, K.C. and W.C. Kwan (1988) 'Export behaviour in small firms in Singapore', *International Small Business Journal*, 6(2), pp. 34–41.

Yeoh, P-L. and I. Jeong (1995) 'Contingency relationships among entrepreneurship, export channel structure and environment: a proposed conceptual model of channel performance', *European Journal of Marketing*, 29(8), pp. 95–115.

Young, S. (1987) 'Business strategy and the internationalization of business: recent approaches', *Managerial and Decision Economics*, 8, pp. 31–40.

Young, S., J. Hamill, C. Wheeler and J.R. Davies (1989) *International Market Entry and Development* (Hemel Hempstead: Harvester Wheatsheaf/Prentice-Hall).

2 The Determinants of Subsidiary Mandates and Subsidiary Initiative: A Three-Country Study

Julian Birkinshaw and Neil Hood

INTRODUCTION

This chapter examines the international responsibilities, or mandates,[1] of foreign-owned subsidiaries in Canada, Scotland and Sweden. The primary focus of the chapter is on the factors associated with mandate formation, but the impact of mandates on subsidiary performance is also examined. The chapter is built on two key premises: (1) that mandates are critical to the long-term growth of foreign-owned subsidiaries; and (2) that they are primarily earned by the subsidiary through the initiative of subsidiary managers. The former assumption has been central to much of the strategic management and public policy literature on subsidiary management (e.g. Etemad and Dulude, 1986; Rugman and Bennett, 1982; Science Council of Canada, 1980), and its implications have been explored. The latter assumption, by contrast, has been frequently mentioned (e.g. Crookell, 1986; Crookell and Morrison, 1990; McGuinness and Conway, 1986) but never studied in depth.

This research builds on a number of recent studies that have looked at the phenomenon of world mandates in foreign-owned subsidiaries (Birkinshaw, 1995; Moore, 1994; Roth and Morrison, 1992). With the exception of Roth and Morrison (1992) prior research has been predominantly case-based and focused on Canada. This study therefore sought to broaden our understanding of world mandates by looking at a large sample of subsidiaries in three countries (Canada, Scotland and Sweden). In relation to the study by Roth and Morrison (1992) this study reassesses their findings in a different set of countries but also goes much further by studying the role of subsidiary initiative in the development of world mandates. The research question driving this study is 'What factors account for the presence/absence of mandates in foreign-owned subsidiaries?' In other words, the study will attempt to understand the reasons why some subsidiaries have gained mandates while others have not. As part of this question, the role of subsidiary initiative as an antecedent to mandates will be carefully considered.

This chapter is organized as follows. The next section outlines previous literature on mandates and subsidiary entrepreneurship. Following this, the theoretical model is put forward and the research propositions described. The research methodology is then outlined, with regard to both sampling procedures and measurement issues. Finally, the findings from the study, and the implications of those findings, are discussed.

LITERATURE REVIEW

While mandates have been utilized for many years, they only received widespread recognition at the beginning of the 1980s, when a Science Council of Canada (1980) report described them as 'An interesting and useful instrument for dealing with the problems posed by a branch plant manufacturing sector'. The report went on to describe four case studies of Canadian subsidiaries that had met with considerable success in winning mandates. A substantial body of research subsequently emerged, from both strategic management and public policy perspectives (e.g. Bishop and Crookell, 1986; Crookell, 1990; Crookell and Caliendo, 1980; Etemad and Dulude, 1986; Poynter and Rugman, 1982; Rugman and Bennett, 1982).

Widespread agreement that mandates were desirable was, however, coloured by a perception that multinational corporation (MNC) parent companies would be reluctant to cede control of strategically important activities to subsidiary companies (Crookell, 1986; Poynter and Rugman, 1982). There were also concerns voiced regarding the competitiveness of a mandate on a sustainable basis (D'Cruz, 1986) and the merits of government actively supporting mandate subsidiaries at the expense of other industrial sectors (Johnston, 1982). Notwithstanding these concerns, mandates became an important feature of the foreign-owned industrial sector in Canada, particularly in the light of free trade with the US (Crookell and Morrison, 1990). Mandate strategy research, furthermore, has not been restricted to Canada. The concept has received explicit attention in Europe (Forsgren and Johanson, 1992; Young, Hood and Dunlop, 1988) and is implicitly at the centre of much recent research on the network conceptualization of the MNC (Ghoshal and Bartlett, 1991).

A world mandate has previously been defined as the full development, production and marketing of a product line in a multinational subsidiary (Rugman and Douglas, 1986). However it has been observed that full-scope mandates, in which the subsidiary has responsibility for development, manufacturing *and* marketing, are relatively rare. Many mandates are constrained both geographically and by function so that some researchers have opted for more generic terms such as specialized mission (Ontario Ministry of Trade and Tourism, 1980) or international responsibilities (Moore, 1994). The preference in this study is to use the generic term mandate with the understanding that sub-types, such as world product mandate and regional manufacturing mandate, can also be identified. This terminology is also consistent with managerial usage.[2] Regardless of scope, however, the primary outcome of the mandate process for the subsidiary is greater specialization, in terms of a focused factory or product responsibility. Full-scope mandates also offer the subsidiary greater autonomy (the right to make strategic decisions without parent company intervention), but, as observed by D'Cruz (1986), manufacturing mandates (such as the Canadian auto plants) actually lead to a lower level of autonomy than that held by Canada-focused operations. A second key point is the recognition that mandates are earned not given (Bishop and Crookell, 1986). Though exceptions exist, the responsibility for identifying the mandate opportunity and pursuing it rests wholly with the subsidiary, because most MNCs are reluctant to yield control of strategic activities to subsidiaries.

Working from the premise that most mandates are earned not given, the broad objective of most studies has been to identify the 'key success factors' associated with the attainment of mandates (e.g. Bishop and Crookell, 1986; Moore, 1994; Roth and Morrison, 1992; Science Council of Canada, 1980). One approach has been to survey a relatively large number of subsidiaries to extract the common features. Moore (1994) represents the most recent example of this, with the following list of success factors emerging: presence of mandate champions, subsidiary competence, early- or late-product life-cycle products, prior export experience, niche capability, flexibility, strong relationships with HQ and other subsidiaries, and government support. A second approach has been to focus on a small number of in-depth case studies in order to understand the causal relationships between factors. The Science Council of Canada (1980) study was definitive in this regard, with its descriptions of Westinghouse Canada, Litton Industries, Black & Decker Canada and Garrett Manufacturing, and it has since been reinterpreted by a number of academics (e.g. McGuinness and Conway, 1986; Pearce, 1992; Rugman and Bennett, 1982).

An earlier study by the first author of the current study (Birkinshaw, 1995) was built on the case-study research tradition. Working again from the premise that mandates are earned not given or allocated, this study identified four distinct processes (i.e. initiatives) that led to the attainment of world mandates, namely: (1) reconfiguration of existing activities; (2) a new business in Canada that is subsequently developed worldwide; (3) bid for a planned corporate investment; and (4) enhancement of an existing mandate. This was an important development because it showed that the key success factors vary according to the process. There is, in other words, neither a generic 'mandate-winning' process nor a generic set of key success factors.

This study was limited in two key respects: first its focus on subsidiaries that had been mostly successful; and second, on its focus on Canadian subsidiaries. The narrow focus was necessary to ensure that the phenomenon was comprehensively researched, but it underscored the need to subsequently examine the broader population of subsidiaries, particularly those that have never pursued initiatives. The broader survey is, as stated above, the thrust of the current study. It should be observed that the insights from the previous study made it possible to undertake a cross-sectional survey with greater precision than was previously possible, because the various mandate-winning processes are now more fully understood.

CONCEPTUAL FRAMEWORK

The dependent variable in this study is the presence/absence of subsidiary mandates – that is, we are interested in understanding those factors that help to predict whether a subsidiary has mandate responsibilities or not. Unfortunately, a simple yes/no answer to the question 'does your subsidiary have any international responsibilities or mandates?' conceals more than it reveals, because mandates vary so much in quality and scope. There is no single measure that captures the complexity of the subsidiary's responsibilities, so a variety of measures were used, as discussed below. Furthermore, subsidiary mandates are not an end in themselves, because they can be poorly managed as well as well-managed. Both the antecedents to and consequences of subsidiary mandates are therefore included in the conceptual framework.

Antecedents to Subsidiary Mandate

It is proposed that subsidiary mandates are gained through three sets of factors: internal subsidiary attributes; aspects of the parent–subsidiary relationship; and the business environment. The traditional approach to subsidiary management, as exemplified by the process school (Bartlett, 1979; Bower, 1970; Burgelman, 1983; Prahalad, 1976), conceptualized a 'structural context' for the subsidiary which consisted of the various facets of its relationship with the parent company. The subsidiary was controlled, according to this model, through the imposition (by head office managers) of an appropriate structural context that induced managers in the subsidiary to behave in desirable ways. In terms of the current study, the suggestion is that by defining an appropriate parent–subsidiary relationship, corporate management can either promote or inhibit mandate development in subsidiaries. Thus, key parent–subsidiary variables such as level of autonomy, communication channels, and access to resources are *ceteris paribus* associated with the presence/absence of mandates in the subsidiary.

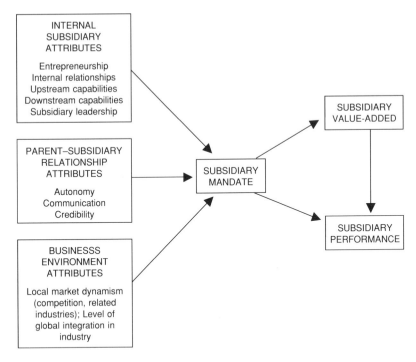

Figure 2.1   Conceptual framework

While most subsidiary behaviour is 'induced' by parent management, Burgelman (1983) showed that there is also a second important category of subsidiary behaviour which he labelled 'autonomous'. Autonomous behaviour falls outside the previously understood strategic domain of the subsidiary, and it arises through the entrepreneurial efforts of subsidiary management. Autonomous behaviour requires a high level of championing and selling by subsidiary management before it is accepted by parent management. While relatively rare in newly-established subsidiaries, the ability of mature subsidiaries to engage in autonomous behaviour is significant, in large part because of the level of specialized resources they control (Prahalad and Doz, 1981). Thus, there is a strong suggestion that the internal attributes of the subsidiary are important predictors of subsidiary initiative, and hence of subsidiary mandates. Figure 2.1 indicates the proposed relationships.

It should be highlighted here that the uni-directional causality between structural context and mandates and between subsidiary attributes and mandates is a simplification of reality. Results from the previous study suggested that subsidiary attributes and subsidiary mandates have a mutually beneficial relationship, while the long-term impact of enhanced subsidiary attributes is (eventually) an enhanced structural context. The suggestion is that all three constructs tend to move together, so that a flow of subsidiary mandates is driven by and should also enhance both internal subsidiary attributes and the structural context. In the current study, however, it is impossible to disentangle causality because the data are cross-sectional rather than longitudinal.

The final element of the basic research model is the impact of the business environment on subsidiary mandates. As proposed by Bartlett and Ghoshal (1986) and others, the subsidiary's role should be a function in part of the opportunities in the local market. Where the local market offers the potential for competitive upgrading (Porter, 1990), the opportunity for taking mandate responsibilities should be greater. There are also issues of industry globalization, in that opportunities for subsidiary mandates will vary according to the need for global integration.

In sum, the conceptual framework implies a number of competing hypotheses regarding the determinants of subsidiary mandates. Is the relationship with the parent the key determinant? Are the attributes of the subsidiary itself more important? Or is the local industrial environment the most important variable? Understanding the relative importance of the three sets of factors is a key objective of this research. The following section explores the specific hypotheses in more detail.

Consequences of Subsidiary Mandate

The long-term expectation for a subsidiary with mandates is that they be effectively managed, and that they contribute to the performance of the subsidiary. Two dependent variables are therefore proposed for the complete framework, both of which should be enhanced by subsidiary mandates. The first is called 'subsidiary value-added' which is a measure of the subsidiary's proven ability to contribute to the strategic imperatives of the corporation. The second is subsidiary performance, measured in terms of conventional estimates such as ROI and market share. Measures will be discussed in a subsequent section, but the idea is that subsidiary mandates, if they are worthwhile, should positively impact on both the financial performance of the subsidiary and on its more intangible role in the corporation.

RESEARCH HYPOTHESES

The Parent–Subsidiary Relationship

There is a long history of research into various facets of the parent–subsidiary relationship. Studies traditionally emphasized specific factors such as the level of autonomy, formalization and control (e.g. Brandt and

Hulbert, 1977; Gates and Egelhoff, 1986; Hedlund, 1981; Negandhi and Baliga, 1981) and their impact on subsidiary performance. More recently the recognition that subsidiaries often have very different roles has pushed researchers towards contingency models in which specific aspects of the parent–subsidiary relationships are hypothesized to predict key behaviours (e.g. Ghoshal and Bartlett, 1988; Ghoshal and Nohria, 1989; Jarillo and Martinez, 1990; Roth and Morrison, 1992), rather than performance *per se*. The latter approach has generally been more successful and it is adopted here.

What aspects of the parent–subsidiary relationship would be expected to increase the subsidiary's contributory role? Ghoshal's (1986) research on innovation in large multinationals is the most relevant previous study. He showed that the creation of innovation in subsidiaries was associated with high autonomy, high parent–subsidiary communication and high normative integration. While the concept of subsidiary mandates is not identical to innovation creation, it is close enough to work with the same set of relationships. More specifically, the subsidiary's ability to pursue mandate opportunities would be expected to increase with greater decision-making autonomy and with high levels of parent–subsidiary communication. Normative integration, that is the extent to which shared values exist across the corporation, is very hard to assess at the subsidiary level (Ghoshal polled head office managers). It was replaced here with a measure of credibility, that is a belief by parent company management that subsidiary management will deliver on its promises. This has been found to be an important factor in world mandate winning strategies (e.g. Bishop and Crookell, 1986; Moore, 1994). It is also a reflection of the extent of normative integration between parent and subsidiary. In summary:

Propositions 1–3 The presence of subsidiary mandates is associated with (1) high strategic autonomy, (2) high parent–subsidiary communication, and (3) high subsidiary credibility *vis-à-vis* the parent company.

Internal Subsidiary Attributes

While the parent–subsidiary relationship defines the broad context in which the subsidiary operates, attributes of the subsidiary itself are potentially at least as important in shaping its contributory role. The literature suggests three aspects in particular. First, strong internal communication between different functions and across management layers increases the level of integration (Lawrence and Lorsch, 1967) and hence opportunities for the cross-fertilization of ideas (Hedlund, 1994). Ghoshal (1986) confirmed the relationship between intra-subsidiary communication and innovation. As shown by Ghoshal and Bartlett (1994), internal relationships can also foster a context in which cooperation, initiative and learning prosper. Second, an entrepreneurial culture (Kuratko *et al.*, 1990), in which risk-taking and entrepreneurial activities are promoted, is liable to be associated with subsidiary value-added. Several clinical studies have documented the presence of an entrepreneurial culture as a key prerequisite for innovation (e.g. Kanter, 1985; Pinchott, 1986; Quinn, 1985), so the expectation here is that the subsidiary's ability to pursue world mandates will also be in part a function of its entrepreneurial culture. Note that Ghoshal and Bartlett's (1994) notion of an internal context that facilitates initiative is closely related to the idea of an entrepreneurial culture. The position taken here is that intra-subsidiary communication is a necessary but not sufficient condition for an entrepreneurial culture, because authority and reward structures also have to be aligned to foster entrepreneurship.

The subsidiary's capabilities are also hypothesized to be an important determinant of subsidiary value added. Previous research has shown that subsidiary capabilities are associated with innovation (Ghoshal, 1986) and the existence of world mandates (Roth and Morrison, 1992). The logic is that for the subsidiary to pursue a world mandate it must have a unique capability to offer to the parent company. This capability has traditionally been thought of as a primary function such as R&D or manufacturing, but it could also be an administrative capability or special expertise with managing international relationships. Note that the key issue here is the relative capability of the subsidiary *vis-à-vis* sister subsidiaries, in that the world mandate is typically awarded to the entity within the corporation that can most effectively undertake it.

Propositions 4–6   The presence of subsidiary mandates is associated with (4) strong internal relationships, (5) an entrepreneurial culture in the subsidiary, and (6) high subsidiary capabilities.

The Business Environment

There are two distinct aspects of the subsidiary's business environment to consider. The 'local' environment consists of the set of suppliers, customers, competitors and regulatory bodies with which the subsidiary interacts in its host country. As observed earlier, several academics have proposed that the nature of the local environment should have a bearing on the role the subsidiary plays in the corporation (e.g. Bartlett and Ghoshal, 1986; Ghoshal and Nohria, 1989). All else being equal, it would be expected that the more dynamic the local business environment, the more opportunities, in the form of potential mandates, it would afford for the subsidiary. Dynamism, in this study, is taken to be the dimensions of the local economy discussed by Porter (1990) – specifically, competitive rivalry, demanding customers and supporting and related industries.[3]

Proposition 7 The presence of subsidiary mandates is associated with local market competitiveness, demanding customers, and strong supporting and related industries in the local business environment.

The second relevant facet of the business environment is its level of globalization. Structural drivers such as the availability of economies of scale make certain industries more prone to global integration than others (Kobrin, 1991). At one end of the spectrum are 'pure global' industries (Porter, 1986) in which the subsidiary's activities are integrated with the rest of the corporate network. At the other end of the spectrum are 'multidomestic' industries in which competition in one national market is not substantially affected by competition in the next. It is proposed here that the presence of subsidiary mandates is directly related to the level of globalization of the industry. Multidomestic industries do not offer much scope for the subsidiary to gain mandates because they tend to be organized as 'miniature replicas' of their parent company (White and Poynter, 1984). Global industries, by contrast, require a high level of specialization from subsidiary companies as each focuses on undertaking certain specific activities on behalf of the MNC as a whole. Full-scope mandates seem rather unlikely in pure-global industries, but reduced scope mandates, such as for manufacturing or R&D only, are strongly predicted. Thus:

Proposition 8 The presence of subsidiary mandates is associated with a high level of industry globalization.

Subsidiary Performance and Subsidiary Mandates

The earlier discussion suggested that subsidiary mandates are believed to be an important component of subsidiary performance (Roth and Morrison, 1992). In this study we considered two aspects of performance. The first is referred to as subsidiary value-added, and it is a perceptual measure of the strategic value of the subsidiary (Bartlett and Ghoshal, 1986). The second is a more traditional estimation of performance in terms of market and financial-based criteria (sales growth, market share, ROI, profit). *Ceteris paribus* it is expected that the presence of a subsidiary mandate will positively relate to both variables.

Propositions 9–10 The presence of subsidiary mandates is associated with (9) high performance in the subsidiary, (10) high subsidiary value-added.

Two additional observations should be made. First, subsidiary performance could potentially be impacted by a number of other variables as well, including any of the independent variables specified in propositions 1 through 8. While not specified formally as research propositions, the analysis below includes an assessment of the association between the eight independent variables, subsidiary value-added and subsidiary performance. Second, it is recognized that subsidiary performance is likely to be a determinant of mandate presence, as well as a consequence of it. In other words, a high-performing subsidiary is far more likely to be awarded a mandate than a low-performing subsidiary (e.g. Birkinshaw, 1995; Moore, 1994; Science Council of Canada, 1980). While the cross-sectional nature of this study obviously precludes testing of causality, the likely reciprocity in this relationship should be borne in mind.

Subsidiary Initiative

As shown in the earlier part of this research programme, mandates can be won in a variety of ways. Two broad types of subsidiary initiative were identified: (1) internal initiatives, which are focused on opportunities within the corporate system such as reconfiguring existing assets and bidding for corporate investments; and (2) external initiatives, which are focused on new product or business opportunities outside the corporate system. The current study was interested in understanding the factors associated with these two types. Furthermore, on the understanding that not all initiatives are successful, the study sought to identify the factors that help to predict initiative success/failure. However, given the lack of prior research in this area, it was thought appropriate to define research questions rather than propositions:

Research questions 1–3 What factors are associated with: (1) internal initiatives; (2) external initiatives; (3) initiative success.

METHODOLOGY

The research propositions were tested using data gathered from a sample of 226 subsidiaries in Canada, Scotland and Sweden. While insights from the earlier studies will be used to interpret the results, the data presented here is exclusively from the questionnaire survey. This section describes how the questionnaire was developed, the specific measures that were used, and the selection of an appropriate sampling frame.

Questionnaire Development

The questionnaire was developed through a three-stage process. First, the draft questionnaire was reviewed by three academicians, who suggested improvements in wording and advice on layout. Second, following a major revision of the questionnaire, it was sent out to the six subsidiary presidents who were involved in the previous study. They all filled out the questionnaire, while the lead researcher did likewise on the basis of his extensive knowledge of the six companies. Responses were then compared, and where the differences between 'actual' (i.e. from the subsidiary president) and 'expected' (i.e. from the lead researcher) were substantial amendments to wording were made. In most cases, however, responses were very similar. At the same time, four pairs of subsidiary and head office managers were also asked to fill out the questionnaire, to ensure that the subsidiary's answers were consistent with the perceptions in head office. No significant differences were found. The inter-rater reliability for these four pairs was 0.61 (using Cohen's Kappa), an adequate but not exceptionally good result. Finally, once the second round of corrections had been made, the questionnaire was sent to a group of three managers in *another* subsidiary. The researcher met with these individuals to discuss their responses, which resulted in a few small changes. It should be observed that this three-stage process was necessary because several measures had to be specially developed for this study. The specifics of these measures are provided below.

Construct Measurement

Existing construct measures were used where possible for this study, most notably from the previous multinational subsidiary studies by Roth and Morrison (1992) and Ghoshal (1986). The appendix provides a detailed description of the measures used for each construct.

Sampling Methodology

Canada, Scotland and Sweden were selected as similar countries along two dimensions: (a) all three are relatively small countries with high standards of living; and (b) all three are 'peripheral' parts of established trading blocs. Our expectation was that subsidiaries in these countries would typically be of the 'implementer' type (Bartlett and Ghoshal, 1986) but with some prospect of becoming a 'contributor' if a mandate was gained. In terms of generalizability, it seems likely that the findings of this study will be meaningful to other 'peripheral' countries in developed areas.

Data was gathered during 1995. Our objective was to sample the population of manufacturing subsidiaries in each country with annual revenues of more than £25 million.[4] In each country a slightly different sampling process was used because of the nature of the available databases. In Canada, the sample was drawn up from a variety of CD-Rom products and directories, including the *Financial Post 500*, *Report on Business 1000*, and the *Disclosure* database. In Scotland we used the database compiled by *Scottish Enterprise*, the inward investment agency, which keeps track of all foreign

Table 2.1   Sample response rates

	Canada	Scotland	Sweden	Total
Questionnaires sent	270	182	221	673
Returned blank, declined to participate	5	5	18	28
Questionnaires returned complete	87	61	78	226
Response rate	32%	34%	35%	34%

Table 2.2   Characteristics of total sample

Average revenues 1994:	£182 million	
International responsibilities:	With	119
	Without	107
Nationality of parent company:	US	115
	UK	13
	Germany	13
	France	13
	Sweden	16
	Netherlands	6
	Switzerland	6
	Finland	20
	South Africa	7
	Norway	1
	Denmark	3
	Belgium	7
	Kuwait	2
	Canada	1
	Australia	1
	Ireland	1

investors in Scotland. Unfortunately this database was stratified by number of employees not revenues, so our cut-off of 100 employees was not exactly comparable to the £25 million. In Sweden we used the databases of foreign-owned subsidiaries compiled by *Veckans Affärer* and *Compass*. Using a standard procedure of mailing the questionnaire to the subsidiary CEO and then mailing a reminder 4 weeks later we ended up with 226 usable responses. Details of response rates and the characteristics of responding subsidiaries are listed in Table 2.1.

The mean size of responding subsidiaries was £182 million, with a range from £15 million through to £1.5 billion. As might be predicted, the parent company was American in a majority of cases, though there were also a large number of European parents. A test of non-response bias was conducted using annual revenues (or number of employees in the case of Scotland) and parent company as dependent variables, and no significant differences were found. Table 2.2 details some of the characteristics of the sample companies.

RESEARCH FINDINGS

Analysis was undertaken using the statistical package SPSS 6.0 for Windows. The propositions were tested using linear regression models, grouped according to the three major dependent variables, namely (1) subsidiary mandate, (2) subsidiary performance and (3) subsidiary initiative. Table 2.3 lists the variables in each of the regression models. These three groups of tests will be considered in turn.

1. Determinants of Subsidiary Mandate

Respondents were asked to state: (1) whether their subsidiary had any mandate responsibilities; (2) if yes, the percentage of their revenues attributable to the mandate; and (3) the percentage of that total that was 'earned' through the entrepreneurial efforts of subsidiary management. In this analysis we used the second answer (*mandate revenues*) and the product of the second and third answer (*earned mandate revenues*) as dependent variables. Both models offered broadly similar findings (see Table 2.4). Upstream capabilities (i.e. R&D and manufacturing) were a very significant predictor of the presence of a mandate, a finding that was further confirmed by the presence of R&D expenditure in the latter model. This is consistent with prior studies (e.g. Roth and Morrison, 1992), underlining that the subsidiary's capabilities are critical to the attainment of mandates. Related to this finding was the presence of subsidiary leadership as a significant variable in the first model. This underlines the importance of internal subsidiary attributes as the driver of subsidiary mandates. Interestingly, downstream capabilities were also significant in the first model but with a reverse sign, which indicates that the presence of downstream capabilities such as marketing and sales is a predictor of the *absence* of a mandate. What this tends to suggest is that those subsidiaries without mandates are particularly strong in the marketing and sales area, rather than mandate subsidiaries being weak in an absolute sense.

The other significant predictor variable, which was actually the most significant in either model, was local market competitiveness, but the curious finding here is that the relationship was the opposite of what was predicted. This suggests that strong local market competitiveness tends to stifle mandates rather than promote them, contrary to what Porter (1990) would predict. It is not obvious how this should be explained. One possibility is that subsidiaries perform better in uncompetitive local markets, and are able to win mandates on the basis of their relative performance.

Table 2.3 Summary of regression models performed in the data analysis

Model	Dependent variables	Independent variables	Which propositions?
1	Subsidiary mandate (mandate revenues, earned mandate revenues)	Autonomy (×3), communication (×2), credibility, internal relationships, entrepreneurial atmosphere, capabilities (×2), percentage R&D, local competitiveness, local factor markets, industry globalization, subsidiary leadership.	Propositions 1, 2, 3, 4, 5, 6, 7, 8,
2	Subsidiary performance (value-added, performance)	Subsidiary mandate, autonomy (×3), communication (×2), credibility, internal relationships, entrepreneurial atmosphere, capabilities (×2), percentage R&D, local competitiveness, local factor markets, industry globalization, subsidiary leadership.	Propositions 9, 10, 11
3	Subsidiary initiative (internal initiative, external initiative, initiative success)	Subsidiary mandate, subsidiary value-added autonomy (×3), communication (×2), credibility, internal relationships entrepreneurial atmosphere, capabilities (×2), percentage R&D, local competitiveness, local factor markets, industry globalization, subsidiary leadership.	Questions 1, 2, 3

Table 2.4 Results of multiple regression analysis: mandate revenues and earned mandate revenues as dependent variables

Variable	Mandate revenues (%)	Earned mandate revenues (%)
Intercept	0.047	11.3
Autonomy		
Communication with parent		
Credibility with parent		
Sub. internal context		
Sub. entrepreneurship index		
Sub upstream capabilities	5.84**	3.93*
Sub down stream capabilities	−5.16*	
Sub R&D as % of sales	1.36**	1.11**
Local market compettiveness	−9.75***	−6.23***
Level of global integration		
Subsidiary leadership	4.29**	
F-value	13.33	10.68
Significance level	0.0000	0.0000
R-squared	0.28	0.16
Adj *R*-squared	0.26	0.14

* $p < 0.05$ ** $p < 0.01$ *** $p < 0.001$.

Another possibility is that mandate subsidiaries are inherently outward-looking, and are therefore unaware of competitive pressures in their local market. We will revisit this issue in the discussion section.

In sum, the analysis of factors associated with subsidiary mandates yielded somewhat surprising results. None of the parent–subsidiary attributes were significant, and the local market competitiveness variable was significant in the unexpected direction. It was, however, confirmed that the subsidiary's capabilities, and specifically its R&D and manufacturing capabilities, are critical predictors of the presence/absence of a mandate.

2. Factors Associated with Subsidiary Performance and Value-Added

The second regression model included all the independent variables from the first model as well as the two measures of subsidiary mandate (Table 2.5). The most important finding from this model was the *absence* of a direct relationship between subsidiary mandate and performance. This is perhaps not surprising, in that locally-oriented subsidiaries can be as well-managed as mandate-holding subsidiaries. A significant result was, however, obtained for the relationship between earned exports and subsidiary value-added, which is a subjective estimate of the strategic importance of the subsidiary to the MNC. Subsidiary value-added, in turn, had a very

Table 2.5 Results of multiple regression analysis: subsidiary value-added and performance

Variable	Subsidiary value-added	Performance
Intercept	−0.907***	0.009
Autonomy		
Communication with parent		
Credibility with parent		
Sub. internal context		
Sub. entrepreneurship index		
Sub upstream capabilities	0.225***	
Sub dowstream capabilities	0.247***	0.353***
Sub R&D as % of sales		
Local market compettiveness		−0.159*
Level of global integration	0.178**	
Exports as % of sales		
% exports 'earned' by subsidiary	0.004*	
Subsidiary leadership	0.169***	
Subsidiary value-added (subj.)		0.283***
F-value	19.2	21.9
Significance level	0.0000	0.0000
R-squared	0.36	0.28
Adj R-squared	0.34	0.26

$* \ p < 0.05 \ ** \ p < 0.01 \ *** \ p < 0.001.$

significant impact on performance, so the implication is that mandates have at least an indirect (and positive) effect on performance.

In terms of the other variables in the equation, subsidiary capabilities were the major driver of subsidiary performance. Upstream capabilities were significant predictors of perceived value-added; downstream capabilities were significant in both models, and – more critically – the most significant predictor of performance. Bearing in mind that subsidiary value-added is itself an important predictor of performance, the implication is that downstream capabilities have both a direct and indirect impact on performance while upstream capabilities have only an indirect effect (via subsidiary value-added).

Subsidiary leadership was associated with subsidiary value-added, as might be expected. The level of global integration was also associated with subsidiary value-added, but this is less easy to explain. The suggestion is that the level of integration of the subsidiary with its parent is somehow related to the perceived contribution it makes to the corporate strategy.

The role of local market competitiveness, again, was contrary to what might be predicted. This finding suggests that stronger performance is obtained in those subsidiaries with relatively placid local markets. This adds some support for one of the arguments put forth in the previous section, but it still begs a convincing explanation. Further investigation is needed in this area.

The most interesting finding from this analysis, in broad terms, is the critical role of subsidiary value-added. From the earlier phases of research, it seems likely that many subsidiaries are undertaking activities that are important for the corporation but which do not directly impact the bottom line of the subsidiary. The current analysis confirms this, by suggesting that there is an underlying sense of qualitative value-added in the subsidiary, that is impacted by a host of factors including mandate responsibilities, subsidiary capabilities and leadership. Importantly, value-added also has a substantive impact on the performance of the subsidiary, though it is impossible to estimate the extent to which that is a fair reflection of perceived value-added.

3. Factors Associated with Subsidiary Initiative

This model included all the variables in the previous regression model. Table 2.6 lists the results of the regression analysis. Note that only 120 of the 228 companies in the sample were able to answer the questions about initiative, in that only they claimed to have international responsibilities. From a methodological perspective, this means that significant relationships are much harder to detect.

The presence of internal initiative was predicted by upstream subsidiary capabilities (consistent with the previous models) and at the 0.10 level by product autonomy and manufacturing autonomy (both negative). We can interpret this to indicate that internal initiative is more likely to transpire when the subsidiary has low autonomy and strong manufacturing and/or R&D. These results are all in keeping with the findings of the clinical study reported in Birkinshaw (1995), though the overall predictive power of the regression equation is rather weak (R-squared adjusted = 10 per cent).

External initiative was predicted by rather different factors, specifically high manufacturing autonomy, low communication (both in terms of quality and frequency), and strong subsidiary leadership. This combination is almost exactly the opposite of the conditions in which internal initiative thrived, a result which is again in keeping with the prior study. It is interesting to note that the facets of the parent–subsidiary relationship had no apparent impact on the existence of world mandates (Table 2.3), but that they are important predictors of the type of initiative. The suggestion is that there are two groups of mandated subsidiaries, defined by the extent of integration with the parent company: (1) those that are relatively autonomous and outward-looking, with strong leaders, focused on developing new products and new markets; and (2) those that are relatively integrated and inward-looking, bidding for corporate investments and reconfiguring existing operations on the basis of their proven capabilities.

Table 2.6 Results of multiple regression analysis: internal initiative, external initiative, success with initiative

Variable	Internal initiative	External initiative	Success with initiative
Intercept	0.017	−0.898	−2.28
Product autonomy	−0.18~		
Organisational autonomy			−0.09~
Manufacturing autonomy	−0.16~	0.21	0.15**
Communication quality		−0.15~	
Communication frequency		−0.17~	
Credibility with parent			
Sub. internal context			
Sub. entrepreneurship index			
Sub upstream capabilities	0.29**		
Sub dowstream capabilities			
Sub R&D as % of sales			
Local market compettiveness			
Level of global integration			
Subsidiary % exports			
% exports 'earned'			
Subsidiary citizenship			0.11*
Subsidiary value-added			
History of strong leadership		0.194**	0.11**
F-value	4.85	5.58	7.16
Significance level	0.004	0.004	0.0000
R-squared	0.13	0.19	0.23
Adj *R*-squared	0.10	0.15	0.20

$\sim p < 0.1$ * $p < 0.05$ ** $p < 0.01$ *** $p < 0.001$.

Finally, respondents were asked how successful their subsidiaries had been in gaining mandates through initiative. The results suggested that strong corporate citizenship, high manufacturing autonomy, low organizational autonomy, and strong leadership were most closely associated with success. Strong leadership has strong face validity and needs no further comment. The conflicting signs of the two autonomy variables is fascinating. Essentially this suggests that success is associated with autonomous manufacturing but fairly close organizational ties. Again, this has face validity, but it is surprising that the data indicates significant relationships in both cases. Finally, the significance of corporate citizenship is probably indicative of a reverse causality, in that successful initiative efforts reflect positively on the perception of the subsidiary in the local community.

In summary, Table 2.7 lists the major findings from the multiple regression analysis. This shows that the majority of the propositions were not

Table 2.7 Summary of findings from data analysis

Model	Dependent variables	Independent variables
1	Subsidiary mandate	Proposition 1 – not supported
		Proposition 2 – not supported
		Proposition 3 – not supported
		Proposition 4 – not supported
		Proposition 5 – not supported
		Proposition 6 – supported
		Proposition 7 – not supported
		Proposition 8 – not supported
2	Subsidiary performance	Proposition 9 – not supported
		Proposition 10 – supported
3	Subsidiary initiative	Research question 1 – Autonomy, upstream capabilities associated with internal initiative
		Research question 2 – Parent communication, autonomy, strong leadership associated with external initiative
		Research question 3 – Autonomy, citizenship and strong leadership associated with initiative success

supported, but this is not entirely surprising because they were set up as 'competing' propositions, not all of which were expected to be confirmed. Nonetheless, several important and interesting results were observed, and these will be discussed in the following section.

DISCUSSION

In essence this chapter's objective was to understand why some subsidiaries have mandate responsibilities while others do not. While the above analysis captures some of the complexities of addressing the research question, this discussion offers a more general interpretation of the evidence, in terms of its implications for subsidiary management and public policy.

Implications for Subsidiary Management

The key observation, from the perspective of subsidiary management, is the primacy of the subsidiary's upstream capabilities, specifically R&D and manufacturing, as the driver of success. Upstream capabilities were associated directly with export responsibilities, value-added, and initiative, and indirectly with financial performance. The message here is that mandate success comes from within the subsidiary. Crookell (1986) and others have long observed that mandates are earned not given, and this study provides solid evidence of this statement. Perhaps the more interesting finding from this study is the role of leadership and an entrepreneurial culture as the driving forces behind subsidiary value-added. This suggests that even if the subsidiary's capabilities are limited, upgrading can be driven by subsidiary management. Certainly there were many cases in the research interviews of subsidiaries that had built mandate responsibilities where none had previously existed. Typically they started small, offering to take responsibility for a single manufacturing run for the North American market for example, but over time their capabilities grew and their ability to take greater responsibilities was enhanced accordingly. Strong visionary leadership, coupled with enthusiasm and involvement throughout the organization were the fundamental drivers of this process.

A second important finding is the relative lack of importance of any aspects of the parent–subsidiary relationship in predicting the presence of subsidiary mandates. Taken in conjunction with the subsidiary capabilities finding, this suggests that comments along the lines of 'we can't win mandates because our corporation is too highly centralized' are not always accurate, reflecting instead the lack of creativity and initiative in the subsidiary itself. The results in Table 2.5, in fact, suggest an even more interesting finding: namely, that aspects of the parent–subsidiary relationship may impact the *type* of initiative that is possible, but not the presence of initiative *per se*. The tentative suggestion is that perhaps tightly controlled subsidiaries should pursue internal initiatives, while more autonomous subsidiaries pursue external initiatives. It would be inappropriate to state the results in simple prescriptive terms, but the evidence leans towards this recommendation. The interview findings are also consistent with this position.

A third issue which is important to both subsidiary and parent-company management is the role of 'perceived value-added'. As this study showed, the presence of a mandate had a positive impact on subsidiary value-added which in turn had a positive impact on subsidiary performance. While there was no direct relationship between mandate presence and performance, there was clearly a sense among subsidiary managers that head-office perception was favourably influenced by mandate presence, and that there were liable to be longer-term links to performance. It is, perhaps, not that important to dwell on the specifics of subsidiary performance, because they depend so much on transfer pricing and the internal success measures that are used. What is probably more important, from the subsidiary's point of view, is its 'strategic importance' to the corporation, because that is a strong predictor of the type of role it will be given (Bartlett and Ghoshal, 1986). In this regard, mandate status must be seen as central to the long-term success of the subsidiary.

Finally, it is important to position this discussion of subsidiary strategy in terms of the broader objectives of the parent company. The entire discussion of subsidiary mandates and initiative is, of course, antithetical to many of the traditional approaches to multinational management, in which subsidiary units are seen as implementing the strategic directives of their parent companies. Our approach is consistent with a number of the more recent models of MNC management (e.g. Ghoshal and Bartlett, 1991; Hedlund, 1986), in that it eschews simplistic assumptions of hierarchy and subordination. However, we should also acknowledge that we are not advocating the emergence of an anarchic system in which subsidiary units are given free rein to pursue opportunities wherever they arise. Such a system would not only encourage opportunistic and self-interested behaviour among subsidiary managers, it would also impair the strategic focus of the parent company. Thus there is need for a clear definition, at a corporate level, of the MNC's business domain, with a consequent understanding that initiatives must fall within that domain to be considered for funding. There is also a need to retain the balance between control and autonomy at the subsidiary level, through both formal processes (e.g. limits on spending, capital allocation systems, budgets) and informal ones (e.g. personal networks, socialization systems, corporate norms), in order to ensure that entrepreneurial energy is channelled into projects that are valued by the MNC as a whole and not just by the subsidiary unit.

Implications for Public Policy

The key insight from this study is that the parent company cannot be 'blamed' if a host country believes the level of subsidiary mandates in their country is too low. Mandates are gained through subsidiary initiative, and this initiative can be directed internally (e.g. bidding for new corporate investment) or externally (e.g. starting a new business locally). In both cases it is the entrepreneurship and leadership of the subsidiary, and its underlying capabilities, that are the drivers of success. Government support, if it is appropriate, should therefore be directed towards ensuring that the quality of local management is enhanced, so that entrepreneurially-minded business enterprises are nurtured, rather than seeking to change the attitudes of parent company managers to host-country investment.

In broader terms, there is reason to believe that subsidiary managers in Canada, Scotland and Sweden are being reasonably successful when it comes to initiative and mandates. Over half the sample companies had a mandate of some sort, the vast majority of which were 'earned' by subsidiary management. Furthermore, anecdotal evidence gained from interviews, industry meetings, and round-table discussions suggests that most subsidiaries in the sample have understood the basic theme of this chapter, i.e. the need to be entrepreneurial. The greater challenge, which many appear to be grappling with at the moment, is the specific steps that need to be taken to enact that theme.

The other important public policy implication in this study is the rather surprising relationship between subsidiary mandate presence and the nature of the local business environment. Simply stated, the survey evidence showed that subsidiaries were more likely to have mandates if domestic market competition was perceived to be weak. This is fundamentally at odds with Porter's (1990) thinking on national competitiveness. Porter's theory predicts that the national or local business environment, and in particular the level of competition within it, drives competitive upgrading by participating firms. To the extent that mandate subsidiaries are more competitive than non-mandate subsidiaries, we would therefore expect to see a higher level of local competition in mandate subsidiaries. In reality we find the opposite.

It is not entirely obvious how to reconcile Porter's theory with the findings of this study. It would appear that Porter's study works best when there are clearly defined 'clusters' of related industries that are recognized as world-class, and which multinational corporations seek access to through their subsidiaries. For the countries in this study, there is little evidence of such clusters: Canada and Sweden both have leading-edge clusters in the natural resource and heavy industry sectors, but these were under-represented in the subsidiary sample; and Scotland has a cluster of electronics companies in 'silicon glen' but this is not a leading-edge cluster in terms of innovation and spin-off companies. Rather than gaining mandates because of the *strength* of the local business environment, the subsidiaries in this study appeared to gain their mandates because of the industry's relative *weakness*. The mandate is awarded in such instances because the subsidiary is in a relatively protected niche – it is strong because it has limited competition, and that is sufficient for the corporation to give it mandate status. This is, of course, very different from a mandate in a leading-edge cluster, but given the relatively small size of the Canadian, Scottish, and Swedish economies it may be that such niche mandates are a more reasonable goal.

In more general terms, this line of argument suggests that Porter's thinking has relatively limited applicability to small peripheral economies such as those represented here. Upgrading of foreign subsidiaries is probably driven by very different factors from those indicated in Porter's diamond model. This study has highlighted the importance of a relatively benign competitive environment for the creation of a niche mandate, as well as the internal drive and entrepreneurship of subsidiary management. It may be that other local-environment factors can also be identified, but this is the domain of future research.

Appendix: Construct Measurement

Subsidiary mandates. Four mandate measures were used. First, respondents were asked to reply yes or no to the question 'Does your subsidiary company have any international responsibilities or world mandates?' Second, they were asked to estimate what percentage, if any, of their total sales revenues were gained through international sales. While the first measure more accurately delineates between subsidiaries with and without mandates, the latter captures information on the scope of mandate responsibilities that is lost in the first. Third, to capture the entrepreneurial element in the mandate-winning process, respondents were asked to estimate what percentage of their international sales were 'earned' by subsidiary management rather than 'given' by the parent.[5] The fourth measure was simply the multiple of the second and third, representing the percentage of sales attributable to earned mandate exports. For example, if 30 per cent of sales were exports and 80 per cent of those exports were earned, this would suggest 24 per cent of exports were attributable to the specific efforts of subsidiary management.

Subsidiary performance. The measurement of subsidiary performance is notoriously difficult for two reasons: (1) performance is a function of the subsidiary's assigned role, so that one may focus on market share growth while the next focuses on profitability; (2) most subsidiaries are wholly-owned, so there is no publicly available data. With these concerns in mind, the measures used by Roth and Morrison (1992) were adopted, in which respondents were asked to assess their subsidiary's performance relative to other subsidiaries for five measures (ROI, profit, productivity, sales growth, market share). Following a principal component factor analysis, we identified a single factor for all five items (KMO measure of sampling adequacy = 0.71).

Subsidiary value-added. It is recognized in the multinational subsidiary literature that each subsidiary has a unique value-adding role, depending on the mix of responsibilities and activities it undertakes for the corporation. Unfortunately, no definitive measures exist for what constitutes value-added. Gupta and Govindarajan (1991) proposed 'resource inflows and outflows'; Bartlett and Ghoshal (1986) suggested 'strategic importance' as a subjective head-office measure; and Roth and Morrison (1992) used a combination of international sales and level of integration with the parent company. For this study three questions were formulated on the basis of answers given in the earlier phase of research: (1) We make a significant value-added contribution to the corporation as a whole, (2) We are globally competitive in our areas of operation, and (3) We are regarded by the parent company as a strategically important subsidiary (responses on a 1–7 scale where 1 = strongly disagree, 7 = strongly agree). Reliability for this scale was found to be acceptable (KMO = 0.62).

Subsidiary autonomy. A seven-item scale was taken from Roth and Morrison (1992) that asked subsidiary managers to identify whether certain decisions were made in the subsidiary, divisional level, or head office. A principal component factor analysis revealed three sub-scales: manufacturing autonomy, product autonomy and organizational autonomy (KMO = 0.68).

Parent–subsidiary communication. Ghoshal's (1986) measures of communication were used, specifically frequency of communication, frequency of business trips to head office, strength of working relations, and sharing of information. Factor analysis suggested that this scale should be divided into two: communication frequency (the first two) and communication quality (the latter two) (KMO = 0.58).

Subsidiary credibility. A three-item scale was developed specifically for this study, with items (1) parent company managers are confident that the subsidiary will achieve what it sets out to do; (2) the subsidiary's capabilities are typically well understood by the parent company managers; and (3) the credibility of subsidiary top management is high (KMO = 0.68).

Internal subsidiary relationships. A four-item scale was developed specifically for this study, based in part on the previous study and in part on the concepts in Ghoshal and Bartlett (1994). Items were: (1) there are strong working relationships between managers within the subsidiary; (2) subsidiary managers interact frequently and share ideas with one another; (3) the subsidiary CEO or president works with managers to focus their efforts towards the subsidiary's objectives; and (4) there is a strong sense of community within the subsidiary. Sampling adequacy was acceptable (KMO = 0.81).

Entrepreneurial culture. The five highest-loading items from the intrapreneurial assessment index of Kuratko *et al.* (1990) was used to measure entrepreneurial culture. Sampling adequacy of this scale was acceptable (KMO = 0.86).

Subsidiary capabilities. The measures used by Roth and Morrison (1992) were used, whereby respondents were asked to state their relative capabilities for eight activities. Factor analysis of these responses yielded two key factors: (1) upstream capabilities (R&D and manufacturing); and (2) downstream capabilities (sales force coverage and marketing) (KMO = 0.50). A measure of R&D intensity was also obtained by asking respondents to estimate their R&D expenditure as a percentage of total sales.

Dynamism of local environment. A seven-item scale was taken from Woodcock (1994). This scale was designed to tap into the four basic attributes of Porter's (1990) diamond model. Following a factor analysis, two factors were identified: (1) local market competitiveness (domestic competition is intense, competition in this country is very intense); and (2) local factor markets (local customers have exacting standards, capabilities of suppliers is very high, relationships between buyers and suppliers are very strong) (KMO = 0.63).

Industry globalization. The scale used by Roth and Morrison (1992) was adopted, but not all items were usable. A factor analysis revealed two factors: (1) global competition (product awareness exists worldwide, international competition is intense, competitors exist in all key markets, business activities are susceptible to scale economies) and (2) market homogeneity (buyer/customer needs are standardized worldwide, competitors market a standard product worldwide, new product introductions occur in all major markets simultaneously) (KMO = 0.76).

Subsidiary initiative. Using the questions developed during the previous phase of research, two scales were extracted. The first, 'External Initiative', described the following four activities: (1) new products are developed in the Canadian market and sold internationally; (2) significant extensions to existing international responsibilities; (3) new international business activities first started in Canada; and (4) enhancements to product lines which are already sold internationally (Alpha = 0.71). The second, 'Internal Initiative', described the following three activities: (1) successful bids for corporate investments in Canada; (2) proposals to transfer manufacturing to Canada from elsewhere; and (3) new corporate investments in R&D or manufacturing attracted by Canadian management (Alpha = 0.64).

Notes

1. Mandate is defined in this study as a business, or element of a business, in which a subsidiary participates and for which it has responsibilities beyond its national market. This is deliberately broader than the definition used in most prior research. The definition of mandate also covers a variety of more-specific terms such as 'world product mandate' and 'regional manufacturing mandate'.
2. Though it should be observed that several managers have expressed their dislike of the term 'mandate'. The objection is typically that mandate implies a paternalistic

head office handing out favours to subsidiaries, when in reality the subsidiary has to work hard to win and retain its responsibilities.

3. Porter (1990) never explicitly discussed foreign-owned subsidiaries in his competitive advantage of nations study. While proposition 7 has some intuitive support, it remains speculative.

4. The £25 million cut-off in size was selected because the strategic imperatives for a large or mature subsidiary are fundamentally different from those of a small and/or growing subsidiary. Many subsidiaries below £25 million in sales are still sales-only operations whose mandate is to maximize sales revenues and little else. In contrast, once a subsidiary starts to receive direct investment in manufacturing, marketing or other functions it has to balance its time between selling and other activities. The question of value-added then comes into play. Certainly £25 million does not represent a definitive boundary, but experience suggests that it is a reasonable one. The manufacturing criterion was to ensure that large importers (e.g. many automobile companies) were excluded, because the notion of subsidiary mandates simply does not apply in such cases. Manufacturing was broadly defined to include, for example, software development.

5. This is a simplification of reality, of course, in that both parent and subsidiary have a role to play in the mandate process. It should be observed, however, that for all six pilot study companies this estimate was made by the researcher and by the subsidiary president with near-identical results, confirming the reliability of the measure. Also, note that this is a 'stock' rather than a 'flow' variable, in that it captures the result of initiative rather than the initiatives themselves. This was necessary for the cross-sectional research design.

References

Barney, J. (1991) 'Firm resources and sustained competitive advantage', *Journal of Management*, 17(1), pp. 99–120.

Bartlett, C.A. (1979) 'Multinational structural evolution: the changing decision environment in international divisions', Unpublished doctoral dissertation, Harvard University.

Bartlett, C.A. and S. Ghoshal (1986) 'Tap your subsidiaries for global reach', *Harvard Business Review*, 64(6), pp. 87–94.

Birkinshaw, J.M. (1995) 'Entrepreneurship in multinational corporations: the initiative process in Canadian subsidiaries', Unpublished doctoral dissertation, Western Business School.

Bishop, P. and H.H. Crookell (1986) 'Specialisation in Canadian subsidiaries', in D.G. McFetridge (ed.), *Canadian Industry in Transition* (Toronto: University of Toronto Press).

Bower, J.L. (1970) *Managing the Resource Allocation Process* (Cambridge, Mass: Harvard University Press).

Brandt, W.K. and J.M. Hulbert (1977) 'Headquarters guidance in marketing strategy in the multinational subsidiary', *Columbia Journal of World Business*, 12, pp. 7–14.

Burgelman, R.A. (1983) 'A model of the interaction of strategic behaviour, corporate context and the concept of strategy', *Academy of Management Review*, 8(1), pp. 61–70.

Crookell, H.H. (1986) 'Specialisation and international competitiveness', in H. Etemad and L.S. Dulude (eds), *Managing the Multinational Subsidiary* (London: Croom Helm).

Crookell, H.H. (1990) *'Canadian–American Trade and Investment Under the Free Trade Agreement* (New York: Quorum Books).

Crookell, H.H. and J. Caliendo (1980) 'International competitiveness and the structure of secondary industry in Canada', *Business Quarterly*, 44, pp. 58–64.

Crookell, H.H. and A.J. Morrison (1990) 'Subsidiary strategy in a free trade environment', *Business Quarterly*, 54.

D'Cruz, J.R. (1986) 'Strategic management of subsidiaries', in H. Etemad and L.S. Dulude (eds), *Managing the Multinational Subsidiary* (London: Croom Helm).

Etemad, H. and L.S. Dulude (1986) *Managing the Multinational Subsidiary* (London: Croom Helm).

Forsgren, M. and J. Johanson (1992) *Managing Networks in International Business* (Philadelphia: Gordon & Breach).

Gates, S.R. and W.G. Egelhoff (1986) 'Centralization in headquarters–subsidiary relationships', *Journal of International Business Studies*, 17(2), pp. 71–92.

Ghoshal, S. (1986) 'The innovative multinational: a differentiated network of organisational roles and management processes', Unpublished doctoral dissertation, Boston: Harvard Business School.

Ghoshal, S. and C.A. Bartlett (1988) 'Creation, adoption and diffusion of innovations by subsidiaries of multinational corporations', *Journal of International Business Studies*, 19(3), pp. 365–88.

Ghoshal, S. and C.A. Bartlett (1991) 'The multinational corporation as an interorganizational network', *Academy of Management Review*, 15(4), pp. 603–25.

Ghoshal, S. and C.A. Bartlett (1994) 'Linking organisational context and managerial action: the dimensions of quality of management', *Strategic Management Journal*, 15, pp. 91–112.

Ghoshal, S. and N. Nohria (1989) 'Internal differentiation within multinational corporations', *Strategic Management Journal*, 10, pp. 323–37.

Gupta, A.K. and V.J. Govindarajan (1991) 'Knowledge flows and the structure of control within multinational corporations', *Academy of Management Review*, 16(4), pp. 768–92.

Hedlund, G. (1981) 'Autonomy of subsidiaries and formalisation. of headquarters–subsidiary relationships in Swedish MNCs', in L. Otterbeck (ed.), *The Management of Headquarters–Subsidiary Relations in Multinational Corporations* (Hampshire, UK: Gower Publishing Co.).

Hedlund, G. (1986) 'The hypermodern MNC: A Heterarchy?' *Human Resource Management*, 25, 9–36.

Hedlund, G. (1994) 'A model of knowledge management and the N-form corporation', *Strategic Management Journal*, 15, pp. 73–90.

Jarillo, J.C. and J.I. Martinez (1990) 'Different roles for subsidiaries: the case of multinational corporations', *Strategic Management Journal*, 11, pp. 501–12.

Johnston, P. (1982) 'The perils of product mandating', *Policy Options*, 3(2), pp. 26–32.

Kanter, R.M. (1985) *The Change Masters* (New York: Simon & Schuster).

Kobrin, S.J. (1991) 'An empirical analysis of the determinants of global integration', *Strategic Management Journal*, 12, pp. 17–32.

Kuratko, D.F., R.V. Montagno and J.S. Hornsby (1990) 'Developing an intrapreneurial assessment instrument for an effective corporate entrepreneurial environment', *Strategic Management Journal*, 11, pp. 49–58.

Lawrence, P. and J. Lorsch (1967) *Organisation and Environment: Managing Differentiation and Integration* (Boston, MA: Harvard University).

McGuinness, N. and H.A. Conway (1986) 'World product mandates: the need for directed search strategies', in H. Etemad and L.S. Dulude (eds), *Managing the Multinational Subsidiary* (London: Croom Helm).

Miller, D. (1983) 'The correlates of entrepreneurship in three types of firms', *Management Science*, 29, pp. 770–91.

Moore, K. (1994) 'Capturing international responsibilities in the Canadian pharmaceutical industry', *Industry Canada Working Paper* (Industry Canada, Ottawa).

Negandhi, A.R. and B.R. Baliga (1981) 'Internal functioning of American, German and Japanese multinational corporations', in L. Otterbeck (ed.), *The Management of Headquarters–Subsidiary Relations in Multinational Corporations* (Hampshire, UK: Gower Publishing Co.).

Ontario Ministry of Industry and Tourism (1980) *The Report of the Advisory Committee on Global Product Mandating* (Ottawa, 1980).

Pearce, J.A. (1992) 'World product mandates and MNE specialisation', *Scandinavian International Business Review*, 1(2), pp. 38–57.

Pinchott, G. III (1986) *Intrapreneuring* (New York: Harper & Row).

Porter, M.E. (1986) *Competition in Global Industries* (Harvard Business School Press).

Porter, M.E. (1990) *The Competitive Advantage of Nations* (New York: Free Press).

Poynter, T.A. and A.R. Rugman (1982) 'World product mandates: how will multinationals respond?', *Business Quarterly*, 46(Fall), pp. 54–61.

Prahalad, C.K. (1976) 'The strategic process in a multinational corporation', Unpublished doctoral dissertation, School of Business Administration, Harvard University.

Prahalad, C.K. and Y.L. Doz (1981) 'An approach to strategic control in MNCs', *Sloan Management Review*, pp. 5–13.

Quinn, J.B. (1985) 'Managing innovation: controlled chaos', *Harvard Business Review*, 63(3), pp. 73–84.

Roth, K. and A.J. Morrison (1992) 'Implementing global strategy: characteristics of global subsidiary mandates', *Journal of International Business Studies*, 23(4), pp. 715–36.

Rugman, A.M. and J. Bennett (1982) 'Technology transfer and world product mandating in Canada', *Columbia Journal of World Business*, pp. 58–62.

Rugman, A.M. and S. Douglas (1986) 'The strategic management of multinationals and world product mandating in Etemad, H. and L.S. Dulude (eds), *Managing the Multinational Subsidiary* (London: Croom Helm).

Science Council of Canada (1980) *Multinationals and Industrial Strategy. The Role of World Product Mandates* (Ottawa).

White, R.E. and T.A. Poynter (1984) 'Strategies for foreign-owned subsidiaries in Canada', *Business Quarterly*, 44 (Summer), pp. 59–69.

Woodcock, P. (1994) 'The greenfield vs. acquisition entry mode decision process', Unpublished doctoral dissertation, Western Business School.

Young, S., N. Hood and S. Dunlop (1988) 'Global strategies, multinational subsidiary roles and economic impact in Scotland', *Regional Studies*, 22(6), pp. 487–97.

3 Locating International Pharmaceutical R&D Subsidiaries: Between-Countries and Within-Countries Determinants

James Taggart

INTRODUCTION

Determinants of the foreign R&D locational decision in the pharmaceutical industry have been described (Terpstra, 1977) and subsequently evaluated (Taggart, 1991) for six major pharmaceutical markets: the USA, the UK, Germany, France, Italy and Japan. The principal determinants were found to be related to national market characteristics and intrinsic R&D resources of the countries concerned, though it has been pointed out that supranational political and economic dimensions may be an overriding factor in the longer term, at least in Europe (Howells, 1987 and 1992). The purpose of this chapter is to evaluate two of the above countries (UK and Germany) against a third (Eire) that is generally recognized to be an infrequent choice for international pharmaceutical R&D; then a more detailed locational analysis will be carried out within one of the countries (UK) as an exploratory comparison between a highly regarded location for drug R&D (Cambridge) and three others (Cardiff, Glasgow, Edinburgh). The cities chosen for this second stage are diverse in many social and economic aspects; thus, in order to produce a locus of comparability, the science park in each of the four has been made the focal point of this research. At both stages the emphasis will be on those determinants that most effectively discriminate between alternative locations. The overall objective of the research, then, is to compare various locations in terms of suitability for inward R&D investments by the international pharmaceutical industry and, as a by-product, to assess policy options for those public bodies that wish to encourage such investments.

It has been suggested that in the 'Post-Business Society' wealth creation revolves around the exchange of intellectual property among collegial networks of knowledge workers (Drucker, 1989). As white-collar workers replaced blue so they, in turn, will be displaced by knowledge workers. The demise of the UK blue-collar worker, particularly since 1980, has followed the relocation of manufacturing to low-cost centres in the Far East. The subsequent globalization of many world markets has intensified the down-stream activities of multinational firms and, in particular, the relative costs of R&D have increased as product life-cycles have shortened dramatically (Howells, 1990c; Drucker, 1992). While manual labour costs have fallen as a proportion of the cost of many consumer and capital goods, intellectual labour costs have not shrunk as a proportion of the R&D expenditures of pharmaceutical multinationals (Taggart, 1993). Constant innovation is the key success factor in the ethical drug industry, and consistently rising pro-ductivity in this area is the philosopher's stone that yields technological advance, product differentiation and sustainable competitive advantage (Taggart, 1989; Howells, 1990b). One industry response has been to locate overseas R&D facilities in countries with low employment costs for tech-nologists (Schnee, 1978), though this is but one parameter in a complex decision process. Howells (1990a) has pointed out that the rapid develop-ment of telecommunications and computer links between the home country laboratory and overseas R&D facilities represents a major new change factor; this trend, by itself, may cause pharmaceutical multinationals to reassess the whole process of R&D globalization.

Having decided to locate a new R&D facility in one particular country, the international pharmaceutical firm is then faced with a more specific locational decision within that country. There is some evidence that R&D facilities are no longer automatically co-located with manufacturing plants and, in the case of the UK at least, science parks are an obvious alternative (Taggart, 1993). The problem of assessing and evaluating the various locational options within a given country is likely to be as complex as deciding between countries, and no such evaluative process has been de-scribed in the literature.

All of this gives use to the broad research questions that underlie this chapter:

- Are the locational determinants evolved by Taggart (1991), based on fieldwork carried out in 1986, still valid parameters for the international pharmaceutical industry in 1994?
- How do Germany and the UK compare to one another as potential locations for international drug R&D, and will the locational determi-nants effectively discriminate between these two and a country like Eire with relatively little international pharmaceutical R&D activity?
- Is there another set of determinants that will effectively discriminate between different locations within one country (say the UK)?
- Can this additional set of determinants be used to evaluate specific loca-tions in rank order?

SCIENCE PARKS AS LOCATIONS FOR
PHARMACEUTICAL R&D

As noted above, science parks in Cambridge, Cardiff, Edinburgh and Glasgow are used as a focal point for locational comparisons in this research; thus, the key characteristics of science parks as described in the literature are outlined below. This is followed by a section that summarizes recent work on the location of international R&D facilities, focusing where possible on the pharmaceutical industry.

While governments and regional development agencies have been keen to foster closer links between industry and academia through the creation of science parks, this mechanism for technology transfer has come under increasing criticism (Van Dierdonck *et al.*, 1991). These authors assess the extent to which science parks have delivered the promised results of new high-technology firms based on the industrial application of scientific knowledge developed at universities. They conclude that science parks have not significantly served to facilitate the transfer of technology, and that spatial proximity is not a requirement even for the transfer of ideas. Rather, the transfer of knowledge is not confined regionally but occurs at a national and transnational level through collegial networks, the plethora of multi-authored research papers, and the burgeoning use of information technology. Indeed, off-park research centres seem to have more links (formal and informal) with academic institutions, and there has been no evidence to suggest that these off-park centres are less innovative than on-park organisations. This confirms earlier work by Monck *et al.* (1988) indicating that, in Britain at least, the primary reason for locating new technology-related enterprises had more to do with the image and prestige of a site rather than the ability to recruit university staff. According to Monck *et al.*, less than 20 per cent of science park tenants in Belgium and the Netherlands claimed that availability of scientific and technical staff was the most important locational factor. Thus, these two papers challenge some aspects of the received wisdom in this area of knowledge:

- Science parks aid the transfer of technology
- Spatial proximity improves the transfer of technology
- Tenants occupy science parks primarily to draw upon local knowledge
- Science parks will have a significant impact on local employment.

The phenomenon of international locational diffusion of multinational R&D has been widely described and analyzed (e.g. Porter, 1990; Cheng and Bolon, 1993). With the increasing trend to internationalization and globalization of business, there has been a parallel movement to locate R&D abroad (Howells, 1990a; Taggart, 1989 and 1991). De Meyer's (1993) case study analysis of sixteen large multinational firms in chemicals, pharmaceuticals, electronics, automobiles and food focused specifically on the internationalization of R&D; ten of the firms were European, four were North American, and two Japanese. Fourteen of the firms had long international experience. The number of foreign R&D facilities per firm ranged from 1 to 17, with a total of over 100. He points out that before 1970 only 27 per cent of all new laboratories were located outside the home country, a figure that has now increased to 65 per cent. Despite this trend, four imperatives for keeping R&D at home are reviewed:

- R&D is characterized by economies of scale and scope (see also Teece, 1987). A key factor is the need for a critical mass of R&D professionals (see also Taggart, 1989). It is more difficult to preserve the historic knowledge base of the firm when R&D is dispersed internationally.
- R&D activities are unstructured and the yields often intangible (see also Clark, 1985). Much of the knowledge built up is tacit and difficult to codify, and this makes it difficult to organize and transfer the knowledge to dispersed centres. Person-to-person communication is extremely important in this context (see also Allen, 1977).
- Secrecy is easier to manage when R&D activities are concentrated geographically. In industries where secrecy is paramount, internationalization of R&D is less desirable (see also Reed and de Fillippi, 1990). This argument clearly applies to the pharmaceutical industry.
- As an invisible asset of the firm, R&D is more difficult to manage when it is dispersed (see also Steele, 1989). Closely aligned to this point is Howells' (1987, 1990a, 1992) emphasis on the critical nature of information and communication technologies in coordinating and controlling international R&D activities.

While he does not specifically discuss the locational problem, De Meyer's results support the traditional view (Ronstadt, 1978; Behrman and Fischer, 1979; Hewitt, 1980) of the foreign R&D locational paradigm, which suggests that multinational firms keep R&D at home until confronted by one or a combination of imperatives that lead to foreign location; each new foreign R&D facility is set up with a closely defined role, and this role may develop in a pre-defined way over time. De Meyer's results also underline the need for an evaluative procedure to choose between alternatives. He contends that the key determinant for establishing international R&D networks is the need to create a structure for 'rapid technical learning'; he sees this concept as having three essential ingredients. First, a newly created R&D centre has to build up knowledge credibility because laboratories tend to be judged subjectively by peers in other similar facilities. It is important for industrial centres to have this kind of credibility because the exchange of information within the network is critical to the multinational's overall need to learn internally. Association with a university is one route to this kind of credibility through the halo-effect of the established institution, but this, by itself, is not enough. Long-term credibility can only be underpinned by substantial and appropriate streams of innovation. Second, diversity in approach to R&D must be actively encouraged; it is essential that laboratories in a network have different approaches to research problems. This creates a portfolio of tactics that increases problem-solving capability for the multinational as a whole and increases the rate of technical learning. Third, face-to-face contact is critical to building up confidence between individuals and R&D sites despite the burgeoning use of telecommunications, electronic mail and video-conferencing (see also Casson and Singh, 1993). In stressing the importance of face-to-face contact, De Meyer is giving implied support to the rationale of science parks where such contact is intrinsic and a factor in enabling exchange of confidence.

In summary, while it is clear that science parks have an important role in the creation and diffusion of new knowledge (a role which seems fairly constant from one science park to another), there are also factors that differentiate between them; some of these relate to pharmaceutical R&D and, more specifically, to the locational decision for a new facility. They include incentives for particular locations, local pre-existing centres of excellence with a strong research focus, image and prestige of particular locations, and availability of R&D professionals. Each of these is assessed by one or more of the locational determinants discussed below (see Tables 3.1 and 3.3).

RESEARCH VARIABLES

The basic approach was to use the list of locational determinants developed by Taggart (1991). From the original list of determinants classified into four groups, the 14 most important (as determined by Taggart) were used in this research (see Table 3.1). These are termed 'locational macro-determinants' (to distinguish them from the factors discussed below), and they are used to differentiate between different countries as locations for R&D facilities. The 'Market Factor' group contained four variables:

- High consumption of pharmaceuticals in terms of total national expenditure. High drug consumption in any particular country is related to a perception of greater locational desirability.
- High growth potential of a particular country market; this is clearly linked to locational desirability.
- High strategic importance of the company's presence in this market; this variable was included to pick up a measure of those aspects of corporate locational strategy that were considered as confidential, and where responses to more specific probing may not have been forthcoming.

- High level of competitors' R&D activity in a particular country market; theoretically, this is a powerful locational determinant for a foreign R&D facility. A high level of competitors' R&D activity suggests an attractive research environment, good availability of resources, and an acceptable regulatory regime.

There was one 'General Regulatory Factor' used:

- Efficient patent law has a markedly positive effect on locational attractiveness, as it yields a degree of security to the incoming multinational corporation's (MNC) internalized technology. While a theoretically equivalent level of patent protection is given in each of the three target countries (UK, Germany, Eire), the perceived level varies between companies and individual observers. Differences in perception may be due to country variations in the application of broadly similar legislation, to the differential impact of similar legislation on individual companies, or to a combination of both.

Four 'Pharmaceutical Regulatory Factors' were included:

- High host-government empathy with the pharmaceutical industry is clearly a desirable attribute to the incoming drugs MNC.
- Helpful regulations for new drug development; these vary widely between countries and have been shown to be a major determinant of pharmaceutical R&D activity. This variable appears to have a positive effect on the locational decision.
- Sympathetic drug safety regulations is also an important determinant of pharmaceutical R&D activity, and is likely to have a positive effect on the locational decision. Subsumed within this and the previous variables is the attitude of pharmaceutical MNCs towards the strength of collaboration with the national body of general practitioners in the testing of new drugs.
- Low control of drug prices; the initial price set by a firm for a new drug in the country where the product was originated is a prime determinant of the overall return to be obtained as it acts as a signal to price regulatory bodies in other countries. The degree of control varies indirectly with locational desirability.

The 'Resource Factor' group contained five variables:

- Excellence of tertiary education system; this variable is a recognized predictor of the future supply of scientists, technologists and engineers, and is a vital consideration in the locational decision. Locational desirability will vary directly with this factor.

- High present stock of scientists, technologists and engineers; no matter what the future position may be as forecast by the previous variable, it is likely that high perceptions for this factor are a desirable condition for the locational decision.
- Low relative costs of scientists, technologists and engineers; the argument here is complementary to that for the previous variable.
- Existence of high local technical expertise (e.g. biotechnology in the UK, fermentation and screening in Japan); where this occurs it is likely to have a positive effect on the desirability of a location for specific types of drugs R&D activity.
- High number of new drugs developed in a particular country; it is likely that a desirable location for a new drugs R&D facility will already have proved its effectiveness as an environment for the successful development of new chemical entities by other firms.

Kotler *et al.* (1993) have described the importance of 'softer' factors relating to quality of life, cultural activities, level of crime, proximity to other facilities, etc. that can have a strong bearing on the locational decision. Following this approach, a list of 24 'locational micro-determinants' was developed in detailed discussions with two researchers in, and one professional observer of, the pharmaceutical industry; the micro-determinants included appropriate factors from the first list (see Table 3.3). These are used to differentiate within a particular country between a number of different locations in terms of suitability for R&D facilities. The locational micro-determinants were classified into three groups – general resource factors, pharmaceutical-specific R&D resource factors, and lifestyle factors. The first group included four factors additional to the corresponding group in Table 3.1:

- Local government incentives; this relates to all financial assistance available at a sub-national level from regional, district or city authorities. In public, firms often claim that such incentives are not decisive; the private view is often different.
- Local government assistance; similar to the previous variable, but relates to non-financial assistance, e.g. facility and personnel search, training, introductions to local suppliers.
- Proximity to international airport; visits from R&D executives from HQ and other parts of the MNC network are a prime means of technology transfer in this industry, so a nearby international airport gives a real advantage to a potential regional location.
- Excellent motorway links; access to other company facilities and external research partners within the region/country is also important at many stages of the development of a new chemical entity, so access to the motorway system may be helpful.

The 'Pharmaceutical Factor' group included:

- Availability of science parks; as noted in the foregoing discussion, science parks make excellent locations for free-standing pharmaceutical laboratories, and they undoubtedly boost the appeal of a region with respect to locational desirability.
- Low cost of lab space; this is the one truly fixed cost where productivity increases are extremely difficult to achieve, so the initial cost may, in some cases, be an important determinant.
- Favourable science park incentives; all other things being equal, the array of financial and non-financial incentives specific to any one science park may tip a decision in its favour.
- Turnkey facilities available; again, the chances of a favourable locational decision may be increased by the availability of partly or fully fitted out laboratory space specific to the needs of the pharmaceutical industry.
- Proximity to centre of excellence; depending on the role of the laboratory concerned, the existence of a nearby centre of excellence (university, college, research establishment) may be a critical factor in terms of access to particular skills and/or knowledge.
- Academic image of local universities; perhaps somewhat surprisingly, pharmaceutical firms seems to be keenly aware of – and put a premium on – the status of local tertiary establishments together with their teaching and research assessments.
- Research grants to local universities; as for the previous variable, drugs firms tend to be conscious and appreciative of overall and pharmaceutical-specific research grants to local establishments, whether or not competitor firms are involved.
- Presence of healthcare industry; this refers to the range of facilities present in the locality, e.g. nature and extent of general practice, existence of acute and teaching hospitals, presence of private facilities, together with any established health research institutes.
- High image of healthcare industry; naturally, this varies from one area to another and this concerns an incoming pharmaceutical MNC as it will become a recognized member of the local network.

All of the 'Lifestyle Factor' variables were included on the basis that the key employees of a pharmaceutical R&D facility are, or have aspirations to be, members of the economically defined middle class with the attendant social aims. Incorporated in this group were:

- Proximity to suburbs; the potential R&D facility benefits by being close to an extensive choice of appropriate housing facilities.
- Proximity to countryside; similarly, access to rural areas and pursuits may be a prime discriminating factor in some cases.

- High quality of life; this variable was included to pick up lifestyle aspects missed by the other factors, though this may present some danger of double counting.
- High image as cultural centre; for middle-class, socially aspiring executives in almost any industry, this has become an important feature in the personal relocation issue.
- Low level of crime; this is almost the antithesis of the previous variable, though what is important here is access to low crime environments for executives and their families rather than general low levels of crime throughout the region in question.
- Good environment for children; choice of high quality education is the base factor here, but other child-oriented facilities and resources have a part to play in increasing locational desirability.

METHODOLOGY

A postal survey was considered to be the appropriate method of gathering data for this initial stage of the research, and a list of some forty pharmaceutical firms active in international markets and represented in the UK was drawn up from industry sources. The questionnaire was directed at the Director of R&D in each UK subsidiary and all but one reply were received from the identified individual; for the exceptional case, the job title emphasized a commercial as well as technical aspect. The Director of R&D was chosen as the recipient of the questionnaire after a number of discussions with industry sources, as this executive was felt to be in the best position to answer the broad range of questions involved. It was pointed out during these discussions that, in the event of a company envisaging a new European R&D laboratory, the Director of R&D would be intimately involved in the process.

The pharmaceutical industry is well known for its secretiveness, and a large response was not expected. In the event, ten firms replied to the postal questionnaire, but only six of the questionnaires were completely answered. To fill the gaps, the other four respondents were contacted on the telephone and the missing data discussed. Two of these questionnaires were rejected because, in the view of the interviewer, the respondents did not have the requisite breadth of knowledge to complete the gaps in the questionnaires. Subsequently, the original six respondents were telephoned for a further discussion on the questionnaire data to ensure that they too had given accurate responses with an acceptable degree of comprehension of the issues involved. This led to a total of eight (20 per cent) complete questionnaires, from which the data is thought to be of good quality; this data is analysed below. Great care was taken with the statistical analysis to allow for the small sample size, and for a similar reason caution must applied in interpreting the results. In all, the data capture stage of the research lasted from June 1993 to July 1994.

Respondents were asked to make a judgement about each locational macro- and micro-determinant on a scale of 1 to 7; the questions were designed in such a manner as to ensure that a high reading on each scale corresponded to a favourable or positive view of any particular determinant. Perspectives of each macro-determinant were sought concerning three European countries – the UK, Germany and Eire. According to Taggart (1993), Germany is the favoured European location for a foreign R&D facility within the international pharmaceutical industry, while the UK comes second. Eire was included as it is marketed abroad by the Irish Development Authority as a low-cost location for multinational R&D. Respondents were also asked to judge each micro-determinant on a similar scale of 1 to 7, with high values again reflecting favourable or positive judgements. Perspectives were sought about four UK locations:

- Cambridge for its prominence in the literature, the anecdotal importance ascribed to it, and for the highly successful Cambridge Science Park;
- Cardiff for the two science parks which serve biomedical R&D needs: Imperial Park and Cardiff Medi-Park;
- Edinburgh because it is acclaimed internationally as a centre of excellence in medicine and the existence of the Heriot-Watt University Research Park;
- Glasgow for the excellence of tertiary education in biomedical sciences and the existence of the West of Scotland Science Park.

The eight respondent companies comprised two UK firms (both with extensive foreign operations, including R&D), one continental European firm, one Japanese firm, and four US firms. Seven of the firms were among the world's top thirty pharmaceutical multinationals; the eighth was about half the size of the smallest of the other seven. Despite the difference in size, the eighth firm was similar to its larger counterparts in terms of its organization, its degree of internationalization and, critically, its apparent approach to decentralization of R&D.

RESULTS

Locational Macro-Determinants

The macro-determinants were examined individually and grouped according to Taggart's (1991) classification and mean values calculated. The grouping procedure was deemed acceptable since a principal factors analysis within each grouping of macro-determinants yielded either a one-factor solution, or a solution that could be reduced to one factor explaining at least half the overall variance. Table 3.1 shows the means for all respondents for the macro-determinants individually and grouped. At the aggregate level, it can be seen that the UK is preferred as a foreign R&D location to Germany for all four groups of factors, though the difference is small in each case. This result conflicts with Taggart (1993).

Both countries are preferred over Eire by a large margin, except in the case of patent laws, where all three are viewed as broadly similar. At the level of individual macro-determinants, Germany is preferred to the UK in terms of consumption of pharmaceuticals, growth potential of the market, and the strategic importance of the market; again however, the differences are not large. Eire is the preferred location only for the low cost of scientists, as expected.

Table 3.2 allows more precision concerning the locational benefits of the three countries and identifies the discriminating macro-determinants. At the aggregate level it can be seen how strongly market factors as a whole discriminate between UK and Eire, and between Germany and Eire ($p < 0.000$).

Table 3.1   Mean values of locational macro-determinants

Locational determinant	UK	Germany	Eire
Market factors			
High consumption of pharmaceuticals	4.63	5.00	2.63
High growth potential of market	3.38	3.63	2.25
Market strategically important	4.88	5.00	1.88
High level of competitors' R&D	5.50	4.13	2.00
Mean value – Market factors	*4.59*	*4.44*	*2.19*
General regulatory factors			
Efficient patent laws	6.13	5.88	5.75
Pharmaceutical regulatory factors			
Host government empathy	3.63	3.00	4.25
Helpful regulations for new chemical entities	4.88	4.63	4.38
Sympathetic safety regulations	3.50	3.50	3.13
Low control of drug prices	3.13	2.38	3.25
Mean value – Pharmaceutical regulatory factors	*3.78*	*3.38*	*3.75*
Resource factors			
Excellence of tertiary education	5.50	5.38	4.13
High stock of scientists	5.63	5.50	3.38
Low cost of scientists	4.75	3.38	5.63
High technical expertise	6.00	5.63	3.38
High number of new drugs developed	5.75	4.38	1.50
Mean value – Resource factors	*5.53*	*4.85*	*3.60*

Source: Research questionnaire.

Table 3.2 t-tests on comparisons of locational macro-determinants

Locational Determinant	UK vs Germany		UK vs Eire		Germany vs Eire	
	t-score	p-value	t-score	p-value	t-score	p-value
Market factors						
High consumption of pharmaceuticals						
High growth potential of market						
Market strategically important	3.667	0.008	6.000	0.000	6.157	0.000
High level of competitors' R&D			13.096	0.000	9.379	0.000
Mean			*6.871*	*0.000*	*10.392*	*0.000*
General regulatory factors						
Efficient patent laws						
Pharmaceutical regulatory factors						
Host government empathy					−3.416	0.011
Helpful regulations for new chemical entities						
Sympathetic safety regulations						
Low control of drug prices	2.393	0.048			−2.497	0.041
Mean						
Resource factors						
Excellence of tertiary education			3.667	0.008	3.416	0.011
High stock of scientists			4.025	0.005	4.123	0.004
Low cost of scientists					−3.473	0.010
High technical expertise			6.251	0.000	4.025	0.005
High number of new drugs developed	4.245	0.004	10.319	0.000	7.221	0.000
Mean	*4.000*	*0.005*	*6.471*	*0.003*	*3.751*	*0.007*

Only p-values <0.05 are shown.
t-test for correlated samples.
Source: Research questionnaire.

Resource factors as a whole discriminate across the board, though somewhat less powerfully, showing the UK preferred to both Germany and Eire, and Germany clearly preferred to Eire. At a more detailed level, two macro-determinants discriminate across the board: high level of competitors' R&D and the high number of new drugs developed. The UK is further preferred over Germany for drug price control and over Eire for the strategic importance of the national market, excellence of tertiary education, high stock of scientists and high local technical expertise. These last four macro-determinants also indicate that Germany is strongly preferred over Eire as a location for pharmaceutical R&D. Finally, there are three macro-determinants that indicate a preference for Eire over Germany: host government empathy, drug price control, and low cost of scientists. Thus, Table 3.2 emphasizes and clarifies the results in Table 3.1: the UK emerges as the clearly favoured location for pharmaceutical R&D followed by Germany, with Eire following in a very poor third place.

Locational Micro-Determinants

A similar analytical procedure was followed with the micro-determinants and the basic results are shown in Table 3.3. At the aggregate level, Cambridge emerges as the most preferred location for pharmaceutical R&D whether measured by general resource factors, pharmaceutical resource factors or lifestyle factors. Similarly, Cardiff is the least preferred location on all three broad parameters. Edinburgh and Glasgow fall between the two with the former a stronger candidate except in respect of general resource factors.

Within the broad groupings of micro-determinants there are some interesting variations from the overall pattern. Cambridge performs relatively poorly (and Glasgow relatively well) in terms of the cost of scientists and lab space, the availability of local government incentives in general and science park incentives in particular, and in proximity to the countryside. Cardiff shows up best for its excellent motorway links and worst for the low level of pharmaceutical R&D current *in situ*. Edinburgh's strengths lie in its proximity to suburbs, its perceived high quality of life, and its image as a cultural centre (all lifestyle factors). Besides the counter-points noted above about Cambridge, Glasgow has the additional benefit of proximity to an international airport; it performs poorly in terms of a low image of the local healthcare industry, proximity to suburbs, and a relatively high perceived level of crime.

Table 3.4 shows the results of a more detailed analysis of the locational micro-determinants; it makes comparisons between the various locations and helps to define the discriminatory micro-determinants. Only statistically significant results ($p < 0.05$) are shown in this table.

Table 3.3   Mean values of locational micro-determinants

Locational determinant	Cambridge	Cardiff	Edinburgh	Glasgow
General factors				
Low cost of scientists	3.88	4.88	4.63	5.00
High stock of scientists	5.75	3.13	4.25	4.50
Excellent tertiary education	5.75	4.13	5.00	5.00
Presence of competitors' R&D	4.13	1.88	2.38	2.13
Local government incentives	3.00	3.50	3.50	4.00
Local government assistance	3.75	3.38	3.75	3.75
Proximity to international airport	3.63	2.88	3.75	4.13
Excellent motorway links	4.38	4.50	3.63	3.88
Mean value – General factors	*4.28*	*3.53*	*3.86*	*4.05*
Pharmaceutical factors				
Availability of science parks	5.13	2.13	3.38	3.38
Low cost of lab space	3.63	5.00	5.00	5.38
Favourable science park incentives	3.13	4.38	4.50	4.88
Turnkey facilities available	4.13	3.00	3.25	3.50
Proximity to centre of excellence	5.88	3.50	4.50	4.13
Relevant areas of excellence	5.50	3.50	3.63	4.00
Academic image of local universities	6.38	3.63	5.00	4.63
Research grants to local universities	4.63	3.00	3.75	3.63
Presence of healthcare industry	3.63	2.13	3.13	3.13
High image of healthcare industry	4.25	3.38	4.00	3.13
Mean value – Pharmaceutical factors	*4.63*	*3.63*	*4.01*	*3.98*
Lifestyle factors				
Proximity to suburbs	4.13	3.88	4.25	3.63
Proximity to countryside	3.88	4.00	4.00	4.13
High quality of life	4.38	3.38	4.38	3.75
High image as cultural centre	5.13	3.00	5.13	3.38
Low level of crime	3.63	3.00	3.50	2.75
Good environment for children	4.63	3.63	4.13	3.75
Mean value – Lifestyle factors	*4.29*	*3.48*	*4.23*	*3.56*

Source: Research questionnaire.

At once, the overwhelmingly strong position of Cambridge can be seen. It is considered to be a better location for pharmaceutical R&D than any of Cardiff, Edinburgh or Glasgow in respect of possessing a high stock of scientists, the presence of competitors' R&D facilities, the availability of science parks and turnkey facilities within them, proximity to a centre of excellence with a high academic image and sub-areas of academic excellence relevant to the pharmaceutical industry. In addition, it is considered to be superior to both Cardiff and Glasgow for research grants to local universities, high image of the local healthcare industry, high quality of life,

Table 3.4 t-test on locational comparisons of micro-determinants

Locational determinant	Camb vs Card		Camb vs Edin		Camb vs Glas		Card vs Edin		Card vs Glas		Edin vs Glas	
	t-score	p-value	t-score	p-value	t-score	p-value	t-score	p-value	t-score	p-value	t-score	p-value
General factors												
Low cost of scientists	-5.292	0.001			-3.211	0.015			-3.274	0.014		
High stock of scientists	5.274	0.001	3.000	0.020	2.758	0.028			-2.497	0.041		
Excellent tertiary education	2.876	0.024	2.393	0.048								
Presence of competitors' R&D	4.277	0.004	3.564	0.009	4.000	0.005						
Local government incentives					-3.742	0.007						
Local government assistance												
Proximity to international airport									-2.758	0.028		
Excellent motorway links												
Mean	*3.174*	*0.016*	*2.958*	*0.021*							*-2.622*	*0.034*
Pharmaceutical factors												
Availability of science parks	4.243	0.004	3.862	0.006	4.782	0.002	-2.546	0.038	-2.376	0.049		
Low cost of lab space	-4.245	0.004	-3.667	0.008	-3.564	0.009						
Favourable science park incentives	-7.638	0.000	-5.227	0.001	-5.584	0.001						
Turnkey facilities available	3.211	0.015	2.966	0.021	2.376	0.049						
Proximity to centre of excellence	4.204	0.004	2.582	0.036	3.862	0.006						
Relevant areas of excellence	2.646	0.033	3.230	0.014	3.000	0.020						
Academic image of local universities	6.068	0.001	5.227	0.001	5.584	0.001	-2.986	0.020				
Research grants to local universities	3.529	0.010			3.055	0.018						
Presence of healthcare industry	3.550	0.009					-3.742	0.007	-2.646	0.033		
High image of healthcare industry	2.966	0.021			2.553	0.038						
Mean	*5.140*	*0.001*	*3.660*	*0.008*	*3.822*	*0.007*	*-4.266*	*0.004*	*-3.918*	*0.006*		
Lifestyle factors												
Proximity to suburbs												
Proximity to countryside												
High quality of life	3.055	0.018			3.416	0.011	-3.055	0.018			3.416	0.011
High image as cultural centre	4.822	0.002			5.584	0.001	-5.338	0.001			4.782	0.002
Low level of crime					2.497	0.041						
Good environment for children	2.646	0.033			3.862	0.006						
Mean	*3.825*	*0.007*			*7.314*	*0.000*	*-2.913*	*0.023*			*3.983*	*0.005*

Only *p*-values <0.05 are shown.
t-tests for correlated samples.
Source: Research questionnaire.

image as a cultural centre, and as a good environment for children. Finally, Cambridge is superior to Cardiff for the presence of a viable local health-care industry and to Glasgow for its perceived level of crime.

Cambridge also has some disadvantages in comparison with the other centres: laboratory space is more expensive and science park occupation incentives are less favourable than any of Cardiff, Edinburgh or Glasgow; and the cost of R&D scientists is significantly lower in Cardiff and Glasgow.

Leaving Cambridge aside, comparisons between the other centres show fewer statistically significant differences. The most noticeable feature of this part of the analysis is that where significant differences do occur they show Cardiff at a disadvantage to either or both of the Scottish locations. Thus, Cardiff appears to compare unfavourably as a pharmaceutical R&D location against both Edinburgh and Glasgow in terms of the local stock of scientists, the quality of its tertiary education, availability of science parks, and presence of a local healthcare industry. In comparison with Edinburgh alone, Cardiff appears to under-perform in the academic image of its universities, its general quality of life, and its image as a cultural centre. The comparison with Glasgow alone is poor only in terms of proximity to an international airport.

Direct comparisons between Edinburgh and Glasgow devolve to lifestyle factors and, in particular, to quality of life and image as a cultural centre. In both cases, Edinburgh is significantly preferred to Glasgow.

DISCUSSION

Locational Macro-Determinants

According to Taggart (1993), Germany is the most favoured location for a new pharmaceutical R&D facility in Europe, closely followed by the UK; the data for that study was gathered during 1986. The data for this chapter, gathered in 1993/94, suggest that the relative positions of the UK and Germany have changed. This may reflect an actual change in the perspective of drug multinationals over the intervening years, it may reflect an effect due to the different firms (and different number of firms) involved in the two studies, or it may embody the impact of a marginal change in research methodology. Perhaps the most likely interpretation is that these two sets of results indicate how similar the two countries are at the aggregate level as loci of pharmaceutical R&D, and how difficult drug multinationals find it to differentiate effectively between the two. It is precisely in this type of situation that appropriate policy responses by national governments and regional development agencies can have a disproportionately positive effect. Governments can have little impact, except in the long term, on any of the four market factors. Regional development agencies, on the other hand, can have a substantial effect by enhancing the positive and playing down the negative perceptions held by multinationals, especially of the strategic importance of the market and of the high level of competitors' R&D within the country. The first of these perceptions encourages non-participating multinationals to 'follow-my-leader' in the sense of Knickerbocker (1973). A perception of high levels of competitors' R&D relates partly to the Knickerbocker effect, but also acts as a clear signal to the prospectively inward investing multinational that other drug firms have already found a particular country to be a very effective locus of R&D operations (Taggart, 1991).

Efficient patent laws must be viewed in the nature of a 'hygiene' factor (Herzberg *et al.*, 1959); if they are not properly structured and policed – that is, if there is dissatisfaction among drug multinationals with the effective working of patent laws – they cease to increase the attractiveness of the country as a potential R&D location and become instead a strong deterrent. The effective policy response to patent law problems will increase protection of intellectual property rights associated with the outputs of R&D. This kind of action may be the result of awareness and self-motivation, it may be at the behest of the numerous and highly effective drug industry pressure groups, or it could even be the outcome of prompting and influence of regional development agencies.

Turning to pharmaceutical regulatory factors, the general level of perceptions of both Germany and the UK is on the low side, and there seems to be a particular need for improved marketing by both governments in terms of empathy with the pharmaceutical industry. It is almost inconceivable that governments actually feel hostile towards a high technology industry that, in both countries, represents a substantial proportion of overall exports as well as being a major employer of high quality labour. Nevertheless, it is evident that drug firms are not happy with industry–government relationships in either country, and this is probably due to governments' attempts to reduce or, at least, stabilize, soaring health care costs over the last fifteen years. There is a clear opportunity for either government to close this gap in perceptions, and an important international competitive advantage could accrue to the country that makes the pharmaceutical industry feel more welcome. Precisely the same argument applies to control of drug prices. Germany has suffered comparatively in this respect due to the pressing need to reduce or control the national drug bill, but the main problem in both countries may be that government action is seen as almost random in its direction and effect, and seems to be carried out with little thought given to the economic impact on the industry or to the future impact on technological development. Regional development agencies may have a part to play in convincing governments that the pleading of industry pressure groups and firms is not altogether self-serving when they look for reasonable price control mechanisms and more encouragement to invest in R&D.

Resource factors are generally highly rated in both countries, though the cost of scientists is a source of some concern to pharmaceutical firms. The obvious response here for governments and regional development agencies is to persuade firms of the higher productivity of more expensive scientists and, in this, the UK currently has a strong argument in the firms' perceptions that a higher number of new drugs has been discovered there than in Germany. At a time when costs of new R&D facilities are growing rapidly and the outputs from pharmaceutical R&D no longer automatically flow from higher front-end investment, this particular macro-determinant operates as a 'feel-good' factor for an international pharmaceutical firm contemplating a new foreign R&D facility. The number of new drugs discovered in a country in the past cannot, of course, reduce current or future risk levels but, in an area where technological forecasting is so difficult, track record may be a critical – if entirely subjective – differentiating variable.

Finally, it is sufficient to note that Eire is so far behind Germany and the UK as to make policy prescriptions almost entirely redundant. It is difficult to envisage what realistic strategy the Irish government could follow that would have any noticeable effect on the perceptions of pharmaceutical multinationals concerning foreign R&D facilities. Table 3.2 shows where the gaps are particularly large and the Irish government would find the market factors virtually impossible to move in its favour; the shift in national resources needed to achieve parity in the resource factors would be wholly disproportionate to any likely economic benefit, and further improvement in pharmaceutical regulatory factors would be unlikely to achieve significant (or any) competitive advantage in terms of footloose drug R&D.

Locational Micro-Determinants

The UK government has no especial desire for a new multinational R&D facility – or any other type of multinational subsidiary – to be located in any particular part of the country, at least if its public pronouncements are to be taken at face value. The task of pleading the case for individual areas is, therefore, almost wholly the preserve of regional development agencies although, in the specific case of pharmaceutical R&D, local government and universities may also have a specialized part to play. It is clear from the results of this research that many of them face difficult, maybe impossible, tasks in persuading footloose drug R&D investments to locate in their areas. Table 3.3 not only demonstrates how far Cambridge is ahead of the other three areas, it also indicates just how clearly pharmaceutical multinationals are able to differentiate between the claims of different locations. Thus, while it cannot be concluded that Cambridge is the most attractive location in the UK, it is obviously a very attractive location indeed. Of the twenty-four micro-determinants, Cambridge has the highest or joint highest score on sixteen, Glasgow on seven, Edinburgh on four, and Cardiff on one. Cambridge's attractions are spread across all three groups of factors, while Glasgow is strong in general factors and Edinburgh on lifestyle factors. Cardiff's case in UK terms is thus as weak as Eire's case on a European scale; its attractions are wholly financial and it is not easy to suggest policy prescriptions that the Welsh Development Agency might follow that would put Cardiff in the frame.

With regard to Edinburgh and Glasgow, Table 3.4 shows the magnitude of the task involved in offering significant counter-attractions to Cambridge. In common with Cardiff, Scottish locations have some financial advantages, but these are not likely to be critical in the inward investment location decision. The most obvious policy prescription would involve the Glasgow Development Agency (GDA) stressing those general factors where Glasgow already has perceived strengths, and Lothian and Edinburgh Enterprise Ltd (LEEL) stressing lifestyle advantages. For both agencies, however, this can be only part of the strategy as, taken alone, these factors would be unlikely to persuade potential inward investors.

These agencies must also give some attention to the 'hygiene factor' dimension of certain of the locational micro-determinants. It should be remembered that the measurements underlying Table 3.4 are perceptions and, as such, are susceptible to improved marketing and focused publicity. Thus, in attempting to increase competitive advantage *vis-à-vis* Cambridge, both GDA and LEEL would be well advised to concentrate on correcting impressions within the international pharmaceutical industry that may be reducing the profiles of Glasgow and Edinburgh; this would include consideration of tertiary education, available local government assistance, availability of science parks and associated facilities, and the excellence and academic image of local universities (particularly in bio-sciences). More particularly, the GDA could devote some attention to the image of the local healthcare industry specifically, perhaps, the damaging publicity over HCI (the troubled private hospital in Clydebank), and to the perennial problem of Glasgow's image in terms of lifestyle factors. This last point is highlighted in the direct comparison between Glasgow and Edinburgh; broadly, they have similar attractions as potential locations for pharmaceutical R&D facilities except in the area of lifestyle factors, where Edinburgh has a highly significant lead in quality of life and cultural activities.

CONCLUSIONS

The first objective of this research was to re-visit the locational macro-determinants evolved by Taggart (1991), using three European countries as a test-bed, to evaluate their continuing utility. Fourteen of the original macro-determinants were used. Three of these were found to be powerfully discriminating between the two most similar countries tested (Germany and the UK); these macro-determinants were the level of competitors' R&D within the country, the degree of drug price control, and the number of new drugs developed. Six other macro-determinants were found to discriminate between Germany and Eire and/or UK and Eire: the strategic importance of the national market to the pharmaceutical multinational, the extent of host government empathy with the industry, helpfulness of regulations governing the testing and introduction of new chemical entities, excellence of national tertiary education, high stock of R&D scientists, and the existence of relevant high technical expertise within the country. Efficient patent laws did not emerge as a discriminating factor, almost certainly because this is viewed in the nature of a 'hygiene factor' by the pharmaceutical industry; unless it exists to an acceptable degree in a particular country, no other combination of locational macro-determinants can make that country an acceptable location for a new R&D facility.

The second objective was to evaluate the three countries as potential locations for new pharmaceutical R&D facilities. Eire emerged in a poor position from this comparison, and no combination of realistic policy initiatives is likely to change this position in the foreseeable future. The UK seems to be viewed more favourably than Germany in the current environment, reversing the position found in earlier research (Taggart, 1993). However, the countries are so close that no firm conclusion could be drawn on the basis of a limited sample of companies. In such a situation, governments and regional development agencies can play an important role in winning footloose R&D investments by marketing more effectively the positive perceptions of their countries, and taking action (where feasible) to improve the negative perceptions. In particular, either country could improve its competitive advantage in this field by improving the general relationship with the pharmaceutical industry, and by re-emphasizing productivity of existing – albeit high-cost – drug R&D facilities.

The third objective was to evaluate the discriminant power of a list of twenty-four locational micro-determinants when used to distinguish between the attractiveness of four UK sites as locations for new pharmaceutical R&D facilities. All ten of those classed as 'pharmaceutical factors' were found to be powerful discriminators. Four 'lifestyle factors' were found to be similarly useful (proximity to suburbs and proximity to countryside did not discriminate) and six 'general factors' (excluding local government assistance and excellent motorway links). Although the sample of companies was not large, the evidence of this research suggests that locational micro-determinants are a most useful supplementary tool to the use of locational macro-determinants.

The fourth objective was to evaluate Cambridge, Cardiff, Edinburgh and Glasgow as potential locations for new pharmaceutical R&D facilities. It should be noted, however, that the results apply specifically to the science park in each city as an R&D location. Cambridge emerged as the undisputed leader and is difficult to envisage how even neglect by local authorities and regional development agencies could erode this position in the medium term. Cardiff is at the opposite end of the scale as determined by the perceptions of the firms that took part in this research, and it is so far behind that effective policy prescriptions are elusive. Edinburgh and Glasgow take up intermediate positions, though they cannot yet be regarded as effective competitors to Cambridge without substantial infrastructure and marketing initiatives by local authorities and regional development agencies. However, in the Scotland-only choice, Glasgow would be likely to emerge ahead of Edinburgh unless undue weight was given to lifestyle micro-determinants.

Finally, the results in this chapter yield little support for the view that cost of R&D personnel is a key macro-determinant of the international location decision for pharmaceutical R&D facilities; in addition, it plays little part in the within-country micro-locational decision. Taken together with other evidence (Casson and Singh, 1993; De Meyer, 1993; Taggart, 1993) it suggests strongly that intellectual labour costs matter little in an industry where long-term competitive advantage and success are limited only by the ability to innovate.

References

Allen, T.J. (1977) *Managing the Flow of Technology* (Cambridge, MA: MIT Press).
Behrman, J.N. and W.A. Fischer (1979) 'The co-ordination of foreign R&D activities by transnational corporations', *Journal of International Business Studies*, 10(3), pp. 29–35.
Casson, M. and S. Singh (1993) 'Corporate research and development strategies: the influence of firm, industry and country factors on the decentralisation of R&D', *R&D Management*, 23(2), pp. 91–107.
Cheng, J.L.C. and D.S. Bolon (1993) 'The management of multinational R&D: a neglected topic in international business research', *Journal of International Business Studies*, 24(1), pp. 1–18.
Clark, K.B. (1985) 'The interaction of design hierarchies and market concept in technological evaluation', *Research Policy*, 4, pp. 235–51.
De Meyer, A. (1993) 'Management of an international network of industrial R&D laboratories', *R&D Management*, 23(2), pp. 109–20.
Drucker, P.F. (1989) *The New Realities* (London: Heinemann).
Drucker, P.F. (1992) *Managing for the Future* (Oxford: Butterworth-Heinemann).
Herzberg, F., B. Mausner and R.B. Snyderman (1959) *The Motivation to Work* (New York: John Wiley & Sons, Inc.).
Hewitt, G. (1980) 'Research and development performed abroad by US manufacturing multinationals', *Kyklos*, 33(2), pp. 308–27.
Howells, J. (1987) *Technology Innovation, Industrial Organisation and the Location of Services in the European Community*, FAST Occasional Paper No. 142, Brussels, Commission of the European Community.

Howells, J. (1990a) 'The internationalisation of R&D and the development of global research networks', *Regional Studies*, 24(6), pp. 495–512.

Howells, J. (1990b) 'The location and organisation of research and development: new horizons', *Research Policy*, 19, pp. 133–46.

Howells, J. (1990c) 'The globalisation of research and development: a new era of change?', *Science and Public Policy*, 17, pp. 273–85.

Howells, J. (1992) 'Pharmaceuticals and Europe 1992: the dynamics of industrial change', *Environment and Planning A*, 24, pp. 33–48.

Knickerbocker, F.T. (1973) *Oligopolistic Reaction and the Multinational Enterprise* (Boston: Harvard University Press).

Kotler, P., G.L. Lilien and K. Sridhar Moorthy (1993) *Marketing Models* (Englewood Cliffs, N.J.: Prentice-Hall).

Monck, C.S.P., P. Quintas, R.B. Porter, D.J. Storey and P. Wynarczyk (1988) *Science Parks and the Growth of High Technology Firms* (London: Croom Helm).

Porter, M.E. (1990) *Competitive Advantage of Nations* (New York: Free Press).

Reed, R. and R.J. de Fillippi (1990) 'Causal ambiguity barriers to imitation and sustainable competitive advantage, *Academy of Management Preview*, 19, pp. 38–102.

Ronstadt, R.C. (1978) 'International R&D: the establishment and evolution of research and development abroad by seven US multinationals', *Journal of International Business Studies*, 9(1), pp. 7–24.

Schnee, J.E. (1978) 'International shifts in innovative activity: the case of pharmaceuticals', *Columbia Journal of World Business*, Spring, pp. 112–21.

Steele, H.W. (1989) *Managing Technology: The Strategic View* (New York: McGraw-Hill).

Taggart, J.H. (1989) 'The pharmaceutical industry: sending R&D abroad, *Multinational Business*, Spring, pp. 10–15.

Taggart, J.H. (1991) 'Determinants of the foreign R&D location decision in the pharmaceutical industry', *R&D Management* 21(3), pp. 229–40.

Taggart, J.H. (1993) *The World Pharmaceutical Industry* (London: Routledge).

Teece, D. (1987) 'Profiting from technological innovation: implications for integration, elaboration, licensing and public policy', *Research Policy*, 15, pp. 285–305.

Terpstra, V. (1977) 'International product policy: the role of foreign R&D', *Columbia Journal of World Business*, Winter, pp. 24–32.

Van Dierdonck, R., K. Debackere and M. Rappa (1991) 'An assessment of science parks: towards a better understanding of their role in the diffusion of technological knowledge', *R&D Management*, 21(2), pp. 109–23.

4 Working with Organizational Complexity and Diversity: An Empirical Study of the Formation and Evolution of a European–Japanese International Joint Venture

Diana Rosemary Sharpe[1]

INTRODUCTION

International joint ventures are becoming increasingly popular as a form of strategic alliance, or cooperative strategy, but their failure rate is widely recognized as being high (Killing, 1982; Kogut, 1988). This form of cooperative strategy involves the interaction of organization systems that bring with them their own cultures, organization and management practices (Shenkar and Zeira, 1987). The influence of environmental factors on the structures and processes of an organization will be more complex in the case of an international joint venture, with the relative influences of parent organization environments and the local environment open to empirical investigation to identify the nature and extent of any national business systems influence (Whitley, 1992, 1994), 'societal effect' on the joint venture's structures and processes (Maurice, Sorge and Warner, 1980; Sorge and Maurice, 1993) or other potential pressures for or against organizational isomorphism (DiMaggio and Powell, 1983; Orru, Biggart and Hamilton, 1991).

The objective of this chapter is to present an in-depth analysis of one international joint venture (IJV) operating across two organizational sites in the UK. As a 'tri-national joint venture' it is particularly interesting, there being little research on this type of joint venture although it has been found to be fraught with performance difficulties (Makino, 1995). The chapter aims to present the challenges faced by the joint venture organization and its members operating in a multi-cultural context and to examine the way that opportunities for learning in the joint venture are managed across both sites.

Methods

Findings are based on a combination of interviews across the organizations with senior managers and an extended period of work over a total of fifteen months in the two organizations as an unskilled shop-floor worker. An Italian–Japanese joint venture in the car industry was chosen for the study, providing an ideal opportunity to explore the interaction of two multinational organizations from very different business systems with different institutional, economic and cultural environments in their home countries. Interest in exploring Japanese activity in international joint ventures also derives from ongoing debates on the transferability of Japanese management practices into Western management systems (for example, Cool and Lengnick-Hall, 1985; Florida and Kenney, 1991; Abo, 1994; Morris, and Wilkinson, 1995; Dedoussis, 1995).

THE CASE ORGANIZATIONS

Structure of the Parent Organizations and the International Joint Venture

The joint venture is a Japanese–Italian joint venture in the car industry. The Japanese parent company, ABC Japan, employs almost 50 000 employees

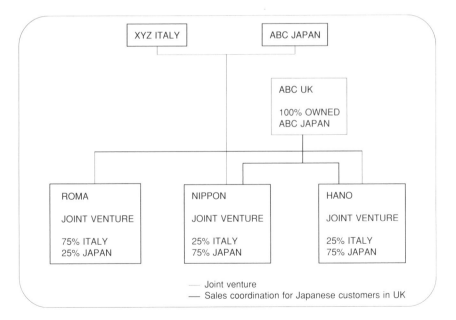

Figure 4.1   An Italian–Japanese international joint venture

world-wide. It currently has three European production facilities including the UK venture. The Italian parent company, XYZ Italy, currently employs approximately 20000 employees world-wide. Figure 4.1 shows the structure of the joint venture. There are three legs to it, with Nippon and Hano located in the UK and a third leg located in Italy. This chapter is based on a study of the two UK legs of the international joint venture.

Nippon and Hano provided an interesting contrast. Nippon was established on a greenfield site following the signing of the international joint venture agreement by the two parent organizations. In contrast Hano was originally purchased by the Japanese parent whilst it was an ongoing concern under British ownership. On entering into the joint venture agreement, the Italian parent became a joint shareholder in the organization. Having a greenfield and a brownfield site has made it possible to research the influence of existing practice on the evolution of structures and processes in the joint venture. This chapter focuses on the challenges faced by management and the way that diversity is received and responded to across the two sites.

The Process of Establishing the Joint Venture

Nippon and Hano are part of a three-legged European joint venture between ABC Japan and XYZ Italy. At the beginning of the 1990s ABC Japan concluded an agreement to form Nippon as a joint venture for production in the car component industry. ABC Japan has a majority shareholding in the Nippon venture, holding 75 per cent of the stock, XYZ Italy holding 25 per cent. As part of the agreement the two parent companies had a reciprocal stock purchase. The Italian parent bought 25 per cent of Hano, the Japanese parent's wholly owned factory in the north of England, and the Japanese parent bought a 25 per cent share in Roma, the Italian parent's wholly owned subsidiary for the production of car components in Italy (see Figure 4.1).

The Strategic Choice of Partner for the Joint Venture

The use of an IJV form of organization, it is often argued, results in additional costs from shared decision-making and coordination of partners, leading to the assumption that an organization typically attempts to form an IJV only if perceived additional benefits outweigh costs (Geringer, 1991). Partner selection is then influenced by the perceived critical success factors that are required to achieve objectives and the extent to which these can be strengthened through entering into a venture with a potential partner. In the joint venture between ABC Japan and XYZ Italy. The offensive strategy (Dunning, 1993), in which Japanese exporters have attempted to turn themselves into 'insiders' in the major markets of the world, characterized the Japanese partner's strategy of gaining entry into Europe with an attempt to build on the locational advantages provided through having a base in Europe and a partner who had firm access to the European market. Factors pushing for local production by the Japanese partner included the long-term thinking regarding the rate of penetration into a market which was seen as impossible by exporting only. There was a perceived need to be present on the ground in the market in which the organization was working, so that the research and development and engineering localized at the same rate as production. The political pressure to increase local content levels in the car industry in Europe (Dunning, 1993) was influential in encouraging the Japanese partner to enter into local production in Europe. The joint venture could be seen as a strategy that captures the locational advantages offered in Europe as a production base brought about by the potential market in the European Community.

An interest in the European market place and a desire to support the Japanese transplants in Europe influenced the Japanese partner's decision to enter into a joint venture agreement with the Italian organization. The Japanese partner did not have the experience in Europe and needed a partner that would help open doors and also provide some extra volume of production to assist the company in the start-up phase, to create the size of facility that could deal with the long-term production plans. The Italian partner considered itself to be lacking in technology within its product base and therefore a technology agreement with the Japanese, and the opportunity for gaining insights into their manufacturing methods, were the motivations behind the Italian partner's interest in the joint venture. The strategic importance of the joint venture for the Japanese partner was seen to lie in the ability to penetrate what was perceived as a totally undeveloped Western European market place. For the Italian partner it meant survival within the product range, as existing technology was not considered sufficient to take them past the end of the decade. Such potential benefits to each partner from the cooperation led to the joint venture being judged as very complementary rather than competitive in nature, although at the most senior level in each parent company the relationship becomes that of Toyota and Fiat who have respective shareholdings in the organizations.

While the Japanese partner's strongest competencies were its product design technology, manufacturing and engineering experience, and ability to relate to and draw upon previous relationships with the Japanese transplants in Europe, for the Italian partner the knowledge of the Western European market was a significant competence. Through the venture the Japanese partner was able to achieve business in Europe that, as one director interviewed outlined, would not have been possible without the venture (Geringer, 1991). The partners have divided Europe into two sections. The technology transfer agreement between the two parents, is less easily analyzed in terms of ownership or locational advantages (Dunning

1993). The agreement could be considered to weaken the traditional ownership advantages of the Japanese production techniques and technological
competencies. However, these are now becoming more difficult to protect
anyway because of replication by competitors. The need to localize production in key markets offering a non-Japanese customer base is increasing the
importance of locational advantages in the industry. If an ownership advantage were to be defined as a competence or potential to develop technology
rather than to possess a specific technology, then the transfer of technology
agreement would not undermine the strength of the Japanese partner,
in this case study, in having the competence to continue to develop and
upgrade its technology. This would support the view of competencies as
information-based invisible assets (Itami, 1987). Knowledge and experience
of the European market would be such a competence for the Italian partner, whilst technological capability would be a competence of the Japanese
partner.

LEARNING TO MANAGE DIVERSITY IN THE JOINT VENTURE

The entry into the joint venture by the two partners provided the opportunity to learn from the organizational practices of the other partner. In this
chapter it is argued that a societal effect (Sorge and Maurice, 1993) may
be interacting with an organizational effect (Mueller, 1994), in a process
where local institutional and value frameworks mediate the degree to which
the organizations can transfer management practices from the parents to
the joint venture.

The Greenfield Site: Nippon

Managing Diversity at Board Level
Following the signing of the joint venture agreement a board of directors
was established, with the chairman, appointed by the Japanese parent,
located in the European HQ in Holland, a Japanese-parent-appointed
managing director on site, and a non-executive director based in Japan.
The Italian parent appointed the director/general manager. The two board
members therefore remaining on site in Nippon were the Japanese-parent-
appointed managing director and the Italian-parent-appointed director and
general manager. The Italian general manager had over nineteen years of
experience in the car industry in Europe with previous experience in international joint ventures in Europe. The Japanese managing director had
considerable experience in setting up the parent organization's operations
outside of Japan including responsibility for the establishment of the
Australian subsidiary. The composition of the board was important in
Nippon, as it led to a situation in which decisions regarding the manage-

ment of the company tended to be made between the Japanese managing director, the Italian representative as director and general manager and the senior management team. The senior management team included a local national responsible for personnel and administration, appointed by the Italian representative on the board, and two expatriates from the Japanese parent responsible for manufacturing and production engineering and finance, appointed by the Japanese parent. On this greenfield site it was considered by the partners as a strategic decision to employ a local senior manager to run the personnel function as there was a realisation that the 'people issue' in the UK was different from that in Japan and therefore they needed someone with experience and knowledge of the local scene. A local manufacturing manager was therefore appointed early on, in line with other Japanese subsidiaries in the area which had followed a similar practice.

The location chosen for the greenfield 'Nippon' site was a growing manufacturing new town in England, offering good road links and an available supply of local labour. Wage rates were favourable in the region compared with other potential areas, and the local labour force was described as very flexible and willing to adapt, the town having had a history of rapid industrial change to become an expanding manufacturing centre.

Creating a position on the board for the Italian minority shareholder, with responsibility for finance and personnel, was a strategic decision to enable the minority shareholder to achieve some influence and control in the organization. In interviews with the two representatives the strategy was said to be working well, and in Japan the venture was said to be looked upon as their most successful to date. A critical success factor identified by the Italian board member was the need for a good personal relationship between the representatives of each partner on the board – 'smoothing troubled waters when any problems occur'. The challenges he was faced with were seen as 'keeping both sides of the fence happy at the same time, in the face of frequently conflicting short-term objectives'.

The conflicts that arose regarding short-term objectives were considered to be driven by the different business systems and cultures of the two organizations. Using the words of the Italian board director:

> Whereas the Japanese culture and ABC Japan says let's treat our baby with kid gloves and support them financially as best we can, give them sufficient cash resources to ensure them a smoother start-up, my Italian colleagues much as they would like me to do it, it isn't in their culture.

Such a board structure does place a lot of pressure on the minority board member. In his own words: 'It is a very difficult role . . . there is the sheer stressfulness of operating a company where you are an outsider, but expected by your parent company to be totally involved'.

The differences in supplier–customer relations between the two parents' ultimate stakeholders, Fiat and Toyota, is reflected in an example given of Fiat unexpectedly increasing orders significantly without giving any pre-advice or warning. In the general manager's words: 'the Japanese can't understand that, you know . . . why weren't we involved back in the early days when they had the first inkling that this was going to happen?'

A further issue to be dealt with by the partners at board level was the management of employment relations. Whilst shareholders of the parent companies were seen as having 'cultural expectations of practices and out-comes', the hands-on operational management problem in the joint venture was again smoothed out between the two key representatives of the part-ners on the board. Though on the surface many employment practices in the company could be interpreted as being associated with a Japanese form of management system, the general manager notes that:

> somewhere along the line things have been modified, things have been changed to suit our requirements here . . . on the Japanese side there are some difficulties in understanding and accepting that the employee rela-tions and the culture, the inherent culture in operator level type of people in this country and specifically in this area, is completely different to that in Japan . . . last year we had an average of 4 per cent absenteeism for example. Now that's not bad by local regional standards, but I don't find it acceptable and the Japanese can't get over it.

The influence of the Japanese partner on the decision-making style at senior management level is clearly highlighted by one senior manager:

> In a British company the managing director would make a decision off the seat of his pants very often you know; people would say it is a crazy decision but at the end of the day they would get on with it. In this company the M.D. may well have his own view but he would not just make a decision, he would get interested parties round the table and spend hours discussing the issues and often after that discussion his view might have started to be modified.

During the research it was possible to explore further the particular decision-making style that was passed down the organization under the influence of the Japanese managing director. This involved the use of interconnecting project teams and interdepartmental work groups respon-sible for sharing their diverse views and understandings of a problem which then would be discussed with the aim of reaching a joint consensus. During my own participation in group meetings with Japanese expatriates I was interested to observe the role of seniority and rank in structuring group dynamics and facilitating consensus. Disagreement would rarely lead to open confrontation or to an explicit challenge to the views of the more senior person. An interesting insight into the interaction of Japanese, Italian and UK directors in meetings was outlined by the experience of one of the UK directors in Hano based on his experience of attending partners' meetings: 'The Japanese are very keen on detail and want to plan every-thing to the minutest detail and time-scale. The Italians have a much more laid-back attitude about it, the English are somewhere in the middle.'

The challenge of multi-cultural team-working is faced at all levels across the three organizations addressed in the research. For partners entering into an international joint venture such as the Japanese and Italian partners in this case study, the ability of employees from board level to the shop floor to operate in a multi-cultural work team is crucial.

The Planned Implementation of Management Practices in Nippon
The influence of the Italian partner on the management practices in the organization were considered by the employees to be largely overshadowed by the influence of the Japanese partner and its particular management practices. With Nippon being established on a greenfield site the partners were faced with decisions on how the organization was to be organized and managed. As the senior personnel manager outlined:

> the challenges from my point of view were to be in at the start of something new and exciting, on a greenfield site, to start with a clean sheet of paper and not to be bound by the custom and practice and the historical factors that may be the case in a brownfield organization.

The situation unfolding at Nippon provides an example of Japanese multinational organizations' strong efforts to institutionalize many aspects of their work organization, supplier relationships and technologies in their overseas transplants (Westney, 1993). At Nippon however there is a recog-nition that some practices that are suitable in the Japanese environment are not suitable in the UK environment. In this sense a hybrid work organiza-tion developed. As the manufacturing manager at Nippon outlined:

> I think the more famous imports that have been here for some time such as Nissan have proved that the British workforce can be trained to work in a different method. They have taken the Japanese culture and the British culture and they have made a hybrid system, but they have proved that it can be done. We are in the process of making a similar environment.

Bringing two cultures together in a third environment was seen as a chal-lenge for the general manager of Nippon, with the need to create best practice for their own environment. Mutual agreements and consensus on what was thought to be best practice for their environment tended to come about only after lengthy discussions, because of previous different environments, different experiences and different preconceptions.

Learning to Manage: The Strategic Deployment of Expatriates at Nippon
In addition to the managing director and two senior managers, seven of the eight managers brought in to run the organization were Japanese. An interesting mechanism set up in the organization was the use of 'coordinators'. Having no line responsibility they were brought in from the Japanese parent organization to act as technical experts. At the time of the research, seven coordinators were employed in the organization. They were seen as being primarily sent over due to their technical expertise that was needed to set up the organization, and they were employed in manufacturing, quality and maintenance. The Japanese employees are seconded to Nippon for four-year periods. The first human resource plan for Nippon was made in the Japanese parent organization and was mainly for the support roles. Over the first twelve-month period on the greenfield site the recruitment of managers, assistant managers and technical engineering staff took place. A strategy used to prepare and train the UK nationals for managerial positions involves placing them in positions as assistant managers under Japanese managers. Following the four-year secondment of the Japanese manager the assistant manager is expected to move up to fill the manager's position.

The current role of the Japanese managers is characterized as being more technical than line related. Whilst the Japanese managers appeared to adjust to the technical side of the business, the products being designed in Japan and the machinery being imported from Japan, the 'people side' of management was seen by the senior personnel and administration manager as more challenging for them. This was considered to be partly due to the language problem. For this reason the assistant managers had a key role to play in the day-to-day line control.

The Brownfield Site: Hano

The Challenge of Managing Diversity on the Brownfield Site
Hano, the second leg of the international joint venture, located in the North of England, is a brownfield site and provides a contrasting approach in the strategic management of the venture by the Japanese parent to that found in Nippon. Hano has a long history, existing previously as a division of a major UK chemicals organization before being purchased by the Japanese parent shortly before the joint venture agreement. Whilst being involved in the manufacture of components for the car industry it operates in a different product group from the Nippon venture. Hano provides the only example in which the Japanese parent has established itself overseas on a

brownfield site.This followed over twenty years of cooperation with the UK organization purchased. The catalyst for the purchase of Hano by the Japanese parent, ABC Japan, was to supply Toyota in the UK. Local manufacture was preferred over supply from Japan. This left the alternatives of setting up an operation in the UK, or purchasing an existing operation. Existing potential organizations manufacturing the product range proved unsuitable and the option of a greenfield site was considered too risky as the market was showing no indication of expansion.

The only change made on the board of directors following the acquisition was that a Japanese chairman was appointed, to be based in the European headquarters in Amsterdam. The management style of ABC Japan, following the purchase, was characterized by a UK national on the board as involving a consultative and approving role rather than a directive role. This was seen largely to be due to the fact that most of Hano's business was with non-Japanese customers. The fact that this was the first experience by ABC Japan of taking over a going concern, rather than starting up an organization that was set up in a specific part of the world to serve specific customers, made the organization's decision-makers cautious. As the local national working in the position of finance director of Hano outlined, there was a hesitation by ABC Japan since they did not want to become involved in the historical business of Hano. As another local director outlined, when ABC Japan bought the company their idea seemed to be that the company would run itself: 'they could bolt a little on the end that would make products for the Japanese customers that they would be involved in maintaining and supporting, and it would just go along like that'.

The timing of the acquisition, however, was bad, in that the market had declined and sales of the organization reflected this, leading to the injection of more ABC Japan expatriates. The strategic role of the Italian general manager adopted in the Nippon leg of the joint venture was not replicated in Hano. Further to the joint venture agreement an Italian director was appointed to the board, but in contrast to the situation at Nippon he is non-resident and non-executive. His role was described by one of the directors as being to keep in touch with developments in the organization. The person appointed also acted as the managing director of Roma, the third leg of the joint venture in Italy.

The strategic deployment of expatriates in Hano by ABC Japan involved the placing of a vice-president from Japan in office. The president was a local UK national, the only non-Japanese president throughout ABC Japan's worldwide network. However he was to retire in the coming months and a Japanese expatriate was placed in the position. A second Japanese expatriate placed on the board filled the newly created position of director of improvement activities. Without any line responsibility he acted as a coordinator and advisor. Over the coming months this position was re-moved and the person moved into a line directorship position with responsibility for production engineering. The board of directors thus stabilized to include five Japanese directors, one Italian director and five local national directors. A further five Japanese expatriates were brought into the organization including a senior design manager and four coordinators in the areas of manufacturing, production engineering, maintenance and company planning. These expatriates were seen to have the important role of working with the local staff in the new investment that had been made following the acquisition, which involved an extension to the existing factory providing a new production area which was to concentrate on serving the prime Japanese customers, Toyota and Honda. As was the practice in Nippon, ABC Japan again appeared to adopt the strategy of utilizing the overseas assignment as a training ground for its junior managers and future managers. In both legs of the joint venture a potential problem area relates to the lack of formal authority that the Japanese coordinators have. They do not possess any line or functional authority. They possess staff authority to act in an advisory role. This provides an intense challenge to the coordinators to 'sell' their ideas to the local nationals in the managerial positions. With performance in the overseas assignment being of critical importance to the career of the expatriate this suggests significant pressures will be placed on the individual within this organizational structure.

Managers Making Sense of Diversity
The fact that this was a brownfield site was considered a challenge for the management of change at Hano. As the manufacturing director, a local national commented:

> Everywhere else has been a greenfield site and trying to change us rather than recruit us and get us to work to the system from day one has actually been quite a problem. . . . What they started doing was to say that we should aim for a blend of the best of the English and the best of the Japanese. The two cultures are fundamentally different and the English people I detect don't want to go all the way. We want to get to a point at which we are successful, but the Japanese culture is so much tougher, so what I think is the two are going to come together a little, but there will always be a gap.

The local human resources director saw the challenge of managing on a brownfield site compared with a greenfield site as being greater:

> If you are a greenfield site, the first thing that you do is define your terms and conditions of employment, company rules. . . . My friends in America [US subsidiary] tell me that all the people coming in through the door have been used to other ways of working, other systems, and you have to convert them if you will. But with an acquisition like ours that has

a history going back sixty years, where you have people whose fathers worked here before them, there is a tremendous amount of ingrained history that this is the way we do things, and especially in terms of industrial relations.

The human resource director continued:

> When the Japanese purchased the company our employees will have been asking Does this mean we have to do exercises every morning? Does this mean we are all going to have to wear uniforms? And we were saying of course, no, there will be no sudden changes, but over time, yes, there are changes. We don't do the exercises but we have introduced work-wear. But the process of changing a company which goes back generations is a very slow process because people don't like change.

The Japanese expatriates were thought to be aware of cultural differences, but, like their English counterparts, were not good at saying precisely what the differences were:

> We may use the same concepts but they may have very different meanings.... I think the Japanese parent company has always recognized that although they have a lot of expertise in developing the product and in manufacturing, they have no specific expertise in relation to employing Western people.

A newly appointed local employee development manager described how he faced both the legacy of the organization culture strongly rooted in the Northern England context and traditions of arm's length employee–employer relations, and the challenge of managing the development of the workforce in the joint venture. He drew on the experience of his counterparts in the US subsidiary of the Japanese parent. In this way the earlier experiences of the US subsidiary provided lessons for the UK subsidiary to learn from:

> Why should the UK subsidiaries have to re-invent the wheel when the US subsidiary had already gone through the learning curve. I can actually take their learning curve, look at it and apply it to our organization in about a tenth of the time, so we learn from good practice, we replicate the good practice that is existing elsewhere.

The employee development manager outlined how he would like to draw on the knowledge of the parent company and the US subsidiary but that the parent company in Japan seemed to give less emphasis on formal management development programmes:

> I wanted to take the best that is available from the States and the best that is coming out of Japan and apply it here so that it becomes neither one nor the other. So I am happy to explore what is coming out of Japan.

His perception was that the Japanese and the local managers could learn from each other:

> The Japanese tend to concentrate very much on the technical programmes and on the health and safety side. So on management development and people development I really do think that the Japanese can learn from what we are implementing.

The development of senior managers in the organization was seen as an important issue. There was no formal development programme in place and the employee development manager felt that a serious obstacle to learning and synergy at board level was the fragmentation of the board, culturally between the local managers and the Japanese, and functionally amongst local senior managers heading different departments. The employee development manager sought to develop communication across functions at board level.

The president of Hano had his own understanding of the differences between the Japanese and English management systems:

> My idea is that in the English system I find that each department is very independent in case there is some mistake or failure in one: they think 'oh that's their problem'; it comes from individualism. In the Japanese system it is like a mesh, there are lots of close connections between departments so if anything happens the other departments will cover and they can recover quicker.

The president outlined how in the parent company in Japan they would develop people and rotate people across departments, which did not happen in the English system where people were specialists in one area. He saw the objective as being the combination of both systems:

> In the English system you have a sort of class system and you judge people by their status. Those at the top in an organization have some leadership and then you go down, so it is top down. In a Japanese company the middle management are very important and their ideas go to the top. So in a Japanese company to make a final decision takes longer. . . . Here we are trying to encourage middle management to think for themselves and not wait for senior managers to make decisions. Until the middle management and supervisory class get stronger the company will not get stronger.

DISCUSSION

Managing Collaboration in the Joint Venture

The surface appearance of complementary relations (Pucik, 1988) in the joint venture presented in this chapter does mask an underlying competitive relationship between the ultimate stakeholders in the two organizations. The issue of strategic control as related to the distribution of benefits from the alliance is especially critical in a competitive alliance utilizing leverage by resources or competencies with the risk that benefits from the alliance may be accrued asymmetrically by the partners, caused potentially by differences in the organizational learning capacities of the partners. Whilst the complementarity of resources provided in the venture by the two partners provides a structural component of trust (Madhok, 1995), the social component of trust is highlighted in the example on the greenfield site of the Japanese and Italian representatives' commitment in Nippon to smoothing troubled waters and providing the 'social glue' to tide over temporary periods where perceptions of inequity in the relationship may exist in the parent organizations.

Joint Ventures and the Expatriate

In tri-national joint ventures the potential for expatriate adjustment difficulties (Beechler and Krazmien, 1996) will be exaggerated. In this case the Italian expatriates were few in number and arguably faced less of a challenge in operating in another European context than did their Japanese counterparts. In this joint venture, discussion with Japanese expatriates indicated that many of the Japanese staff sent over were hand-picked for the job, and their success in the joint venture would be of much importance for their future career opportunities in the parent organization. In addition to placing pressure on the employees to succeed, such an arrangement is also likely to create some conflict of loyalty for the expatriates between the parent organization and the joint venture (Shenkar and Zeira, 1987). With the management team including employees on secondment, working relations would have to be built up from the beginning again with any changes of staff. This was identified as a source of anxiety at both sites. At board level the strategic deployment and re-deployment of people is also a source of uncertainty about the future. From discussions in Nippon, Hano and the Japanese parent's UK holding company, ABC UK, it is clear that the Japanese parent is still in the early stages of developing any clear strategy for the utilization of the expatriate assignment as a means of organizational learning in the home country or as part of an ongoing management development programme. The vast majority of research on expatriate adjustment has been on American expatriates (Black and Porter, 1991; Black and

Mendenhall, 1990) adjusting to overseas assignments. In addressing the issue of Japanese expatriate adjustment raised in this research, it is necessary to consider the specific cultural and institutional context in Japan shaping the social relations and expectations of the employees in their work. In the context of the joint venture studied it appears that work-related values are important factors to explore in assessing the difficulties of adjustment for the Japanese expatriates. In discussion with several Japanese expatriates, language difficulties and issues relating to raising children in a Western context were also experienced as challenging for them.

The venture has been influenced by a large number of forces including parent environment influences (Westney, 1993; Di Maggio and Powell, 1983; Meyer and Rowan, 1991), local environment influences, the interpretation of these forces by decision-makers in the parent organizations in developing strategy, the intangible assets of the organization which have influenced its ability to adapt in different ways, and the ways in which the local and expatriate managers have sought to manage the opportunities provided through the collaboration. Conflicting short-term objectives were seen to emerge from the different business expectations and understandings (Whitley, 1994) between the Japanese and Italian partners in the venture. It can be argued that multinational organizations operating outside of their home country will consider taking with them their specific management style, management practices, form of work organization and technology where these are considered to be a source of their competitive success. However the extent to which these can be successfully transferred will be influenced by the local environment in which they operate.

My period of research in the organizations as a general operative on the shop floor, confirmed that the actual application of management initiatives coming primarily from the Japanese parent organization were modified across the brownfield and greenfield sites according to the local context. On the brownfield site the existence of tradition, norms and conventions on the shop floor influenced the degree to which new management initiatives could be implemented. This was particularly the case in attempts to change formal work groups and authority relations on the shop floor.

The study indicates that setting up a tri-national joint venture on a brownfield site is much more complex than on a greenfield site due to existing organizational culture, local management practices, worker expectations, norms and conventions. In Nippon, the greenfield site, there was a direct attempt to apply many of the technical and social features of the work organization found in the Japanese parent organization. The Italian partner in the venture adopted a mediating role in adjusting practices to the local environment. Such a synergistic cooperative strategy utilizes the knowledge of the European partner of the local work environment. In Hano pressures for local isomorphism and internal organizational consistency can be seen to mediate the ability to implement management initiatives (Rosenzweig and Nohria, 1994). Within Hano, in the oldest sections of the shop floor, management practices that evolved under local national ownership are being gradually adapted, but many practices evolved and are embedded in the local institutional and social context which the manufacturing manager considers requires a revolutionary new way of thinking by the workforce to facilitate change. In the newest parts of Hano, built following the acquisition by the Japanese parent and the joint venture agreement, management practices and technical organization have been introduced that resemble many of the features of the Japanese parent organization's practices. A history of previous unionization and strong demarcations on the shop floor is important in explaining the resemblance of human resource management practices in Hano to local practices. In Nippon the role of the Italian representative on the board has been important in adapting human resource management practices to the local environment and it has been in this role that the insights of the Italian partner have been most valuable in shaping management practices.

The case highlighted that many management practices can most easily be transferred on a greenfield site not influenced by existing organizational customs and practices. On a brownfield site, organizational inertia may lead to practices that more closely resemble local practices than on a greenfield site. This was particularly the case with human resource management practices at Hano in the early period of Japanese ownership, with some resembling local practices – for example wages and benefits – but also some being adapted from the Japanese parent organization practices, such as participation in decision-making, communications and training. Pressures for internal consistency in practices (Evans and Lorange, 1989) across organizations owned by ABC Japan were seen in the area of health and safety. Recruitment practices in Nippon were seen to resemble other local organizations rather than the parent organizations, through adaptation to the local labour market and the customs and expectations of organizations working in the local community. In Nippon the Italian partner has often provided the local insights for the joint venture to mediate and adjust to the competing pressures experienced by the Japanese partner and to a lesser extent by the Italian partner in the UK environment.

A collaborative joint venture partnership in a fiercely competitive industry may be maintained where two organizations identify mutual benefits from such an agreement. In this study locational advantages and technology transfer opportunities were identified. The study indicated the critical importance of relations at board level in managing such a cooperation. Particularly in a tri-national joint venture crossing different business systems and cultures there is a high possibility of misunderstanding and fragmentation of the board unless opportunities for synergy and organizational learning through the venture are identified. The study has highlighted the particular challenges of operating an international joint venture at a brownfield site compared with a greenfield site. Ingrained traditions and practices at the brownfield site studied added to the complexity of managing the venture, particularly for the expatriates seeking to make sense of local practices and work with local directors at board level.

Note

1. The author is grateful for the opportunity given by Nippon, Hano and ABC UK to carry out work in these organizations. There are many people to thank both on the shop floor and in the office at Nippon and Hano. I am grateful for the comments of Monir Tayeb, Paul Beamish, Ray Loveridge and Jos Benders on earlier drafts of this chapter. I also wish to acknowledge and express appreciation for the guidance and encouragement provided by Richard Whitley in the course of my research and doctoral studies which were made possible by funding kindly provided by Manchester Business School.

References

Abo, T. (1994) 'The analysis of Japanese factories located overseas', in T. Abo (ed.), *Hybrid Factory: The Japanese Production System in the United States* (Oxford: Oxford University Press).

Bartlett, C.A. and S. Ghoshal (1989) *Managing Across Borders: The Transnational Solution* (Cambridge, MA: Harvard Business School Press).

Beechler, S. and M. Krazmien (1996) *The Relationship between Expatriates, Parent Company–Affiliate Integration and HRM Control in the Overseas Affiliates of Japanese and American MNC's*, Working paper no. 103, Center on Japanese Economy and Business, Columbia Business School, New York.

Black, J.S. and M. Mendenhall (1990) 'Cross- cultural training effectiveness: a review and a theoretical framework for future research', *Academy of Management Review*, 15(1), pp. 113–36.

Black, J.S. and L.W. Porter (1991) 'Managerial behaviors and job performance: a successful manager in Los Angeles may not succeed in Hong Kong', *Journal of International Business Studies*, 22(1), pp. 99–113.

Cool, K.O. and C.A. Lengnick-Hall (1985) 'Second thoughts on the transferability of the Japanese management style', *Organization Studies*, 6(1), pp. 1–22.

Dedoussis, V. (1995) 'Simply a question of cultural barriers? The search for new perspectives in the transfer of Japanese management practices', *Journal of Management Studies*, 32(6), pp. 731–45.

DiMaggio, P.J. and W.W. Powell (1983) 'The iron cage revisited: institutional isomorphism and collective rationality in organizational fields', *American Sociological Review*, 48, pp. 47–160.

Dunning, J.H. (1993) *The Globalisation of Business: The Challenges of the 1990's* (London: Routledge).

Evans, P. and P. Lorange (1989) 'The two logics behind human resource management', in Y.L. Doz and A. Laurent (eds), *Human Resource Management in International Firms: Change, Globalization, Innovation* (London: Macmillan).

Florida, R. and M. Kenney (1991) 'Transplant organizations. The transfer of Japanese industrial organization to the US', *American Sociological Review*, 56, (June), pp. 381–98.

Geringer, J.M. (1991) 'Strategic determinants of partner selection in international joint ventures', *Journal of International Business Studies*, 22(1), pp. 41–62.

Itami, H. (1987) *Mobilising Invisible Assets* (Cambridge, MA: Harvard University Press).

Killing, J.P. (1982) *Strategies for Joint Venture Success* (New York: Praeger).

Kogut, B. (1988) 'Joint ventures: theoretical and empirical perspectives', *Strategic Management Journal*, 9, pp. 319–32.

Kogut, B. (1993) 'Learning, or the importance of being inert: country imprinting and international competition', in S. Ghoshal and D.E. Westney (eds), *Organization Theory and the Multinational Corporation* (London: Macmillan).

Kristensen, P.H. (1994) 'Strategies in a volatile world', *Economy and Society*, 23(3) (August), pp. 305–34.

Madhok, A. (1995) 'Revisiting multinational firms tolerance for joint ventures: a trust-based approach', *Journal of International Business Studies*, 26(1), pp. 117–38.

Makino, S. (1995) 'Joint venture ownership structure and performance: Japanese joint ventures in Asia', Doctoral dissertation, University of Western Ontario.

Maurice, M., A. Sorge and M. Warner (1980) 'Societal differences in organizing manufacturing units: a comparison of France, West Germany and Great Britain', *Organization Studies*, 1(1), pp. 59–86.

Meyer, J.W. and B. Rowan (1991) 'Institutionalized organizations: formal structure as myth and ceremony', in W.W. Powell and P.J. DiMaggio (eds), *The New Institutionalism in Organizational Analysis* (London: University of Chicago Press).

Morris, J. and B. Wilkinson (1995) 'The transfer of Japanese management to alien institutional environments', *Journal of Management Studies*, 36(6), pp. 719–30.

Mueller, F. (1994) 'Societal effect, organizational effect and globalization', *Organization Studies*, 15(3), pp. 407–28.

Orru, M., N.W. Biggart and G.G. Hamilton (1991) 'Organizational isomorphism in East Asia', in W.W. Powell and P.J. DiMaggio (eds), *The New Institutionalism in Organizational Analysis* (London: University of Chicago Press).

Pucik, V. (1988) 'Strategic alliances, organizational learning and competitive advantage: the HRM agenda', *Human Resource Management*, 27(1), pp. 77–93.

Rosenzweig, P.M. and N. Nohria (1994) 'Influences on human resource management practices in multinational corporations', *Journal of International Business Studies*, 25(2), pp. 229–51.

Shenkar, O. and Y. Zeira (1987) 'Human resource management in international joint ventures', *Academy of Management Review*, 12(3), pp. 546–57.

Sorge, A. and M. Maurice (1993) 'The societal effect in the strategies of French and West German machine tool manufacturers', in B. Kogut (ed.), *Country Competitiveness: Technology and the Organization of Work* (Oxford: Oxford University Press).

Westney, D.E. (1993) 'Institutionalization theory and the multinational corporation', in S. Ghoshal and D.E. Westney (eds), *Organization Theory and the Multinational Corporation* (London: Macmillan).

Whitley, R.D. (1992) *Business Systems in East Asia: Firms, Markets and Societies* (London: Sage Publications).

Whitley, R.D. (1994) 'Dominant forms of economic organization in market economies', *Organization Studies*, 15(2), pp. 153–82.

Part Two

Competitive Advantage in an International Context

Introduction to Part Two

David Wilson

The chapters in this section variously address the questions of appropriate strategies for firms operating in an international context. What is striking about all four chapters is that each emphasizes the softer, less tangible and more process-oriented aspects of strategic management in securing competitive success and organizational performance. In Chapter 5, Sher, Wong and Shaw focus on learning, training and education; Fahy (Chapter 6) points to the importance of intangible capabilities; Taggart (Chapter 7) emphasizes the importance of organizational structures and cultures; whilst Casson, Loveridge and Singh (Chapter 8) show the impact and influence of national cultures on multinational corporations (MNCs).

It is only a few years ago that papers emphasizing such relatively intangible resources would have been in the minority in any discussions of internationalization. One paper, perhaps, might have hinted that global strategies or international trade theory may not be so generic as their proponents implied. Perhaps there were country-specific differences and, in any case, were we measuring the right factors both in firms and in industries? But the rest of this stereotypical conference would have been burgeoning with papers on strategic planning, industry analysis and portfolio technique. That imbalance has seen a dramatic change over the last five years or so. Today, a whole section of this book (and with similar concepts spilling over into other sections) argues that what were, until recently, taken to be central aspects of competitiveness, such as industry structure and tangible assets, may not be the crucial factors by which firms operating internationally gain and sustain competitive advantage.

Of course, it is not solely in international management that such a transition has taken place. The same emphasis on processual and intangible factors has been seen in the fields of strategic management and organization theory. The notion of competitive advantage as a concept in strategic management is arguably only a little over thirty years old, beginning with the two 'Alfreds' (Sloan and Chandler). Basing their work in a context of economic growth and at a time when the USA was an economic leader in the world economy, their seemingly immutable laws of strategy and structure paved the way for a whole host of analytical tools, panaceas and strategic models. These include the experience curve, the growth-share strategic portfolio matrix, industry structure and competitive analysis (especially the work of Michael Porter). The result was inevitable. Managers could employ such analytical tools to their advantage and adopt generic strategies to suit particular market, industry and competitive conditions. Thus, contingent certainty came to dominate strategic management for almost three decades.

It is no surprise, therefore, that this particular form of contingency theory proved attractive to those scholars analyzing international business. If such contingent factors applied so readily to individual firms in their operating context, then it was surely logical to extend the analysis to firms formulating strategies in an international context? Just as in strategic management, these paradigms predominated until it became evident that neither strategic planning nor industry analysis seemed to be accounting for much of the unexplained variance in the performance of firms engaged in international management. Times have changed, as each of the following chapters describes. For example, the ownership of multinational firms is no longer solely in the hands of the few economically dominant nations such as the USA and UK. The rise of the so-called 'tiger' economies and the stimulation of world trade by successive reductions in tariff barriers (GATT); the growth of countertrade from previously under-developed nations; the speed of technological development and increased communication patterns; the changing profile of education and training world-wide and the shift from emphasising the *capacity* of a firm to produce to its *capability* to innovate and sustain competitive advantage, have all confounded the paradigms of relatively simplistic, often ethnocentric, contingency approaches. Each chapter in turn deals with different aspects of the emerging process and resource-based view of the firm in its international context.

Sher *et al.* focus on Taiwanese information technology firms. The question is how do such firms develop new knowledge through technology transfer, and what are the key criteria to enhance the process? Using the concept of absorptive capacity, Sher *et al.* studied Taiwanese firms at the project level of analysis. Data were collected from multiple sources using multiple methods, ranging from telephone surveys, through interviews to informal discussions. Analysis of the data reveals two strong factors which Sher *et al.* call technological effectiveness and economic effectiveness. Comparing these against more effective and less effective projects, they conclude that more effective projects are more closely associated with the incidence of the factors. For these authors, effectiveness reflects a range of organizational achievements such as the quality of materials or machinery to the relative ease of introducing process innovations. Controlling for function by analyzing the same function in different geographical areas, the consistent finding is that technological diffusion is greater in the more effective projects. Sher *at al.* are especially concerned to emphasize the role of learning in this process. By this, they mean the capability to transfer product technologies, modify them and match them to existing production systems rather than try and create new systems. The learning is in the process of transfer which some firms do well and others less well. The key processes which underpin this learning are difficult to specify precisely, since they involve interpretation, learning and training. For example, one of the key processes appears to be the accurate interpretation of externally sourced information. Again, effective projects are also those where bottom-line benefits are apparent to senior managers and where training is group-based rather than individually centred on specific skills. This is what Sher *et al.* call learning by doing, Taiwanese style. Finally, although the main level of analysis is at the project level, Sher *et al.* comment on two organizational factors which also seem to distinguish the effective processes of technology transfer. These are the level of interpersonal processes and the internal politics of the firm. For those of us involved in the study of strategy formulation at the firm level, these factors are no surprise. We would expect such contextual variables to play an influential role in mediating the outcomes of any technology transfer at the project level. Nevertheless, Sher *et al.* rightly point out that one has to start somewhere to analyze the nostrums of technology transfer, and examining these at the project level reveals key disjunctures with prevailing paradigmatic orthodoxies. Future research in this area might fruitfully try and combine the project and the organizational levels of analysis.

Fahy explicitly notes the swing away from 'Porterian' contingency economics towards a more resource-based view of the firm. The term 'resource-based' can, of course, mean all things to all people if it remains unspecified. Fahy is helpful in guiding us toward some precision in this regard. He firstly distinguishes between assets and capabilities. The argument is that, for too long, contingency views have emphasized assets. Fahy argues that tangible assets posses an immediate attraction to empirical researchers. Assets such as plant, land, capital goods or financial deposits not only show up visibly on the balance sheet, but are also easily measurable and comparable. Intangible assets, such as trademarks, intellectual property, patents and reputation can also be reflected in relatively high stock market valuations of publicly quoted companies. Taking a 'Porterian' perspective toward such assets, Fahy argues that we could construct a scale of theoretical competitiveness of the firm. This is based on the assumption that tangible assets can only underpin relatively weak competitive strengths. They can be imitated and easily substituted for, even in the short term. Intangible assets, Fahy warns, are perhaps not quite as intangible as we might think. Although they resist duplication in the short term (unlike tangible assets), they can be copied, refined or substituted in the longer term. Even where intangible assets are legally protected, such as intellectual property rights, such protection is ultimately imperfect and subject to inherent limitations against its abuse and appropriation.

The key to competitiveness, argues Fahy, lies primarily in the capabilities of a firm. These include the level and type of skills possessed by its members, the nature and extent of teamwork utilized and the receptiveness and support of organizational structures and cultures. Fahy regards such capabilities as providing the highest degree of competitiveness which is sustainable since they cannot be visibly assessed or measured and are inherently difficult to duplicate exactly. So far, so good at the level of the firm. Fahy then uses this framework of the capabilities model to the international context. Comparing assets at the international level (such as location or climate) with capabilities (such as a country's stock of knowledge), Fahy concludes that we would be better abandoning the idea of international competitiveness based solely on assets and concentrate instead on knowledge, learning, technological development and management practices-in-use at the level of the nation state. He assesses this theoretical model against a range of international strategies, ranging from the multinational to the transnational, concluding that in each case the capabilities view provides a better analytical tool for assessing and gaining competitive advantage in the international context.

Taggart concentrates on technology as a single factor, but one which Sher *et al.* and Fahy argued was central in their own analysis. Looking at Research and Development (R&D) strategy in the multinational affiliate, Taggart reveals the growing centrality of technological factors in the overall strategy of the firm. Previously considered to be operational or, at best, a tactical factor in decision-making, technology is now at the forefront of strategic management, especially in multinational corporations. One of Taggart's conceptual foundations for his subsequent arguments in the chapter is that innovation and new technology are inextricably interlinked. He gives evidence for this by showing that technology pervades strategy across the board, ranging from 'first-movers' in markets to 'me-too' followers.

Based on data from the Scottish electronics industry, Taggart investigates the above propositions as they apply to multinational affiliates. His results are wholly congruent with those of Sher *et al.* and Fahy. He first concludes that technology alone as a factor is not enough to differentiate firms in terms of performance. The link is neither so obvious nor so direct. Mediating variables of organization structure and culture come into play. These, argues Taggart, allow (or prevent) efficient and effective technology transfer in subsidiaries to allow them to develop and innovate further. Deeper investigation, however, reveals that variables of the receptiveness and supportiveness of organizational structure and culture are by no means unitary or homogeneous. For example, Taggart reveals that there is an inevitable trade-off which occurs in the decentralized structure/heterogeneous culture combination. Such a nexus may foster innovation. But it will also serve to stifle the efficiency of strategic implementation to some degree. The key question is to what degree – and does this matter? But the answer to this question is outside the scope of Taggart's research.

Taggart also reveals that wholly technology-led strategies perhaps are properly placed in the land of organizational myths. They are a theoretical luxury which no firm can afford. They have to deal with a range of other powerful contingencies, not least the demands of customers. Patterns do emerge from the data, however. Organic, flexible forms of organization both in terms of structure and culture outperform the rigid organizations. Although much talked about, few firms have in fact created much R&D 'space' for innovation and development and most firms were stronger in the implementation of technological developments rather than in the basic innovation process. This finding highlights the persistent tension between creativity (basic innovation) and the implementation of new ideas (the innovation process). More successful firms appear to be those in which the role of R&D is embedded in and congruent with the general strategy of the firm rather than being tangential to it. Such findings have their limitations which Taggart notes himself. The limitations of the sample raises questions of how industry-specific such findings are and whether different sectors or different ownership patterns of affiliates may reveal differences. As Taggart notes, ownership, too, from different countries is likely to bring into play the cultural influences of different national cultures on affiliates, a subject addressed squarely by Casson *et al.* in the final chapter of this section.

Casson *et al.* encapsulate a series of surveys and data collection carried out in MNCs. These include postal surveys and interviews conducted mainly with managers from the personnel functions of the firms studied. This chapter takes the perspective of corporate culture and places it in an international context. The central question is, since MNCs need to establish and capitalize on their abilities to transfer knowledge and competencies world-wide, then some forms of control are clearly necessary over this process. Culture is viewed as potentially a key method of achieving and securing such control in the long term. Like Fahy's capabilities, such cultures can be firm-specific and, at least in the short term, non-substitutable.

Once again, intangible factors are emphasized in this chapter. This is particularly so in Casson *et al.*'s emphasis on the 'fit' between the firm and its national context. Eschewing 'Porterian' tangible factors of competitiveness and raising questions over the perspective of the institutional economists' view of competitiveness, Casson *et al.* examine to what extent the firm–national context interrelationships are influential in being a potent resource for yielding sustainable competitive advantage. They are careful, however, to point out that the adoption of a culturally-bound explanation of relative performance raises a number of conceptual issues. Unidirectional causality cannot merely be assumed and nor can the possibility of intervening variables. Noting such caveats, the data reveal some identifiable patterns of national culture over such factors as job security, the notion of career, business strategies and human resource management in general.

Yet, individual multinational corporations also display features which do not seem to correspond to national cultural stereotypes. Nevertheless, such features group together in patterns. Casson *et al.* reveal three such group-ings, ranging from the incremental innovators, through the acquisition and merger strategists to what is termed the 'conservative' firm. These firm-specific features when grouped together provide an alternative pattern to that predicted by national cultural stereotypes. Yet, Casson *et al.* also find that notions of organizational culture, such as normative commitment, tend to be congruent with wider social values in various countries, fitting better where the wider institutional patterns of education and social values are in line with business objectives.

Ending this section with the chapter by Casson *et al.* brings the debates between hard and soft measures, tangible and intangible assets and the importance of culture at the organizational and societal levels of analysis to the forefront of debate. International business has, for some decades, borrowed from economic and strategic management approaches. Taking models of the firm in its sector and transposing to the international level of analysis has been a dominant theme in much writing about international business. Yet the empirical data which are beginning to emerge indicate that such approaches seem to suffer from severe limitations in explaining competitive advantage as well as the ability of new firms from the rising economies to compete and dominate some markets in a very short time. The problem, of course, is one which is familiar to any social scientist. It is one thing to theorize about the 'soft' factors of international business. It is another to operationalize and measure them in a holistic and comparable way. Empirical work, based on this theorizing would seem to be an urgent need for the next phases of research in international business. Perhaps then we will be able to assess the relative explanatory power of the softer, more processual factors against the hard empiricism of economics and strategic planning.

5 Absorptive Capacity and Learning in Technology Transfer: The Case of Taiwanese Information Technology Firms

Peter Sher, Veronica Wong and Vivienne Shaw

INTRODUCTION

Technology transfer has been considered as an effective facilitator of technology development for late industrializing countries (Chanaron and Perrin, 1987). Kogut and Zander (1993) note that technology transfer lies at the heart of the issue of the growth of firms, domestically and internationally. Firms grow on their ability to create new knowledge and to replicate this knowledge so as to expand their market. Their advantage lies in being able to understand and carry out technology transfer more effectively than other firms. Kedia and Bhagat (1988) argue that the practice of adopting and implementing Western technologies in newly industrialized countries (such as South Korea and Taiwan) has not been a simple case of 'borrowing' or imitating. Technologies are transferred to these economies for cultivating indigenous technological capability and establishing competitive advantage. This research, therefore concentrates on the facilitative role of technology transfer in the specific context of Taiwanese information technology firms.

The performance of Taiwanese information technology firms has been remarkable in recent years. In 1994, the product value of the Taiwanese information technology industry ranked fourth in the world, after the USA, Japan, and Germany. The hardware product value was US$ 11.579 billion; this had grown 19.5 per cent from the previous year. The world market shares of major hardware products manufactured in Taiwan are: monitors (56 per cent), portable PC (28 per cent), desktop PC (8 per cent), motherboard (80 per cent), scanner (61 per cent), power suppliers (31 per cent), graphic cards (32 per cent), terminals (22 per cent), network cards

(34 per cent), mice (80 per cent), keyboards (52 per cent), sound cards (11 per cent), net hubs (18 per cent), and video cards (24 per cent).[1]

The latter figures imply that Taiwanese information technology firms have secured outstanding performance in international markets. This is a remarkable achievement given the late industrial development of Taiwan. Taiwan started its industrialization process in the 1950s after the nationalist government in China was defeated by the communist government and retreated to Taiwan. Consequently, the industrial infrastructure of Taiwan lags behind those of industrialized countries. The Index of Technology Capability[2] of Taiwan in 1992 was 7.28, while that of South Korea was 7.41, France 29.60, Germany 54.21, Japan 69.50, and the USA 100.00.

That Taiwanese information technology firms have achieved outstanding performance in the global information technology market is surprising considering the investment by Taiwanese companies. The aggregate R&D expenditure of Taiwan's industry accounts for 1.7 per cent of Taiwan's GNP, far less than the 2.2 per cent in South Korea, 2.8 per cent in the USA, and 3 per cent in Japan. Worse, the R&D expenditure in the private sector accounts for only 0.93 per cent of GNP in Taiwan, far less than the 2.02 per cent in South Korea and 3.47 per cent in Japan.[3] It is likely that Taiwanese information technology firms' recent ascendancy in international markets has been based on their ability to assimilate needed technologies through a variety of sources and acquiring technological capability to develop new products rather than developing their own products from scratch. This chapter focuses on selected aspects of a wider study into technology transfer in Taiwanese information technology firms: issues relevant to absorptive capacity, barriers and patterns of intra-firm technological diffusion, and learning (see Figure 5.1).

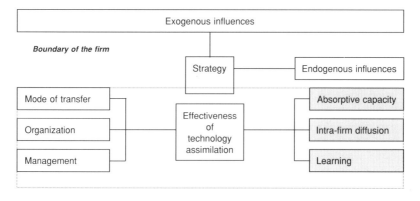

Figure 5.1   Research scope

LITERATURE REVIEW

Absorptive capacity is the organization's ability to recognize the value of new external information, assimilate it, and apply it to commercial ends (Cohen and Levinthal, 1990). It refers not only to the acquisition or assimilation of information by an organization but also to the organization's ability to exploit it. Atuahene-Gima (1992) notes that absorptive capacity has three components: (1) a firm's characteristics such as R&D, manufacturing and marketing expertise, (2) the firm's prior relevant knowledge in relationship to the external technology acquired, and (3) the R&D unit's awareness of developments in external technologies and its ability to play a facilitative role.

At a conceptual level, absorptive capacity is considered by various researchers as one of the most important factors that determine the effectiveness of technology transfer (e.g. Baranson, 1970; Atuahene-Gima, 1992). Cohen and Levinthal (1990) argue that absorptive capacity represents an important part of a firm's ability to create new knowledge. Kedia and Bhagat (1988) also point out that the lack of a sophisticated technical core (implying weak absorptive capacity) makes the utilization of imported technologies harder for innovation to occur in technologically inferior firms. However, these researches did not empirically examine the impact of absorptive capacity on technology transfer; as such the present research seeks to investigate, from an empirical base, the effect of absorptive capacity on the technology transfer outcome. Specifically we pose our first proposition:

Proposition 1   Companies with a high level of absorptive capacity are able to transfer technology more effectively.

Sheen (1992) highlights two problems in external information acquisition. The first is concerned with resource allocation and volume of information acquired. It is often difficult to avoid information overload or to ensure that individuals do not spend time where the groundwork has been done. Second, there is a perennial problem in multidisciplinary input and the difficulty of communicating particularly technical information across disciplines. As such the project team must attempt to strike a balance between internal cross-functional communication and the coordination of information captured and external sourcing of new information.

Chatterji and Manuel (1993) also identified several major barriers to successful acquisition of external technologies: (1) obtaining internal consensus on technologies that should be assigned top priority or targets for acquisition; (2) resource limitation which reduces the firm's ability to purchase appropriate technologies; (3) locating and establishing relationships sources with the suppliers of the specific technology required by the firm;

(4) evaluating the technology *vis-à-vis* relevant targets that should be set by the firm; and (5) internal organizational blocks such as management's aversion to risk, the 'not-invented-here' syndrome resulting in reluctance to accept external ideas, and an inappropriate structure leading to poor coordination of the technology transfer process and failure to internalize the technology.

Additionally, from the innovation diffusion literature, Vandermerwe (1987) draws attention to several barriers to in-house diffusion of new ideas which have relevance to our understanding of organizational acceptance of new or acquired technologies. These are: (1) difficulties in making observable benefits clear to others; (2) the perception by others that the risks are too high; (3) resistance from departments and lack of agreement on benefits accruing to the firm; (4) political and psychological obstacles; (5) idea generator's inability to get access to the power base and secure top management's support for its implementation; (6) the 'not-invented-here' syndrome; and (7) failure to justify project costs and return on investment. If we consider the adoption of external technologies to be synonymous with the acceptance of new ideas or information, then it would not be unreasonable to offer the following proposition:

Proposition 2 Companies which are able to overcome the barriers of intra-firm technology diffusion will be more effective at technology transfer.

Learning to utilize technological knowledge requires management's commitment to the deployment of appropriate resources in the firm. Lall (1980) develops a six-fold classification of learning: learning by doing, learning by adapting, learning by designing, learning by improving, learning by setting up a production system, and learning by designing new processes. Bell (1984) offers a more proactive scheme which includes learning-by-training when technology training programmes take place, learning-by-hiring where specialized tasks require the hiring of individuals, and learning-by-searching where disembodied knowledge and information are sought and acquired by the firm.

The extensive literature on technology transfer shows the great importance of R&D in achieving successful international technology transfer. Emphasis has also been focused on the role of technical education and the provision of appropriate training to engineers in recipient countries (usually meaning less developed or developing nations) (Madu, 1989). Training is found to be a key success factor in both international technology transfer (Lasserre, 1982) and transferring core manufacturing technologies within a firm (Galbraith, 1990). Lorriman and Kenjo (1994) note that training is considered to be one of three key factors underpinning Japan's economic success. They consider that human resource development systems facilitating the rapid post-war growth of the Japanese economy were based on on-the-job training. Madu (1989) argues that the ability to modify and improve technology can only be achieved through education and training. As such, we offer the next proposition:

Proposition 3   Companies which facilitate learning and training are more likely to implement effective technology transfer.

Measurement of Effectiveness

Effectiveness is defined by some researchers as 'the degree to which organisational goals are reached' (Ruekert *et al.*, 1985). Measurements of technology transfer effectiveness are drawn from both the technology transfer and new product development literature (e.g. Teece, 1977; Davidson, 1980; Cooper, 1984; Hagedoorn and Schakenraad, 1990). Seventeen measures of effectiveness are commonly used: capturing technical ability, getting access to desired technologies, achieving technical complementary, improving product quality, improving products performance, reducing cost, averting risk, pooling resources, shortening lead time, increasing market share, achieving economies of scale and scope, achieving vertical integration, monitoring technical change, initiating internationalization, pursuing company growth, and attaining a larger return on investment (ROI). This research, therefore, uses these variables to measure the effectiveness of technology transfer within Taiwanese firms.

METHODOLOGY

Data Collection

The unit of analysis of this exploratory research is the project level. Data was obtained using a structured questionnaire and variables measured using five-point Likert scales. Firms in the sample were selected in combination by the simple random sampling method from three sources: (1) the *Largest 1000 Manufacturing Firms of 1994 in Taiwan* and the *Largest 300 Service Firms of 1994 in Taiwan*,[4] (2) the *1994 Directory of Taipei Computer Association*, and (3) the *1994 Directory of Hsinchu Science-based Industrial Park*. The sample covers two groups of technology-oriented firms: (1) native Taiwanese firms, and (2) foreign direct investors that deploy both R&D and manufacturing functions in Taiwan. Four sub-industries relating to information technology, semiconductor, and software, computer & peripherals, telecommunication, are included in the sample.

A telephone survey of 80 firms was conducted in the first phase to check whether or not the firm had transferred technologies in the past five years.

Fifty of the surveyed firms (63 per cent) had undertaken the activity in the past five years. All but one of these firms agreed to participate in the present study. The second phase involved personal interviews, lasting one to one and a half hours, with managers who were conversant with technology transfer and new product development issues in the 49 participating companies. Each company offered to discuss two cases of technology transfer, with two companies offering, in addition, a third case, giving a total of 100 projects. Interviewees were targeted at a level no lower than R&D (or project) manager. Informants ranged from company presidents, associate vice presidents, and R&D vice-presidents, to senior engineers and R&D managers. One key informant in each company was interviewed and the same informant provided information with respect to all the technology transfer projects selected for study. In addition to the formal interview with the primary informant, there were informal discussions about focal projects with other members involved with the projects. These enabled the interviewer to obtain qualitative judgements as well as check, and correct for, any inconsistencies in managerial responses.

Table 5.1   Varimax-rotated matrix of effectiveness variables

Effectiveness	*Factors*		*Communality*	*Cronbach's alpha*
	(1) Technological effectiveness	*(2)* Economic effectiveness		
Capture technical capability	0.84892	0.38246	0.86693	
Monitor technical change	0.84695	0.24573	0.77770	
Get access to desired technology	0.83785	0.37271	0.84090	
Achieve technical complementary	0.81451	0.41041	0.83186	
Improve product quality	0.78863	0.43121	0.80788	0.9663
Improve product performance	0.78337	0.39619	0.77063	
Avert potential risk	0.75443	0.42101	0.74642	
Pool resources	0.70463	0.51359	0.76028	
Shorten lead time	0.68793	0.50841	0.73172	
Achieve vertical integration	0.60235	0.55258	0.66846	
Attain larger ROI	0.32488	0.88013	0.88017	
Achieve company growth	0.34725	0.87687	0.88948	
Achieve scale of economies	0.37540	0.87496	0.90649	0.9726
Achieve scope of economies	0.41625	0.86990	0.92842	
Increase market share	0.46737	0.81565	0.88371	
Initiate international expansion	0.50189	0.77499	0.85250	
Reduce delivery cost	0.54267	0.67620	0.75173	
Eigenvalue	12.56535	1.32995		
% of Variance	73.9	7.8		
Cumulative % of variance	73.9	81.7		

Kaiser-Meyer-Olkin Measure of Sampling Adequacy = 0.93350.
Barlett's Test of Sphericity = 2390.1864, Significance = 0.00000.

Data Analysis

Factor analysis was used to reduce the seventeen effectiveness variables to more manageable dimensions. Two key factors emerged: which we call technological effectiveness and economic effectiveness (see Table 5.1).

The sample was then split into more effective and less effective projects according to the median of aggregate effectiveness score. Following Doyle *et al.* (1992), a 3.5 score was used as the cut-off point – those with a score above 3.5 were rated as being more effective and those below as being less effective. The resultant groups were validated using multiple discriminate analysis. Ninety-two per cent of grouped cases are correctly classified (see Table 5.2).

In exploring the differences between less and more effective projects, the *t*-test for two independent samples was applied. In selecting significance levels, most behavioural research would consider the 0.01 and 0.05 levels of significance to be appropriate; however, in exploratory research, the 0.10 and 0.20 levels were regarded as acceptable (Roscoe, 1975). As the current study is exploratory in terms of its focus on technology transfer by Taiwanese information technology companies, the 0.10 level was used in this research.

RESULTS

Profile of the Sample

The computer and peripherals industry accounted for most of the cases in this research (48 per cent), followed by telecommunication (25 per cent), software (14 per cent), and semiconductors (13 per cent). Eighty-nine per

Table 5.2 Classification matrix for multiple discriminant analysis of effectiveness

Actual group	Number	Predicted group membership	
		More effective projects	*Less effective projects*
More effective projects	40	40 (100%)	0 (0%)
Less effective projects	60	8 (13.3%)	52 (86.7%)

Percent of 'grouped' cases correctly classified: 92%.

cent of the sample projects came from indigenous Taiwan firms. Others were subsidiaries of multinational corporations from the USA, France, and the Netherlands. In all, 2 presidents (3.8 per cent), 2 vice-presidents (3.8 per cent), 10 associate vice-presidents (19.3 per cent), and 37 R&D managers (71.2 per cent) were interviewed. All were conversant with the technology transfer project selected for study.

More Effective and Less Effective Projects

Table 5.1 shows the results of the factor analysis of the 17 effectiveness variables. Two factors account for 81.7 per cent of the total variance. Validity (communality) and reliability (Cronbach's alpha) are also shown. The Cronbach's alphas of the ten variables tapping 'technological effectiveness' and the seven describing 'economic effectiveness' are respectively 0.9963 and 0.9726. Both confirm the reliability of the two performance constructs. Face validity is high because all measurements are easily interpretable. Capturing technical capability, monitoring technical change, getting access to desired technologies, achieving technological complementary, improving product quality, improving product performance, averting potential risk, pooling resources, shortening lead time, and achieving vertical integration tapped the technological dimension of effectiveness. Attaining larger ROI, achieving company growth, scale and scope of economies, increasing market share, initiating internationalization, and reducing delivery cost tapped the economic effectiveness dimension.

Absorptive Capacity and Effectiveness of Technology Assimilation

The results in Table 5.3 support previous conceptual work which suggested that absorptive capacity was important in achieving effective technology transfer. Firms reflect stronger absorptive capacity in more effective projects than in less effective ones, thus lending support to proposition 1. Compared with the other variable sets, absorptive capacity in our sample firms is the most important dimension in successful technology assimilation. If a firm develops a strong capacity to adapt and to apply externally sourced technologies in production, it is more likely to be successful in leveraging its resources to secure effective technology transfer.

In terms of adaptation, there is a better capacity in more effective projects to interpret acquired information, identify possible modifications, to substitute and adapt acquired technologies. There are significantly better capabilities in more effective projects to improve quality and performance of products which embody transferred technologies. Acquired technologies may not initially fit the organizational needs and objectives, and therefore adaptive modification is important to allow actual exploitation of acquired technologies. Value engineering (or value analysis) is commonly applied in

Table 5.3 Absorptive capacity in more and less effective technology transfer projects

Absorptive Capacity	Sample (n = 100)	Less effective project (n = 60)	More effective project (n = 40)	t-test two-tailed significance
Interpret acquired technical information	3.69 (1.52)	3.1000 (1.492)	4.5750 (1.083)	0.000***
Identify possible modification	3.47 (1.57)	2.8833 (1.627)	4.3500 (0.975)	0.000***
Identify possible substitution	3.17 (1.61)	2.5667 (1.555)	4.0750 (1.248)	0.000***
Identify possible adaptation	3.20 (1.58)	2.6667 (1.526)	4.0000 (1.301)	0.000***
Ensure quality of machinery, construction, and materials, etc.	3.01 (1.71)	2.3667 (1.540)	3.9750 (1.510)	0.000***
Inspect the conformity with specification and standards	3.32 (1.64)	2.6167 (1.508)	4.3750 (1.213)	0.000***
Debug	3.32 (1.50)	2.7167 (1.508)	4.2250 (0.920)	0.000***
Revise QC operation	2.60 (1.58)	2.0167 (1.384)	3.4750 (1.450)	0.000***
Set up maintenance and test facility	3.00 (1.71)	2.3667 (1.594)	3.9500 (1.431)	0.000***
Adjust plant design	1.75 (1.27)	1.4000 (0.887)	2.2750 (1.569)	0.002***
Improve quality	3.12 (1.70)	2.2333 (1.489)	4.4500 (0.959)	0.000***
Improve performance	3.19 (1.64)	2.3167 (1.479)	4.5000 (0.751)	0.000***
Find alternative use for the assimilated technology	2.44 (1.47)	2.1000 (1.285)	2.9500 (1.584)	0.006***
Develop new product using assimilated technology	2.75 (1.59)	2.1167 (1.354)	3.7000 (1.436)	0.000***
Develop new application using assimilated technology	2.73 (1.60)	2.1167 (1.379)	3.6500 (1.477)	0.000***
Introduce process innovation	1.64 (1.15)	1.3833 (0.846)	2.0250 (1.423)	0.013**
Fuse assimilated technology with other technologies	2.72 (1.52)	2.1333 (1.321)	3.6000 (1.374)	0.000***

* $p < 0.1$ ** $p < 0.05$ *** $p < 0.01$.
Means are shown in each cell and correspondent standard deviations are shown in brackets under means.

all Taiwanese information technology firms. The skill not only facilitates the substitution of materials and components thereby reducing overheads, but also provides diversification opportunities for products that embody acquired technologies.

Technologies are not always ready for product development especially those technologies transferred from public research institutions. A lack of marketing input in public research institutions means that technologies transferred from these institutions generally need to be further developed to meet the specific requirements of the individual firm's product lines. Sometimes new applications are developed in an attempt to adapt technologies to fit a firm, which ultimately increases business success. One Taiwanese visual technology firm acquired technology from the Industrial Technology Research Institute and converted it into a leading technology in the field, thus superseding the original technology. With respect to the capability of developing applications, there is a significantly better capability of finding alternative uses, and developing new products and applications for transferred technologies in more effective projects than less effective ones.

Compared with less effective projects, more effective projects reflected significantly better capacity to (1) ensure the quality of machinery, construction and materials, (2) inspect conformity with existing specifications and standards, (3) set up maintenance and test facilities, (4) revise quality control operations, (5) adjust plant design, and (6) introduce process innovation (see Table 5.3). This implies that more effective technology transfer required greater involvement of production and benefited from superior proficiency at process-related activities. As Rosenberg (1982) notes, through direct involvement in manufacturing, a firm is better able to recognize and exploit new information relevant to a particular product market. Production experience provides the firm with the background necessary to recognize the value of, as well as implement methods to recognize or automate, a particular manufacturing process. This observation partly illustrates that for many Taiwanese information technology firms, their strength lies in the area of production and in their conversion of manufacturing capacity. Both, in turn, influence their absorptive capacity.

Barriers to Intra-firm Technology Diffusion and Effectiveness

Barrier levels in less effective projects are significantly higher than those in more effective projects (see Table 5.4). Our results suggest that barriers to intra-firm technology diffusion will reduce the competitive edge of firms in high growth lucrative markets like information technology markets. The findings concur with Vandermerwe (1987) who argued that organizational blocks to new ideas resulted in opportunity costs in both time and money because of delays in the firm's response to its environment and innovation opportunities.

Risks are perceived in less effective projects to be higher than those in more effective projects. Interdepartmental resistance is significantly higher in less effective projects than in more effective ones. There is a significantly

Table 5.4 Intra-firm diffusion in more and less effective technology transfer projects

Intra-firm diffusion	Sample (n = 100)	Less effective project (n = 60)	More effective project (n = 40)	t-test Two-tailed significance
Barrier level	1.65 (0.88)	1.8500 (0.988)	1.3500 (0.580)	0.002***
Risk perceived too high	1.48 (0.92)	1.7167 (1.075)	1.1250 (0.404)	0.000***
Interdepartmental resistance	1.46 (0.81)	1.6500 (0.917)	1.1750 (0.501)	0.001***
Hard to transmit benefit	1.63 (0.92)	1.7333 (0.989)	1.4750 (0.784)	0.150
No consensus on benefit	1.69 (0.97)	1.8333 (1.011)	1.4750 (0.877)	0.063*
Political barrier	1.22 (0.61)	1.2667 (0.660)	1.1500 (0.533)	0.353
Psychological barrier	1.27 (0.66)	1.3667 (0.802)	1.1250 (0.335)	0.041**
No access to power base	1.24 (0.59)	1.3667 (0.712)	1.0500 (0.221)	0.002***
Not-invented-here syndrome	1.31 (0.76)	1.4000 (0.867)	1.1750 (0.549)	0.116
Threat to present projects	1.69 (1.07)	1.6167 (0.958)	1.8000 (1.224)	0.427
Hard to justify ROI/cost	1.82 (1.18)	2.1000 (1.285)	1.4000 (0.841)	0.001***
Structural barrier	1.29 (0.71)	1.3667 (0.802)	1.1750 (0.549)	0.159
Same region same function diffusion	2.86 (1.78)	2.8333 (1.679)	2.9000 (1.945)	0.860
Same region different functions diffusion	1.56 (1.12)	1.6000 (1.182)	1.5000 (1.038)	0.665
Different regions same function diffusion	2.69 (1.81)	2.0000 (1.438)	3.7250 (1.840)	0.000***
Different regions different functions diffusion	1.07 (0.29)	1.0500 (0.287)	1.1000 (0.304)	0.406

* *p* < 0.1 ** *p* < 0.05 *** *p* < 0.01.
Means are shown in each cell and correspondent standard deviations are shown in brackets under means.

lower degree of consensus on perceived benefits of assimilated technologies in less effective than in more effective projects. Returns on investment are significantly harder to justify in less effective than in more effective projects. The difficulties of achieving a coherent perspective on risks and benefits tend to hinder the cost-effective transmission of acquired technologies. The capability to make correct judgements about technologies relies on the technological capability of the firm as a whole. Not only R&D but all relevant departments in new product development are responsible for cultivating technological capability so as to contribute positively in screening and implementing technologies.

There is significantly less access to the power base in less effective projects than in more effective ones. Psychological barriers in less effective projects are significantly higher than those in more effective projects. Personal bias and self-interest can get in the way of an individual's judgement of new ideas and collaborative activities with other people. Political barriers break up teamwork and can leave people in isolation. Furthermore, if political barriers arise from interdepartmental causes, firms will definitely encounter stagnation in terms of the speed of new product development and growth, and will consequently lose their competitiveness and ability to survive. Therefore, proposition 2 finds strong support here.

Pattern of Intra-firm Technology Diffusion and Effectiveness

Intra-firm technology diffusion within the same function across different geographical regions is significantly greater in the more effective projects than in less effective projects (see Table 5.4). The diffusion of technical knowledge within the same function, in the context of this research in the R&D department, is very important to the effectiveness of technology transfer.

Learning and Effectiveness of Technology Transfer

In more effective projects, there is significantly greater emphasis on learning-by-doing than in the less effective ones (see Table 5.5). In the qualitative discussions with key informants, it emerged that learning-by-doing in sample firms involved multi-level learning consistent within Lall's (1980) notions of 'multi-layered learning'. The latter covered: (1) learning-by-adapting in which assimilated technologies remain unchanged but their utilization becomes more efficient either through the experience of workers or through minor changes made in a plant; (2) learning-by-designing whereby assimilated technologies are replicated which involves the setting up of a capital goods industry; and (3) learning-by-improving designs such that assimilated technologies are specifically adapted to recipient's materials, production conditions, and skills. Responses indicate that Taiwanese firms rarely learn by setting up radically new production systems and designing new processes. They tend to transfer product technologies and modify these to meet existing production systems instead of introducing new process innovations which might be inherently rigid for them.

Learning-by-doing in Taiwanese industries, therefore, has a quite different connotation from that in Western industries. Although both processes

Table 5.5 Learning in more and less effective technology transfer projects

Learning	Sample (n = 100)	Less effective project (n = 60)	More effective project (n = 40)	t-test Two-tailed significance
Individual learning	3.46	3.4000	3.5500	0.541
	(1.19)	(1.278)	(1.061)	
Group learning	3.79	3.5000	4.2250	0.007***
	(1.32)	(1.334)	(1.187)	
Firm learning	1.90	1.7667	2.1000	0.106
	(1.01)	(0.998)	(1.008)	
Learning by doing	4.17	3.8667	4.6250	0.000***
	(0.96)	(1.065)	(0.540)	
Learning by training	2.73	2.6167	2.9000	0.245
	(1.19)	(1.166)	(1.215)	
Formal on-job training	2.83	2.6167	3.1500	0.014**
	(1.11)	(1.166)	(0.949)	
Informal on-job training	3.74	3.4333	4.2000	0.000***
	(1.05)	(1.125)	(0.723)	
R&D training	3.95	3.7333	4.2750	0.040**
	(1.36)	(1.460)	(1.132)	
Manufacturing training	1.89	1.6167	2.3000	0.012**
	(1.27)	(1.091)	(1.418)	
Marketing training	1.47	1.3333	1.6750	0.060*
	(0.89)	(0.857)	(0.917)	
QA training	1.65	1.3667	2.0750	0.001***
	(1.00)	(0.802)	(1.118)	

* $p < 0.1$ ** $p < 0.05$ *** $p < 0.01$.
Means are shown in each cell and correspondent standard deviations are shown in brackets under means.

involve trial-and-error, learning-by-doing in Taiwanese industries stresses knowledge replication while Western industries place greater emphasis on knowledge creation. In Taiwanese firms, this implies a hands-on approach whereby engineers learn to adapt, design, improve, set up production systems, and re-design processes.

Collective learning is another success factor in technology assimilation in the Taiwanese information technology industry. Group-level learning is significantly more emphasized in more effective than in less effective projects. Kedia and Bhagat (1988) note that in Japan, Singapore, Hong Kong, and Taiwan, successful examples of technology diffusion are strongly collectivistic. There are also function-wide discussion groups which are discipline based (normally within R&D functions) but very little learning at firm level is organized. Mean values show that group- and individual-level learning are more emphasized than firm-level learning (see Table 5.5).

The mean value of 'learning-by-training' (2.73) is apparently lower than that of 'learning-by-doing' (4.17). It would seem that training is less important in facilitating the learning process in Taiwanese information technology firms than hands-on experience. This finding contrasts with research findings regarding the importance of training in the rapid post-war economic development of Japan. One reason is that Taiwanese industries rely far more on informal on-the-job training than formal training programmes. This is confirmed by the observation that the mean value of 'informal on-the-job training' (3.74) is significantly higher than that for 'formal on-the-job training' (2.83). Informal on-the-job training refers to engineers seeking the expert opinion and advice of senior engineers or managers, thus learning in an informal way; this is facilitated by the master–apprentice relationship. Tacit knowledge is passed on through the process of demonstration from masters to apprentices.

Training is one success factor of technology transfer although Taiwanese information technology firms do not acknowledge this importance explicitly. More effective projects reflect significantly more training than the less effective ones. Training in R&D, manufacturing, marketing, and quality assurance departments is significantly greater in more effective than in less effective projects. With respect to the training of various functions, people from the R&D department participate in more training than do manufacturing, marketing, or quality assurance staff.

According to Sheen (1992), there are relatively few formal mechanisms for diffusing knowledge in an industry. Some companies employ leading-edge research experts to conduct seminars. Some of these experts are taken on as long-term consultants but they are approached in an *ad hoc* manner. This research supports her findings. Taiwanese information technology firms hire engineering professors from both domestic and foreign universities and Chinese ethnic engineers to conduct engineering seminars or training programmes. Engineers who attend external training programmes are also responsible for passing acquired knowledge to their colleagues through seminars and other informal media. Together, the research findings offer a great deal of support for proposition 3.

CONCLUSION

The study findings provide strong support for the three research propositions posed in this chapter. First, there is strong evidence to confirm that companies displaying a higher level of absorptive capacity are able to transfer technology more successfully than those that lack this skill. Importantly, successful cases in the study invariably show a stronger ability to interpret externally sourced information and to selectively modify acquired technologies to enhance product quality and performance while improving production proficiency.

Second, in the effective cases of technology transfer in sample firms, project leaders are more able to surmount the barriers which retard intra-firm diffusion of technology than in the less effective projects. Furthermore, effective cases are significantly more adept at justifying financial (ROI and cost) benefits to the firm. Clearly, this helps to reduce management's perceived risk and to overcome multi-functional resistance to the adoption of new technologies/ideas.

Thirdly, the study findings confirm the role of learning and training in facilitating technology transfer in sample firms. Specifically, managers emphasize group-based learning and learning-by-doing more heavily in the effective than in the less effective cases.

The results confirm the significance of informal on-the-job training and its impact on technology acquisition and implementation outcome in sample firms. Further, the emphasis on technical (i.e. R&D, production, quality assurance) training was significantly more pervasive in the more successful than in the less successful projects.

Future Research

The current research focuses on three key elements – absorptive capacity, intra-organizational diffusion of information, and learning – that govern the effectiveness of technology transfer in a sample of Taiwanese IT firms. The specific industry and national context of the study mean that the empirical findings may not be generalizable to Taiwanese firms in all types of industry or to technology transfers undertaken by firms in other newly industrialized countries (NICs). Future research should examine the propositions concerning effective technology transfer in firms operating in a wider range of industries as well as across different industrializing or newly industrialized economies.

In high-tech and rapidly changing technological environments, businesses must increase their speed and adeptness at responding to changes in these environments. Few businesses, however, have unlimited resources to cultivate indigenous or state-of-the-art technologies. Technology acquisition and adaptation arguably offer an alternative route to build technological advantage. There is, however, little empirical research into how companies, in both industrializing and developed Western economies, should leverage resources and capabilities to accomplish fast, effective assimilation and exploitation of externally sourced technologies in a global business context. Further investigations focusing on international businesses in technology-intensive industries would yield valuable insights into cross-border technology transfer and the implications for global business management.

Notes

1. Source: *Commercial Times*, 23 December 1994, p. 14.
2. Source: *An Overview of Industrial Technology Development*, 1994, the Ministry of Economic Affairs, Republic of China. The index is calculated by four criteria: the number of patents filed, the value of technology trading, the export value of technology-intensive products, and the add-on value of manufacturing industry.
3. Source: *Commercial Times*, 14 February 1995, p. 14.
4. Special Edition, *Commonwealth*, 10 June 1994.

References

Atuahene-Gima, K. (1992) 'Inward technology licensing as an alternative of internal R&D in new product development: a conceptual framework', *Journal of Product Innovation Management*, 9, pp. 156–67.

Baranson, J. (1970) 'Technology transfer through the international firm', *American Economic Review Papers and Proceedings*, pp. 435–41.

Bell, R.M.N. (1984) 'Learning and the accumulation of industrial capacity in developing countries', in M. Fransman and K. King (eds), *Technological Capability in the Third World* (London: Macmillan).

Chanaron, J.J. and J. Perrin (1987) 'The transfer of research development and design to developing countries', *Future*, October, pp. 503–12.

Chatterji, D. and T.A. Manuel (1993) 'Benefiting from external sources of technology', *Research-Technology Management*, November–December, pp. 21–6.

Cohen, W.M. and D.A. Levinthal (1990) 'Absorptive capacity: a new perspective on learning and innovation', *Administrative Science Quarterly*, 35, pp. 128–52.

Cooper, R.G. (1984) 'How new product strategies impact on performance', *Journal of Product Innovation Management*, 1, pp. 5–18.

Davidson, W.H. (1980) *Experience Effects in International Investment and Technology Transfer* (Ann Arbor: UMI Research Press).

Doyle, P., J. Saunders and V. Wong (1992) 'Competition in global markets: a case study of American and Japanese competition in the British market', *Journal of International Business Studies*, 23(3), pp. 419–42.

Galbraith, C.S. (1990) 'Transferring core manufacturing technologies in high-technology firms', *California Management Review*, Summer, pp. 56–70.

Hagedoorn, J. and J. Schakenraad (1990) 'Strategic partnering and technological cooperation', in C. Freeman and L. Soete (eds), *New Exploitations in the Economics of Technical Change* (London: Pinter), pp. 1–37.

Kedia, B.L. and R.S. Bhagat (1988) 'Cultural constraints on transfer of technology across nations: implications for research in international and comparative management', *Academy of Management Review*, 13(4), pp. 559–71.

Kogut, B. and U. Zander (1993) 'Knowledge of the firm and the evolutionary theory of the multinational corporation', *Journal of International Business Studies*, Fourth Quarter, pp. 625–45.

Lall, S. (1980) 'Developing countries as exporters of industrial technology', *Research Policy*, 9(1), pp. 24–53.

Lasserre, P. (1982) 'Training: key to technological transfer', *Long Range Planning*, 15(3), pp. 51–60.

Lorriman, J. and T. Kenjo (1994) *Japan's Winning Margins* (New York: Oxford University Press).

Madu, C.N. (1989) 'Transferring technology to developing countries – critical factors for success', *Long Range Planning*, 22(4), pp. 115–24.

Roscoe, J.T. (1975) *Fundamental Research Statistics for the Behavioural Sciences*, 2nd edn (New York: Holt, Rinehart & Winston, Inc.).

Rosenberg, N. (1982) *Inside the Black Box: Technology and Economics* (New York: Cambridge University Press).

Ruekert, R.W., O.C. Walker and K.J. Roering (1985) 'The organisation of marketing activities: a contingency theory of structure and performance', *Journal of Marketing*, 49(Winter), pp. 13–25.

Sheen, M.R. (1992) 'Barriers to scientific and technical knowledge acquisition in industrial R&D', *R&D Management*, 22(2), pp. 135–43.

Teece, D.J. (1977) 'Technology transfer by multinational firms: the resource cost of transferring technological know-how', *The Economic Journal*, 87(2), pp. 242–61.

Vandermerwe, S. (1987) 'Diffusing new ideas in-house', *Journal of Product Innovation Management*, 4(4) (December), pp. 256–64.

6 The Role of Resources in Global Competition[1]

John Fahy[1]

INTRODUCTION

World trade since the end of the Second World War has been characterized by dramatic levels of growth in both scale and scope. For example, since 1950, world exports of manufactured goods have risen by a factor of sixteen compared with output growth of around seven (Buckley and Brooke, 1992). With this increasing trade has come new centres of economic power. If the World Bank's forecast for economic growth to the year 2020 is correct, China will overtake the United States as the world's largest economy and, in addition, India, Indonesia, South Korea, Thailand and Taiwan will all feature in the world's top ten economies (*The Economist*, 1994). Institutional developments have helped foster these changes. Regional harmonization is continuing in Europe since its landmark year of 1992 and also in North America and East Asia. Growing levels of democracy have created new factor and product markets in Central and Eastern Europe.

These changes have meant that, at the level of the individual firm, the issue of global competition continues to become increasingly important. Of the approximately 7000 multinational corporations (MNCs) operating in 1970, over half were accounted for by just two countries, namely, the United States and Britain. By 1986, there were over 37 000 MNCs and furthermore, four of the world's richest countries – the United States, Japan, Germany and Switzerland – accounted for less than half of them. Competition for resources and markets is intense, new challengers are appearing from different parts of the world and formerly secure national industries and firms are being subjected to realities of competition. For example, in 1930, the United States held over 80 per cent of the world market for automobile production, but by 1980 this share had dropped to just over 20 per cent despite the fact that much of the production in US plants was foreign-owned (Aliber, 1993).

Global competition has historically captured the interest of a range of scholars, most notably in the fields of economics and management. However, a great deal of work remains to be done in terms of fully understanding inter-firm competition at the global level and particularly the question of how firms can attain a competitive advantage at this level. To date, the substantial volume of literature within the field of international business has not been explicitly concerned with these two questions. Contributions from economics have evolved from early trade theory (Ricardo, 1817; Hecksher, 1919) which put the nation rather than the firm at the centre of its analysis of trade patterns and competitiveness. Subsequent work, such as that grounded in industrial organization economics (Hymer, 1960; Kindleberger, 1969) and transaction cost economics (Buckley and Casson, 1976; Rugman, 1981) have proposed alternative explanations for the existence of the multinational firm, while the eclectic paradigm and its extensions (Dunning, 1981) have sought an integrated explanation for international production. Extant management-based contributions have tended to focus on process issues (Bartlett and Ghoshal, 1989; Ghoshal and Nohria, 1993), and where competition has been addressed, it has tended to have been within the confines of the global/local dichotomy (Porter, 1986). Therefore, the purpose of this chapter is to build on and integrate the literature from the fields of economics, international business and strategic management with the view to specifically tackling the question of how the firm can attain a sustainable competitive advantage in a global environment.

SOURCES OF COMPETITIVE ADVANTAGE

One of the principal concerns of the strategic management literature is the question of how some firms manage to consistently outperform others in the marketplace. As this literature has developed, alternative explanations have been proposed. In the early 1980s, the dominant view, reflected by the work of Porter (1980) and grounded in Bain/Mason Industrial Organization (IO), was that superior performance was a function of industry structure and barriers to entry. Porter proposed that superior performance lay in understanding industry structure which could be analyzed in terms of five key forces, namely the rivalry among existing competitors, the threat of entrants and of substitutes and the bargaining power of buyers and suppliers. Firms could earn monopoly rents by either selecting industries which were 'structurally attractive' or by manipulating the forces driving competition in their favour through the selection of generic strategies. The normative implication of Porter's model was essentially a contingency one. He suggested a typology of generic strategic alternatives, the suitability of which was dependent on industry structure and stage of development (Porter, 1980).

However, in the late 1980s, a growing body of empirical work testing Porter's ideas ironically began to cast doubt on their validity. Researchers observed performance differences not only between firms in the same industry (Hansen and Wernerfelt, 1989; Rumelt, 1991), but also within the narrower confines of strategic groups within industries (Cool and Schendel, 1988). For example, Hansen and Wernerfelt's (1989) study assessed the relative impact of economic and organizational factors on firm performance and found that organizational factors explained about twice as much of the variance in firm profit rates as economic factors. These findings coincided with and complimented a conceptual swing away from the industry as the focus of interest. The beginnings of this swing can be seen in the work of economists such as Wernerfelt (1984) and Barney (1986) and management theorists such as Coyne (1986). What followed has been something of an explosion of interest in the firm and its resource endowments, popularly labelled the 'resource-based view of the firm'. The basic proposition of this view is that the performance differences of firms are more effectively explained by their idiosyncratic resource endowments rather than the structure of the industries in which they operate. As Barney (1991) puts it, if the firm possesses resources which are valuable, rare, inimitable and non-substitutable, then these resources should be deployed in the marketplace and a position of sustainable competitive advantage will be attained.

Aside from its current popularity as an explanation for performance differences between firms, the resource-based view of the firm has particular appeal in the context of firms operating in a global environment. A review of the international business literature demonstrates that, over time, resources have been a central theme and key element of the different schools of thought. Trade theory is founded on country resources and how asymmetries between countries in terms of their resource endowments leads to absolute and comparative advantages. Prevailing theories of the multinational firm, such as the industrial organization theory of Hymer (1960), the eclectic paradigm of Dunning (1981) and the evolutionary economic theory of Kogut and Zander (1993) rely heavily on the notion of firm-specific resources and the importance of these resources in global competition. Additionally, there is also the recognition that a globally-scaled firm has at its disposal a very large resource pool upon which competitive strategies can be based.

Therefore, the following section proposes to adopt the resource-based view of the firm as a theoretical framework to provide insights into the nature of competitive advantage in a global environment. This approach holds promise on a number fronts. First, to date, conceptual and empirical work on the resource-based view of the firm has taken place in a largely 'domestic' context and without due attention to the unique challenges faced by firms operating internationally. Given the ubiquitous nature of global competition in the 1990s, as noted at the outset, this oversight needs to be redressed. Second, there are the potential benefits to be gained from the two-way exchange of ideas. In other words, not only does the resource-based view of the firm hold potential for informing our understanding of global competition, but in reverse, testing its fundamental tenets in the global context may also help to refine and clarify the ideas implicit in the resource-based view. Finally, extending the resource-based view to the global context responds to repeated calls for a multi-disciplinary approach to international business research (Buckley, 1991; Daniels, 1991; Dunning, 1989). In the following section, the key insights of the resource-based view are delineated and the necessary extensions and additions to take account of the global environment faced by many firms are provided. In particular, new insights into the nature of competition and competitive advantage are highlighted.

THE RESOURCE-BASED VIEW IN A GLOBAL ENVIRONMENT

As a first step, it is necessary to review the basic propositions of the resource-based view of the firm. Its logic is a relatively simple one. It starts with the assumption that the desired outcome of managerial effort within the firm is a sustainable competitive advantage (SCA). Achieving an SCA allows the firm to earn economic rents or above-average returns. In turn, this focuses attention on the question of how firms achieve and sustain advantages. The resource-based view contends that the answer to this question lies in the possession of certain key resources, that is, resources having the characteristics of value and barriers to duplication. An SCA can be obtained if the firm effectively deploys these key resources in its product-markets. Therefore, the resource-based view emphasises strategic choice, charging the firm's management with the tasks of identifying and deploying key resources to maximize returns. In summary, the essential elements of the resource-based view are (i) the possession/development of key resources, (ii) the deployment of those resources via competitive strategies and (iii) the attainment of an SCA leading to superior performance measured in conventional terms such as profitability and return-on-investment. Each of these elements are now examined in greater detail with specific reference to the case of firms operating in a global environment.

Resources

The list of resources in any given firm is likely to be a long one. One of the principal insights of the resource-based view of the firm is that not all resources are of equal importance or possess the potential to be a source of sustainable competitive advantage. Much attention in the literature, therefore, has focused on the issues of value and barriers to duplication, the two defining characteristics of advantage-creating resources. Barney (1991) defines a valuable resource as one which permits the firm to conceive of or implement strategies which improve its efficiency and effectiveness by meeting the needs of its customers. There has been somewhat less agreement in and around the issue of barriers to duplication which has been the focus of several contributions (Barney, 1991; Dierickx and Cool, 1989; Coyne, 1986; Hall, 1992; Peteraf, 1993; Reed and DeFillippi, 1990).

Barriers to duplication may take many forms and may vary in terms of the type of resource under consideration. For example, Grant (1991) notes that resources may inherently possess barriers which prevent their imitation, acquisition or substitution by competitors. Furthermore, resources may be difficult to duplicate due to tacit qualities (Reed and DeFillippi, 1990) which are a feature in many skills-based industries where value-creating activities are difficult to identify and codify. Equally, many value-creating resources are complex and embedded in team-based experiences and organizational routines implying that few individuals, if any, within an organization, possess the depth of knowledge to grasp an overall understanding of the sources of superior performance (Nelson and Winter, 1982). This information is immobile even though particular employees may be recruited by competitors. Additionally, even in situations where value-creating resources are clearly identifiable they can be protected from duplication through the legal system of property rights (Hall, 1992).

Therefore, in terms of identifying and deploying its resources effectively, the firm must understand the relative strength of each resource in terms of its barriers to duplication by competitors. Several classification schemes have been recommended in the literature, but for simplicity it is proposed that resources be divided into three generic groupings, namely, tangible assets, intangible assets and capabilities. Tangible assets refer to the fixed or current assets of an organization which have a fixed long-run capacity (Wernerfelt, 1989). Examples include plant and equipment, land, other capital goods and stocks, debtors and bank deposits. Tangible assets have the property of ownership and their value is relatively easy to measure (Hall, 1992). The book value of these assets is assessed through conventional accounting mechanisms and this value is usually reflected in the balance sheet valuation of companies. However, such assets are transparent (Grant, 1991) and are therefore relatively weak in terms of their barriers to duplication by competitors. Thus, though assets such as plants or land may be geographically immobile, they are relatively imitable and substitutable. In summary, tangible assets possess weak barriers to duplication and are therefore likely to be poor sources of sustainable competitive advantage in a global environment.

Firms may possess a variety of intangible assets including trademarks, patents, trade secrets, networks and reputation (Hall, 1992). These intangible assets often account for the significant differences which can be observed between the balance sheet valuation and stock market valuation of some publicly quoted companies (Grant, 1991; Hall, 1992). These differences are particularly pronounced in industries like pharmaceuticals where patents are critical, consumer goods where trademarks and brand reputation are critical and service firms where company reputation is critical (Grant, 1991). Intangible assets have relatively unlimited capacity (Wernerfelt, 1989). For example, Nayyar (1990) demonstrates how service firms can diversify on the basis of reputation where consumers face significant information acquisition costs. Intangible assets are relatively resistant to duplication efforts by competitors due to either regulatory or position gaps (Coyne, 1986). Intellectual property is afforded legal protection and though this protection is not without its limits in international markets, recent years have seen some improvements, particularly with property rights agreements arising out of the completion of the Uruguay round of GATT talks. Others, such as networks and reputation are examples of accumulated assets (Dierickx and Cool, 1989) which resist duplication in the short run. Therefore, it would be expected that intangible assets will be a more important source of sustainable competitive advantage in a global environment than tangible assets.

Capabilities represent a broad grouping and have been variously described as skills, invisible assets (Itami, 1987) and intermediate goods in the production process (Amit and Schoemaker, 1993). Typical capabilities include, teamwork, organizational culture and relationships between workforce and management. Capabilities have relatively limited capacity in the short run due to learning and change difficulties but have relatively unlimited capacity in the long run (Wernerfelt, 1989). They do not have clearly defined property rights as they cannot be the subject of a transaction (Hall, 1992) resulting in difficulties in their valuation and acquisition. However, such difficulties represent a potent barrier to duplication. Because they are either skill-based or interaction-based, capabilities possess varying levels of tacitness and complexity (Reed and DeFillippi, 1990) making them difficult to duplicate and hence a very important source of competitive advantage in a global environment.

In summary, it is possible to conclude that in a global environment capabilities will represent a more important source of competitive advantage than intangible assets which in turn will represent a more important source of advantage than tangible assets. However, this three-way classification of resources which derives from the economic and management literature does not describe the full picture for the firm trading internationally. The three groups of resources defined above are all essentially firm-specific resources. However, the company operating across national boundaries has access as well to country-specific resources in both its home country and in each of the countries in which it does business. Fully understanding the resource endowments of the internationally-traded firm requires consideration of these country-specific resources.

In an effort to outline the role played by country-specific resources in the global competitive advantage of firms, it is also helpful to distinguish two types of country-specific resource, namely country-specific assets and country-specific capabilities. Country-specific assets include a country's location and climate, its natural resources, its costs of labour and capital, and its government incentives which have traditionally been seen as important determinants of international production decisions (Dunning, 1981; Doz, 1978). Such assets are relatively transparent and tangible and in the cases of natural resources, location and climate, they are inherited and fixed. By definition, country-specific assets are unique to each particular country and are available to all firms on an equal basis (Dunning, 1981). As such, it is possible to duplicate a competitor's stock of country-specific assets and consequently they are a relatively unimportant source of competitive advantage in a global environment.

On the other hand, country-specific capabilities refer to a country's stock of knowledge of technological and management practices (Kogut, 1991). These capabilities tend to be culture-bound, developed slowly over time and diffuse across the boundaries of the firm easier than across national borders (Kogut, 1991). Therefore, firms are likely to have easier access to country-specific capabilities in their country-of-origin and engage in horizontal foreign direct investment to gain access to capabilities in other countries. Country-specific capabilities are similar to Dierickx and Cool's (1989) concept of asset stocks at the firm level implying that they cannot be adjusted instantaneously but only slowly and over time as a country invests in developing its education levels or market infrastructure. Because of the complexity and culture-bound nature of country-specific capabilities, the likelihood is that it will be more difficult to both identify and duplicate a competitor's stock of country-specific capabilities, meaning that the latter are likely to be more important than country-specific assets as a source of competitive advantage in a global environment.

In summary then, the issue of competitive advantage in a global environment is complicated by the fact that firms operate across multiple national boundaries. Models of competitive advantage must take this into account. In particular, resource classifications must be extended to take account of resources available in both the country-of-origin and host countries of global competitors. Country-specific resources are diverse and complex and may be an important source of advantage. Added to firm-specific resources, the globally-scaled firm has access to a complex and diverse resource pool. However, we noted above that resources are only a source of competitive advantage if they are identified and deployed by the firm via its competitive strategies. We now turn to this question.

Strategy

Business or competitive strategy in a global environment has traditionally been viewed in terms of the challenge of managing the conflicting demands of responding to local needs while at the same time searching for global efficiencies. These twin themes have evolved from the unification/fragmentation debate (Fayerweather, 1969) through the integration/responsiveness debate (Prahalad, 1976) to the global/local debate (Levitt, 1983). The task of strategy has been seen as one of trying to balance the efficiencies to be gained from the integration of cross-border operations with the need for flexibility and local responsiveness in different markets. Over time, different sides of the argument have been emphasized. Throughout the 1960s and 1970s the need for local responsiveness was emphasized due to differences between countries in terms of tastes, industry structures, distribution systems and government regulations. This was followed in the 1980s by a distinct shift in emphasis to looking at the possibilities and benefits of global integration. This position was perhaps most forcefully argued by Levitt (1983) who proposed that markets were homogenizing due to technology and communications, a trend which made the 'multinational corporation obsolete and the global corporation absolute'. This thesis spawned a controversy which remains ongoing.

Towards the late 1980s, the global/local dichotomy was considered to be too simplistic to capture the full complexities of business strategy in a global environment (Ghoshal, 1987). What effectively emerged was a contingency view reflected in the popular strategic typology proposed by Bartlett and Ghoshal (1989). Though primarily concerned with issues of organizational structure and managerial process, these authors identified four distinct approaches which they deem to be appropriate given certain industry conditions. Firms pursuing a *multinational* strategy are those which seek to build a strong position in many markets by responding to local conditions and demands. An *international* strategy is one in which the firm competes on the basis of leveraging domestic strengths in foreign markets. Firms pursuing a *global* strategy seek to increase efficiency through the integration, rationalization and standardization of worldwide operations. Finally, a *transnational* strategy gives equal emphasis to and seeks to balance the pressures for integration and responsiveness as well as transferring learning and innovations across borders (Bartlett and Ghoshal, 1989). The adoption of each of these strategies has subsequently been empirically validated (Leong and Tan, 1993).

What is of interest for our purposes is understanding how the pursuit of each of these global business strategies is likely to influence or be influenced by the firm's resource endowments. Given the differences between each of the strategic types it is to be expected that they would place different demands on the firm's resource pool. The relationships between resource compositions and competitive strategy in a global environment are outlined in the following paragraphs.

Multinational firms are characterized by what can be described as a polycentric orientation (Perlmutter, 1969). In other words, the management of multinational firms is described as having a view of the world which sees foreign markets as potentially very different, requiring relatively high levels of localization of both products and strategy. Though these levels of localization may not be cost-effective, they are deemed to be necessary given market differences. Consequently, foreign subsidiaries are considered to 'know what's best' for their local regions and are afforded high levels of autonomy and responsibility. What are the likely implications of this orientation/strategy for the firm's resource endowments? It is to be expected that resources located in host countries would be considered to be relatively more important by multinational firms than by the other strategic typesidentified by Bartlett and Ghoshal (1989). Furthermore, this emphasis is likely to extend both to resources which are specific to the host countries and to assets and capabilities which are specific to the firm's foreign subsidiaries. This important role played by subsidiaries in the overall competitiveness of the firm is further highlighted in Chapters 4 and 10 of this book.

International firms are those in which control is maintained by headquarters in the country-of-origin and where operations in foreign markets are seen as being appendages to the domestic corporation (Bartlett and Ghoshal, 1989). Consequently, these kinds of firms might be said to be characterized by a somewhat parochial or ethnocentric managerial philosophy (Perlmutter, 1969) where the home country is of greatest importance and concern. In terms of competitive strategy, the home country is viewed as the key source of new developments which lead to advantages in domestic and foreign markets. This orientation is likely to be most prevalent in firms with large domestic markets and/or those at an early stage of international development. In terms of their resource deployment, international firms are likely to contrast sharply with multinationals, emphasizing instead both home country-specific resources and the firm-specific resources of the parent firm.

The global firm has much in common with the international firm but is more likely to be exhibited by experienced competitors and particularly those operating in industries where there is homogeneity of customer needs and pressure for cost efficiencies. Global firms typically view the world as one market and seek to produce globally standardized products or modular products which can be easily and cheaply adapted to local conditions (Porter, 1986). The marketing of such standardized products, in turn creates the possibilities for centralized production facilities enabling global economies of scale. Indeed global firms are likely to locate their value adding activities such as R&D, design, production and marketing wherever in the world they deem it to be most cost-effective to do so (Porter, 1986). Therefore, the global firm is likely to adopt a mixed approach to its resource deployment. Home country firm-specific assets and capabilities are likely remain important to the global firm as these are typically the bases upon which initial advantages are gained in world markets (Bartlett and Ghoshal, 1989). However, in seeking to continue to be competitive, global firms are also likely to put a premium on host country-specific resources such as natural resources, the costs of labour and capital and/or government incentives which enable them to gain cost efficiencies.

Finally, transnational firms are likely to adopt a very balanced approach to resource deployment. The transnational strategy is a complex one, seeking to incorporate and maximize the strengths of the other three forms, namely, the responsiveness of the multinational, the ability of the international firm to transfer resources and the cost efficiencies of the global firm (Bartlett and Ghoshal, 1989). This means that the firm will operate on the basis that some activities are best centralized in the home country, that others are best centralized in diverse world locations and that others are decentralized locally. Thus, the firm operates as a coordinated network with flows of people, information, resources and products to and from headquarters and subsidiaries as well as between subsidiaries (Bartlett and Ghoshal, 1989). No part of the organization is seen as being more important than another, and therefore the firm-specific resources of both the parent and subsidiaries are likely to be considered to be of equal importance. A similar lack of distinction exists at the level of the country, implying an equal weighting for both home and host country-specific resources.

To conclude, the firm's strategic posture is likely to place unique demands on its resource endowments. The impact of this relationship on the performance of the firm in a global environment is examined in the next section.

Performance

One of the central concerns of academics and business practitioners has been in attempting to understand the determinants of success and failure of a business enterprise and, in particular, what enables certain firms to attain consistently high performance levels. A fundamental assumption in organization theory holds that the performance of an organization is influenced by the level of fit that it has with the environment in which it is operating. This is analogous to the issue of strategic fit in the strategy literature where performance is viewed as being influenced by the existence of a fit between the firm's strengths and the key success factors in its industry (de Vasconcellos E Sa and Hambrick, 1989).

The discussion in this chapter elaborates on the nature of this relationship in the context of firms operating in a global environment. It has demonstrated that even though resources may be valuable and difficult to duplicate, this does not in itself confer a sustainable competitive advantage on the firm. The resources must be identified and used by management to create products and service outputs which are valuable to customers (Barney, 1991). It was shown in the previous section that the pursuit of different strategies in a global environment imposes different demands on the firm's resource pool. Therefore, it is to be expected that firms which display a consistency or fit between their resources endowments and their strategic choices will outperform those where such congruence does not exist. In other words, not only must there be a fit between the firm's resources and the environment in which it is operating but there must also be a fit at another level, namely, that between the firm's resources and its competitive strategies.

CONCLUSION

This chapter has sought to provide an understanding of the nature of sustainable competitive advantage in a global environment. The current environment imposes many demands on today's managers. For many firms, factor, production and market locations can now be anywhere in the world and the technological infrastructure is increasingly being put in place to facilitate the coordination of disparate activities. Strong competitors are emerging from different parts of the world with different views on how 'the game should be played'. Advances in technology and communication foster the potential for integrated competitive strategies on a worldwide basis. Much of the extant international business literature does not adequately address this practical reality. The focus of the traditional economic literature is at the macro level of the country or is concerned with explaining the existence of multinational firms. The international management literature is predominantly concerned with process issues such as structure and control systems or human resource issues in the multinational firm. Yet for many firms, survival and prosperity in this environment means being able to attain competitive advantages not just locally but on a global basis.

The resource-based view of the firm which has evolved in an essentially 'domestic' context has a great deal to inform us about the nature of global sustainable competitive advantage (GSCA). It provides an illuminating framework for assessing the relative merits of the different resources available to the firm. Competitive advantages are attainable when the resources used to gain those advantages are unique and difficult to duplicate. On this basis, firm-specific capabilities, though highly intangible and often difficult to understand, represent perhaps the most potent source of advantage available to the firm. Managers must make the investment necessary to identify and develop these capabilities and to effectively transfer them throughout the organization if a global competitive advantage is to be attained. But this application of the resource-based view to the global context has also helped to highlight some existing deficiencies in its content. In particular, it has demonstrated that the classification schema used to identify resources have been incomplete and need to be extended to take account of the different country-specific resources available to the globally-scaled firm. These types of resources have long been viewed as being of critical importance in the international business literature.

Finally, this chapter has also emphasized the important role of strategic choice. Resources in and of themselves, no matter what their characteristics, do not confer a competitive advantage. They must be identified and correctly deployed by the firm's management team. This means that we must extend our view of strategic fit in order to understand the determinants of superior performance in a competitive marketplace. When it was first proposed, many commentators viewed the transnational as the ideal organizational form for today's competitive environment. This view has subsequently been rejected by Ghoshal and Nohria (1993) who instead argued in favour of a 'horses for courses' approach, with the best strategy being contingent on industry conditions. The analysis presented in this chapter suggests that there is a further 'resources for courses' contingency which must also be considered. Firms that attain a congruence between their resource endowments and their competitive strategy as well as between their competitive strategy and their industry conditions are likely to be the superior performers in today's globally competitive marketplace.

Note

1. The author gratefully acknowledges the support of the Arts and Social Sciences Benefactions Fund, University of Dublin, Trinity College.

References

Aliber, R.Z. (1993) *The Multinational Paradigm* (Cambridge, MA: MIT Press), pp. 4–5.

Amit, R. and P.J. Schoemaker (1993) 'Strategic assets and organisational rent', *Strategic Management Journal*, 14, pp. 33–46.

Barney, J.B. (1986) 'Strategic factor markets: expectations, luck and business strategy', *Management Science*, 32, pp. 1231–41.

Barney, J.B. (1991) 'Firm resources and sustained competitive advantage', *Journal of Management*, 17, pp. 99–120.

Bartlett, C. and S. Ghoshal (1989) *Managing Across Borders: The Transnational Solution* (Cambridge, MA: Harvard Business School Press).

Buckley, P.J. (1991) 'The frontiers of international business research', *Management International Review*, 31, pp. 7–22.

Buckley, P.J. and M.Z. Brooke (1992) *International Business Studies: An Overview* (Cambridge, MA: Blackwell Publishers).

Buckley, P.J. and M. Casson (1976) *The Future of the Multinational Enterprise* (London: Macmillan).

Cool, K. and D. Schendel (1988) 'Performance differences among strategic group members', *Strategic Management Journal*, 9, pp. 207–33.

Coyne, K. (1986) 'Sustainable competitive advantage – what it is and what it isn't', *Business Horizons*, 29, pp. 54–61.

Daniels, J.D. (1991) 'Relevance in international business research: a need for more linkages', *Journal of International Business Studies*, 22, pp. 177–86.

Dierickx, I. and K. Cool (1989) 'Asset stock accumulation and sustainability of competitive advantage', *Management Science*, 35, pp. 1504–11.

Doz, Y. (1978) 'Managing manufacturing rationalisation within multinational companies', *The Columbia Journal of World Business*, 11, pp. 82–94.

Dunning, J.H. (1981) *International Production and the Multinational Enterprise* (London: George Allen & Unwin).

Dunning, J.H. (1989) 'The study of international business: a plea for a more interdisciplinary approach', *Journal of International Business Studies*, 20, pp. 411–36.

Economist, The (1994) 'The global economy', 333, S1–S46.

Fayerweather, J. (1969) *International Business Management: A Conceptual Framework* (New York: McGraw-Hill).

Ghoshal, S. (1987) 'Global strategy: an organising framework', *Strategic Management Journal*, 8, pp. 425–40.

Ghoshal, S. and N. Nohria (1993) 'Horses for courses: organisational forms for multinational corporations', *Sloan Management Review*, 34, pp. 23–35.

Grant, R. (1991) 'The resource-based theory of competitive advantage: implications for strategy formulation', *California Management Review*, 33, pp. 114–35.

Hall, R. (1992) 'The strategic analysis of intangible resources', *Strategic Management Journal*, 13, pp. 135–44.

Hansen, G.S. and B. Wernerfelt (1989) 'Determinants of firm performance: the relative importance of economic and organisational factors', *Strategic Management Journal*, 10, pp. 399–411.

Hecksher, E.F. (1919) 'The effects of foreign trade on the distribution of income', *Economics Tidskrift* (1919). Reprinted in H.S. Ellis and L.A. Metzler (eds), (1965) *Readings in the Theory of International trade* (Homewood, IL: Richard D. Irwin).

Hymer, S. (1960) *The International Operations of National Firms: A Study of Direct Foreign Investment* (Cambridge, MA: MIT Press, (1960) 1976).

Itami, H. (1987) *Mobilizing Invisible Assets* (Cambridge, MA: Harvard University Press).

Kindleberger, C.P. (1969) *American Business Abroad* (New Haven and London: Yale University Press).

Kogut, B. (1991) 'Country capabilities and the permeability of borders', *Strategic Management Journal*, 12, pp. 33–47.

Kogut, B. and U. Zander (1993) 'Knowledge of the firm and the evolutionary theory of the multinational corporation', *Journal of International Business Studies*, 24, pp. 625–45.

Leong, S.M. and C.T. Tan (1993) 'Managing across borders: an empirical test of the Bartlett and Ghoshal (1989) organisational typology', *Journal of International Business Studies*, 24, pp. 449–64.

Levitt, T. (1983) 'The globalisation of markets', *Harvard Business Review*, 61, pp. 92–102.

Nayyar, P.R. (1990) 'Information asymmetries: a source of competitive advantage for diversified service firms', *Strategic Management Journal*, 11, pp. 513–19.

Nelson, R. and S. Winter (1982) *An Evolutionary Theory of Economic Change* (Cambridge, MA: Harvard University Press).

Perlmutter, H.V. (1969) 'The tortured evolution of the multinational corporation', *Columbia Journal of World Business*, 10, pp. 9–18.

Peteraf, M.A. (1993) 'The cornerstones of competitive advantage: a resource-based view', *Strategic Management Journal*, 14, pp. 179–91.

Porter, M.E. (1980) *Competitive Strategy* (New York: The Free Press).

Porter, M.E. (1986) 'Competition in global industries: a conceptual framework', in M.E.

Porter, *Competition in Global Industries* (Boston, MA: Harvard Business School Press), pp. 15–60.

Prahalad, C.K. (1976) 'The strategic process in a multinational corporation', Unpublished doctoral dissertation. Graduate School of Business Administration, Harvard University.

Reed, R. and R.J. DeFillippi (1990) 'Casual ambiguity, barriers to imitation and sustainable competitive advantage', *Academy of Management Review*, 15, pp. 88–102.

Ricardo, D. (1817) *On the Principles of Political Economy and Taxation*, edited by P. Sraffa (Cambridge: Cambridge University Press, (1817) 1951).

Rugman, A.M. (1981) *Inside the Multinationals* (London: Croom Helm).

Rumelt, R.P. (1991) 'How much does industry matter?', *Strategic Management Journal*, 12, pp. 167–85.

de Vasconcellos E Sa, J.A. and D. Hambrick (1989) 'Key success factors: test of a general theory in the mature industrial-product sector', *Strategic Management Journal*, 10, pp. 367–82.

Wernerfelt, B. (1984) 'A resource-based view of the firm', *Strategic Management Journal*, 5, pp. 171–80.

Wernerfelt, B. (1989) 'From critical resources to corporate strategy', *Journal of General Management*, 14, pp. 4–12.

7 R&D Strategy in the Multinational Affiliate

James Taggart

INTRODUCTION

One of the key objectives in determining a firm's corporate strategy is to match its own internal competencies and resources to the complex and ambiguous external environment in which it finds itself. In an increasingly competitive and internationalized business world, success is grounded in uniqueness and commercial advantages that must be continually updated. For the multinational corporation (MNC), the processes of strategic analysis, option evaluation and implementation are further complicated by the fact that the company may operate across a diverse range of geographic environments and markets. This introduces additional demands on the organization in terms of establishing a suitable control structure. The way it configures its various subsidiary operations around the world and how it coordinates activities between them become important issues for the MNC.

In appraising the external business environment, technological factors have traditionally been perceived as an important consideration. In the past, however, technology has often been relegated to peripheral importance when developing an actual strategy. The management of technology has been regarded conventionally as a tactical rather than a strategic issue. However, there is now a growing acceptance that technological factors are of strategic importance and should be intrinsic to the process of formulating overall business strategy. This is particularly so for MNCs. Technology is often the single most important source of competitive advantage that an international firm can possess, and not simply for those who are directly associated with high technology or advanced R&D. Technological developments drive new products and processes, and MNCs can be extremely efficient in transferring innovation quickly throughout their network of subsidiaries.

The aim of this chapter is to address some of the issues surrounding the strategic management of innovation and new technology in the Scottish electronics industry, based on an empirical investigation of a selection of MNC subsidiaries.

REVIEW OF CONCEPTS

The perception that technological decisions need to be made in the context of overall corporate strategy is a fairly recent one. Kantrow (1980) notes that much of the relevant literature up to the 1970s was concerned with the specialized application of technology within the separate functional areas of business; there was little guidance on the 'total process' by which companies translate a technological development into new products or services. This has changed considerably. A large number of authors have since assessed the strategic implication of technology in achieving ownership-specific competitive advantage (Porter, 1985; Maidique and Patch, 1989; McGee and Thomas, 1989; Pavitt, 1990; Dodgson, 1991; Merrifield, 1991; Berry and Taggart, 1993 and 1994). The review here necessarily concentrates on those aspects of the subject relevant to this study. Although the discussion generally considers the development of manufactured products, many of the points are equally applicable in service industries.

Technology and Corporate Strategy

Erickson *et al.* (1990) regard management of technology as covering the management of research, product and process development, and manufacturing engineering. Basic and applied research expand the firm's grasp of scientific and engineering skills, development makes this knowledge relevant to the firm's business, and manufacturing engineering translates technology into desirable products for the customer. Technology now plays an increasingly important role in achieving and maintaining competitive advantage (Porter, 1983), and technology strategy must be developed and implemented within the content of overall corporate strategy (Wilson, 1986). Further, a unified technology strategy should address three interrelated business areas – product development, process development and information systems. For a technology-intensive MNC, such a strategy should cover the critical issues of technology acquisition, the method of exploiting technological advantage, and the diffusion of technology within the organization and beyond (Taggart and McDermott, 1993, p. 85). MNCs are prolific creators and diffusers of technology, and the typical multinational technology portfolio is likely to consist of a combination of technologies from a variety of sources. For a wider review of these issues, see Berry and Taggart (1994).

The Strategic Management of Technology

Porter (1983) claims that the study of technological innovation is too often decoupled from the study of competition, and vice versa. Emphasis on the management of technology is largely restricted to the internal conditions for achieving success in individual R&D projects, and to ensuring the required linkage between innovation and customer needs. More fundamental though, is the possibility that technological change can alter the rules of competition in an industry, and can be used by firms as the basis for sustained competitive advantage. The competitive significance of technological change does not depend on its scientific merit or on its effect on the ability of the firm to serve market needs *per se*, but on its unique power to impact on industry structure (Kodama, 1992). This occurs via any of the five fundamental competitive forces at work in all industries: threat of entry, substitution, bargaining power of suppliers, bargaining power of customers and rivalry between existing competitors (Porter, 1980).

Technological change is a key strategic variable in competitive positioning. It can be the great equalizer that nullifies the advantages of market leaders and creates opportunities for new entrants and followers. 'Technological change is perhaps the single most important source of major market share changes among competitors for this reason and is probably the most frequent cause of the demise of entrenched dominant firms' (Porter, 1983). Even in low-tech firms, technology can rapidly move from a supporting role to become central to competitive strategy. It is often assumed that new process technologies are primarily cost-oriented, aimed at supporting a broad competitive strategy of low-cost leadership. Similarly, new product developments are considered to support a stance based on differentiation. However, both types of technological change can have a significant role in supporting each of these generic strategies.

Goodridge *et al.* (1988) describe two alternative viewpoints in the research literature relating to the growth of firms and the development of technology strategies:

- The 'traditional' or market-driven viewpoint: here, profit is the primary corporate concern within the firm, followed by market objectives. Market needs drive business strategy, and technology assumes the relatively minor role of facilitator. It is not regarded as a key strategic resource and is therefore not incorporated into strategic thinking.
- The technology-driven viewpoint: this approach focuses heavily on technology, which is seen as providing the stimulus for growth through the introduction of new products and processes. Technology is therefore promoted to centre of the corporate stage.

Empirical investigations by Perrino and Tipping (1989) identified two parameters that significantly affected R&D deployment decisions; technological maturity and customer interface requirements. They found that where core technologies are mature, then customer interface requirements are high. Alternatively, where technologies have low maturity, then customer interface requirements are also low. Hence, the level of technological maturity within the product or process will determine whether the firm's approach should be market or technology-driven. Adler *et al.* (1992) claim that an effective overall business strategy should be buttressed by explicit and complementary strategies in each of the firm's functional areas. Management experts have developed powerful conceptual frameworks for analyzing the key functional strategies in manufacturing, finance and marketing. But as yet, technology managers have not received comparable guidance, and there is no broadly accepted framework for the strategic assessment of R&D functions.

Innovation Strategy

Depending on a variety of internal and external factors, firms necessarily adopt different stances with regard to innovation and the accumulation of new technology. A number of authors have attempted to categorize the range of strategic postures (Ansoff and Stewart, 1967; Freeman, 1982; Sethi, 1985; Maidique and Patch, 1989; McGee and Thomas, 1989; Erickson *et al.*, 1990). Freeman (1982) identifies six basic types of innovation strategy, which he labels offensive, defensive, imitative, dependent, traditional and opportunist. These reflect a range of different approaches or choices, such as outright technical leadership or follower, copier or adapter, technology-driven or market-driven, low-cost producer or niche market specialist. Ansoff and Stewart (1967) suggest that the formulation of technological strategy should be based on a systematic analysis of the 'technological profile' of the firm, where a technology-intensive business has five characteristic parameters: the research versus development mix, the degree of downstream coupling, the length of the product life-cycle, the R&D investment ratio, and a measure of the company's proximity to state-of-the-art technology. They identify four principal alternatives for competitive positioning:

- First-to-the-market: this is based on a strong R&D programme with talented research personnel, technological leadership, close downstream coupling and an acceptance of risk-taking.
- Follow-the-leader: this is based on alert and accurate competitive intelligence, strong development resources, and an ability to react quickly as the market starts its growth phase.
- Me-too: this is based on superior manufacturing efficiency, cost control, no R&D.
- Application engineering: this is based on product modifications to fit the needs of particular customers in a mature market, minimal development but using technically perceptive salespersons working closely with designers.

Maidique and Patch (1989) attempt to develop a similar framework to aid in the formulation of an innovation strategy for a technology-intensive firm. They describe the firm's technological policy as consisting of a portfolio of choices and plans that enables it to respond effectively to technological threats and opportunities. They suggest the firm must make choices in at least six areas:

- Technology selection, specialization and embodiment in new products.
- Level of competence required in a particular technology.
- Sources of technology, either internally generated or externally acquired.
- R&D investment level.
- Competitive timing, whether to lead or lag competitors in product introduction.
- R&D organization and policies – e.g., central R&D lab or dispersed locations, project teams or matrix structures, patent policy, publication policy.

As we have seen above, the context of these choices within alternative corporate strategies is illustrated with reference to four broad competitive stances, which clearly parallel those of Ansoff and Stewart: First-to-market; Second-to-market or Fast-follower, Late-to-market or Cost Minimization; and Market Segmentation or Specialist. For each approach to stand a chance of being successful, there are inherent implications for the resources and capabilities required in the different functional areas of the business. In particular, the technological choices must be consistent with and mutually reinforce other dimensions of the corporate strategy such as the manufacturing and marketing policies.

There should be a strong commitment to state-of-the-art R&D to achieve technological leadership in a First-to-market strategy. Fast-following requires more nimble development and engineering strengths, with less emphasis on basic or applied research. Late-to-market strategies are based on cost advantages through product and process engineering skills, to achieve economies of scale in manufacturing; there is little R&D effort in the late entry strategies. The Specialist approach requires strong competencies in product modification, applied engineering and flexibility in short-run manufacturing.

MNC Organization of R&D

In general, the problems of establishing a suitable organizational structure and culture of R&D are significantly compounded for MNCs within which operations may be dispersed over a range of environments and markets. MNCs initially retained much of their basic and applied research close to the home country. Overseas R&D locations were largely technology transfer units that adapted manufacturing techniques or performed local customer technical service. Over time, the R&D functions in some of these locations have evolved to take on responsibility for developing new and improved products for host country markets or even new products for the world market. As the rate of technological advance increases and product life-cycles shorten, new technologies must be transferred within the MNC's network very quickly to optimize the competitive advantage. This is made simpler if the key subsidiaries in the main regional markets have their own facilities for further adaptation and development.

Gresov (1984) claims that proper organizational design for international firms can greatly enhance their ability to generate, adopt, implement and market innovations. He considers the two basic phases of innovation and implementation separately. While large MNCs are often good at generating innovation within the organizational network, there can be deficiencies in diffusing or internally marketing knowledge for the purposes of implementation.

Gresov describes two dilemmas relating to the structure and culture of the organization. In cases where the firm has a centralized structure, the process of innovation is inhibited by a lack of lateral communication within the organization and a lack of awareness of other developments in the wider environment. However, it is better equipped to develop a planned and unified approach to implementation. For more decentralized, complex organizational structures, the reverse is true. A similar argument applies for different types of organizational culture (a more relevant issue for international firms than for a wholly domestic one). A homogeneous culture favours the discipline of implementation over innovation. On the other hand, heterogeneous cultures offer a more open and tolerant environment in which innovation can develop, but at the expense of implementation efficiency.

His solution is presented as a traditional 4-box matrix that considers simultaneously the effects of structure and culture. The implication is, for example, that the poorer innovative capacity of the centralized structure may be compensated for by promoting a more diverse and heterogeneous culture. Similarly, other implementational weaknesses of a complex organizational structure could be improved by promoting a more homogeneous cultural pattern. In either case, the overall capacity of the organization to manage both aspects of its technology can be improved.

Strategy in MNC Subsidiaries

Strategy at subsidiary level has been a particular focus of research for the past fifteen years. Hedlund (1981) identified the link between subsidiary autonomy and the degree of informality in the HQ–subsidiary relationship. Subsequently, a number of other strategic dimensions have been investigated. Porter (1985), Prahalad and Doz (1987), Jarillo and Martinez (1990), and Roth and Morrison (1990) have all studied integration of activities within the multinational network. Coordination of activities has been the focus of Porter (1985) and of Prahalad and Doz (1987). Localization/local responsiveness has been assessed by Prahalad and Doz (1987) and by Jarillo and Martinez (1990). Of particular interest here is the paradigm developed by White and Poynter (1984) using data from MNC subsidiaries in Canada, subsequently developed with Scottish data by Young *et al.* (1988) and Taggart (1992 and 1996a). This model rests on three dimensions – market scope, product scope, and value-added scope. These give rise to five strategy options for the multinational subsidiary, each with implications for the nature and scope of R&D carried out by the subsidiary:

- Marketing Satellite: these subsidiaries do not manufacture, neither do they carry out R&D.
- Miniature Replica: these are small-scale replicas of the parent that concentrate on the local market; in some cases they may have an R&D capability.
- Rationalised Manufacturer: manufactures specific components or sub-assemblies for the parent; there is no product R&D, and even process R&D is unlikely.
- Product Specialist: these subsidiaries are likely to have a significant R&D component, especially if world or regional product mandates are involved.
- Strategic Independent: these subsidiaries are autonomous in R&D, production and marketing.

Organization of International R&D

There is a clear tendency for multinational R&D to remain centralized in the home country (Taggart, 1989), even though production and marketing are widely internationalized. However, there are significant and growing pressures to disperse R&D activity (Terpstra, 1977), and these have been particularly strong in the last twenty years. OECD (1977) derived a tripartite classification of international R&D activity in the pharmaceutical industry: Sun and Satellites, Functional Decentralization, 'Let Several Flowers Bloom'. Behrman and Fischer (1979) developed an R&D taxonomy based on market orientation: Home Market firms, Host Market firms, World Market firms; the likelihood of decentralized R&D increases from Home to World firms. Both paradigms are useful, but less so when we consider the integration of technology strategy and corporate strategy. In this case, Ronstadt's (1978) paradigm is perhaps more useful as it indicates how technology strategy must develop as the firm moves into higher taxonomic areas of R&D complexity. Ronstadt suggests four types of overseas R&D:

- Transfer Technology Unit (TTU): established to help particular foreign manufacturing units to transfer manufacturing technology from the corporate parent, and to provide related technical services for overseas customers.
- Indigenous Technology Unit (ITU): established to develop new and improved products expressly for foreign markets; these products are not the direct result of new technology supplied from the home country.
- Global Technology Unit (GTU): established to develop new products and process for simultaneous application in the MNC's world markets, including the home country.
- Corporate Technology Unit (CTU): established to generate new knowledge of a long term exploratory nature for the corporate parent.

Ronstadt's work is particularly helpful in understanding the evolution of international R&D activity, subject to two basic imperatives. First, there is a pronounced tendency to change purpose and continue operations at the same location, while increasing the number of R&D professionals involved. Second, there is a tendency towards slow growth and reduced investment if a change of purpose does not occur.

RESEARCH PROBLEM

As noted earlier, the aim of this exploratory study is to examine some of the key issues involved in the strategic management of innovation and new technology within subsidiaries of major manufacturing MNCs. This gives rise to four specific research questions, and focuses attention on the linkages between them:

- Is the management of technology actually considered in the conscious strategic sense, or is it simply the tactical implementation of a more market-driven approach (cf. Goodridge *et al.*, 1988)?
- How may the general subsidiary operation be characterized, integrated within the overall corporate network, and linked to the nature of R&D activity (cf. White and Poynter, 1984; Ronstadt, 1978)? In particular, what is the impact of varying levels of subsidiary autonomy in the development of technology strategy?
- Is the subsidiary's strategy for technology accumulation and innovation recognizable as belonging to a distinct category such as technological leadership, fast follower, etc. (cf. Maidique and Patch, 1989; Ansoff and Stewart, 1967)?

- To what extent is technology strategy effectiveness determined by organizational aspects (cf. Gresov, 1984)?

This exploratory investigation was carried out within the Scottish electronics industry where effective management of technology is clearly of major significance. There are 90 MNC electronics subsidiaries located in Scotland (Scottish Enterprise, 1995), of which 20 carry out a significant degree of technology development. Plants engaged primarily in defence-related work were excluded, as they operate within a different set of commercial priorities and driving forces. This reduced the original pool of firms to 14, though they include the largest and most influential manufacturers within the Scottish electronics industry. Nine of these firms agreed to a personal interview, seven being US-owned and two European-owned. Personal interview was deemed the most suitable method as much of the desired data was qualitative in nature. Thus, semi-structured interviews of up to one and a half hours were held with the chief technical officers of the firms between May and July 1995. In six firms, separate interviews were conducted with two technical officers, and with three in the remainder. Where subsequent evaluation of interview responses appeared to indicate a substantive difference between respondents in any particular affiliate, a series of telephone discussions were undertaken in an attempt to resolve such variances. In all cases, respondents were asked to focus on products that had gone through the complete development cycle in the previous five years and to ignore those projects that were currently being implemented.

RESULTS

A brief summary of the interview results is given in Table 7.1. In several of the columns of this table, firms with different areas of business may be classified in more than one way. Where appropriate, an overall 'aggregate' role is defined for the purposes of this study; otherwise multiple classification of a firm's activities in terms of idealized forms or theoretical models is often difficult in practice; real life behaviour is much less clear. For example, when the Maidique and Patch paradigm was discussed with respondents, some confirmed that they had used all of the strategies on different occasions and in response to different situations. This tends to cloud some of the potential relationships and linkages between factors.

The age of the plants ranged from 11 to 35 years, with an average of 25 years. The size of firms ranged from 100 to 2000 employees, with an average of around 800. Similarly, the size of the firms' R&D group varied considerably within the sample, from 18 to 300 employees. As a proportion of the total, the number of employees that are normally in 'development' ranges from a few per cent to a maximum of 20 per cent across the sample. It

Table 7.1 Summary of research results

Firm	Total	'R&D' staff		Years in UK	Parent co. nationality	Product or process	Market or tech driven	White and Poynter subsidiary role	Ronstadt R&D role	Innovation strategy	Innovation vs. implemetation
A	1500	300	20%	26	USA	Product	Market (Tech)	Strategic Independent	GTU	1st-to-Market	Implementation
B	100	18	18%	13	USA	Process	Market	Strategic Independent	GTU	2nd-to-Market	Innovation
C	1000	100	10%	19	USA	Both	Market (Tech)	Miniature Replica – adopter/innovator	TTU GTU	2nd-to-Market and Late-to-Market	Implementation
D	1100	180	16%	29	USA	Product	Market	Miniature Replica – adopter (innovator)*	ITU (GTU)*	1st-to-Market and Late-to-Market	Both
E	750	28	4%	35	USA	Process	Market	Miniature Replica – adapter + Rational Manuf	ITU	1st-to-Market and 2nd-to-Market	Both
F	2000	50	2.5%	26	USA	Both	Market	Miniature Replica – innovator*	ITU*	1st-to-Market and Market Segmentation	Implementation
G	470	75	16%	32	European	Product	Market	Product Specialist (MinRep-adaptor)	ITU	All	Implementation
H	200	35	17.5%	31	European	Both	Market	Strategic Independent	GTU	Market Segmentation	Innovation
I	190	20	10%	11	USA	Both	Market	Rationalized Manufacturer	ITU GTU*	2nd-to-Market	Implementation

* Indicates that classifications apply to only part of firm.

should be noted that the R&D figures are not always directly comparable, since there is inevitably some looseness in the definition of development activities, and in the extent to which the figure includes the full spectrum of engineers, technicians, support staff, etc. Overall, development activities were aimed at product and process technologies in roughly equal measures. In practice, it was often difficult to separate the two, since most process advancements are intimately related to improvements in the overall product as well. Generally, the semiconductor fabrication companies had a more obvious focus on process technologies, as expected.

Strategic Importance of Technology

The need for a strategic approach to innovation and new technology was strongly advocated by all respondents. There was repeated confirmation of trends such as decreasing product life cycles, increasing global competition, and particularly the growing financial imperative to bring new products to the market quickly and regularly. There is an increasing need to be aware of technological trends in the wider environment (and in some cases predict future trends), in order that the right technologies are identified and pursued. For large MNCs with numerous Miniature Replica plants around the world, the choice of development location is increasingly critical, as is the method of technology distribution prior to manufacture for a global market.

On reflection, it is no great surprise that the strategic importance of technology is readily accepted in these firms. The electronics industry is so immersed in and so dependent on technology that it cannot be divorced from the decisions that affect the strategic direction of the firm. (On a simplistic level, these nine MNCs were all established many years ago, and the fact that they are still in existence today makes this point self-evident.) In this sense, the evangelical message about the central importance of technology is already taken for granted by the firms.

Another reason why technology is already regarded as vital at the highest corporate level is the fact that the founders of most of these companies were themselves engineers. Typically, as the firm grew from a backyard operation to an international corporation, they maintained a strong technical input and a keen awareness of technological issues. Although most of these original entrepreneurs have since departed, their influence is still felt indirectly through their immediate successors. In general, the nature of the industry is such that there will always be individuals with a strong technical background at corporate and subsidiary board level, and a high technological profile is guaranteed.

Although the importance of innovation and new technology has long been recognized in these firms, this does not necessarily mean that technology has been managed strategically. On the contrary, the majority of interviewees claimed that in the past, their firms probably placed too much importance on technology and R&D for its own sake. This is much in line with Levitt's (1965) view. Development projects were sometimes selected on the basis of how interesting they appeared to engineers, rather than their potential to generate new business (also noted by Erickson *et al.*, 1990; and Wheelwright and Clark, 1992). However, as commercial pressures have increased in recent years, the relative importance of technology in driving the firm's strategic direction has decreased. Technological forces are now tempered by a much more overtly market-driven approach.

According to Table 7.1, the rejection of a technology-driven approach to innovation is virtually unanimous. It seems that a technology-driven philosophy of the sort described by Goodridge *et al.* (1988) is regarded as something of a luxury in today's business climate. Certainly, the only interviewees to hint at a more fundamental driving role for technology were from two of the largest firms in the survey. Again, it should be pointed out that some of the largest MNCs have separate and dedicated research labs that are much less concerned with the direct application of their efforts to marketable products (cf. Ronstadt's CTU). In practice, most interviewees went on to say that their intention was to balance the necessity to satisfy customers needs with the requirement to be fully aware of the possibilities offered by emerging new technologies. This is much more in line with the pragmatic matching process described by Freeman (1982). There appears to be little chance of any of these particular technology managers becoming distracted by the attraction of their own pet projects.

The general extent to which technology is embedded within the core of business strategy is reflected in the fact that a separate technology strategy was thought to be unnecessary in most of the companies. A 'technology road map' was used by several firms to highlight the strategic direction of new developments.

Roles of Subsidiaries and R&D Units

The White and Poynter (1984) model was used here to classify the subsidiary strategies of respondents. As mentioned previously, it is sometimes difficult to categorize the strategic role of the entire plant, especially if it is involved in different business areas. In some cases, two different categories are given, and secondary roles may be shown in brackets. It can be seen that all of the possible categories are represented here in at least one case (with the exception of Marketing Satellite, which is automatically excluded, since the initial selection criteria focused attention on plants with manufacturing operations). There are:

- Three Strategic Independents.
- Four (five) Miniature Replicas – one adopter, two (three) adapters, two (three) innovators.

- Two Rationalised Manufacturers.
- One Product Specialist.

The incidence of all these strategic types in Table 7.1 implies a diversity of subsidiary roles within the sample firms. It also indicates the merit of the bases on which the framework is constructed, i.e. the dimensions of product scope, market scope, and value-added scope. The general attraction of frameworks such as White and Poynter's is that they allow a complex set of subsidiary functions and responsibilities to be encapsulated into a simple phrase that produces a clear mental picture of the plant's purpose. This process of consolidating information then makes relationships with other factors easier to handle and identify.

It is notable than the Strategic Independent plants have the three highest proportions of R&D employees in their firm (17.5–20 per cent). Presumably, the fact that these plants are almost entirely responsible for their own strategic direction means that there is a greater onus on supporting themselves in the R&D functions (since no one else will). A similar argument applies for the Product Specialist plant, which has the next highest proportion of R&D staff.

In general, the plants which have these 'higher level' roles tend to be older than average, possibly because the greater responsibility has to be earned over time. (However, one Strategic Independents is among the youngest firms in the sample.) In terms of size, Strategic Independents fit no obvious pattern since they are drawn from both extremes of the range.

The Ronstadt classification assigned to each of the nine firms is listed in Table 7.1. As above, in circumstances where it is difficult to determine a single category for the whole R&D function, a second category has been indicated. Three additional points should be made in connection with this classification:

- Ronstadt's original work considered the reasons for creating the R&D facility. In this study, the focus of attention is on its function at the present time, with no explicit concern for its original purpose.
- No distinction has been made between R&D units that were acquired by the parent company and those that were initiated by them.
- The role of Indigenous Technology Units in developing new and improved products for the host country market has been extended in this consideration to include host region markets (i.e. Europe as a whole).

The R&D units of the nine firms were divided fairly evenly into two main categories; Global Technology Units and Indigenous Technology Units. There were no Corporate Technology Units, which is not surprising given that all of the subsidiaries here were firmly linked to manufacturing operations. Only one firm showed any significant Technology Transfer element; again, this is undoubtedly a consequence of the original selection criterion which eliminated firms that did not undertake a 'significant' amount of R&D.

It might be expected that a firm's R&D role would develop in parallel with and in support of general changes in the overall subsidiary strategy. In this respect, it can be seen that all three of the Strategic Independent plants are serviced by their own Global Technology Units. This is indicative of the level of the firm's responsibility and independence from the parent company and other subsidiaries. As noted previously, this role also appears to demand a higher proportion of R&D staff to sustain it. The Miniature Replica plants were generally associated with Indigenous Technology Units. This reflects the more regional focus which these plants observe.

In some interviews, it became apparent that the role of both the subsidiary and the supporting R&D unit had changed over time. Ronstadt's classifications are particularly useful in highlighting the nature of the process. Typically, the plant had been established as a Miniature Replica (adopter or perhaps adapter), with a R&D unit that was operating as a Transfer Technology Unit. The subsequent growth in the status of a firm's R&D unit is in line with the view that R&D activities tend to evolve gradually into higher value roles. However, the details of the particular evolution are likely to be different in each case. In this sample, there appears to be no obvious correlation between the age of a firm and its R&D role. One firm (C), whose R&D unit has successfully made the transition from Transfer to Indigenous to Global Technology Unit, is one of the youngest in the sample.

Strategies for Technology Development

As noted above, most interviewees found it difficult to categorize the approach to innovation and new technology acquisition as belonging to only one of Maidique and Patch's (1989) four strategies. Firms necessarily accumulate many different product or process technologies over time, possibly in support of different business areas. The optimum strategy for each is contingent on a range of internal and external factors. Unfortunately, without reference to a particular example, it was difficult for interviewees to remember or elucidate the general determinants in the decision-making process. On many occasions, a deliberate strategy was not consciously considered, and developments simply 'happened'.

Most of the firms have used all of these standard approaches at one point or another and, as such, it is often impractical to develop specific functional characteristics in, say, marketing or manufacturing to suit a particular strategy. However, for key technologies, some firms clearly went through a process of assessing the most feasible strategic approach in relation to their present internal resources, or to highlight future improvements that might be required in recruitment or training. This is where the real power lies in frameworks such as Maidique and Patch's or Ansoff and Stewart's (1967). Like most strategic management tools, their strength is not in producing the 'right' answer, or unveiling a startling revelation, or in categorizing previous actions. It is simply that they encourage managers to think about the complex range of issues that surround their key decisions, and arrange them within a meaningful and helpful framework. They are primarily intended as forward-looking devices, rather than backward-looking, as used here.

The Maidique and Patch matrix is most useful in the way that it sets out alternative strategic directions and identifies a logical set of functional characteristics that would support each strategy best. None of the interviewees disagreed with any of these functional requirements, and in some cases, they struck a particular resonance with their own experiences. According to Table 7.1, all but one of the respondents were able to nominate one or two Maidique and Patch classifications that best represented their firm's aggregate approach to technology acquisition. The main conclusions may be summarized as follows:

- Each strategy has been substantially used by at least two different firms.
- In general, the sample is slanted towards the early-to-market strategies. This coincides with the widely held view that development cycles and time-to-market are now critical issues in the electronics industry, and continuous innovation of new products is essential.
- In particular circumstances, some care may need to be taken in following a first-to-market strategy. Potential customers may perceive that there is a risk in being too dependent on a single supplier. In certain cases, it may be advisable to wait until technical standards have been set within the industry, rather than risk going out on a limb too early.
- Following the introduction of a new product, a late-to-market/cost minimization strategy was sometimes employed to improve the efficiency of the manufacturing process, before the next generation of products was developed. There are no instances where a late-to-market strategy was applied to a new product introduction.
- On the basis of these results, there appears to be no clear relationship between a firm's aggregate innovation strategy and either its subsidiary or R&D classification. This may be a consequence of the subjective nature of the interpretation, or the fact that subtle relationships may be lost in the aggregation process. In any case, the limited sample size means that only the most obvious relationships would stand out.

In connection with the firms' innovation strategies, the following related issues were identified:

- The effectiveness of patents and non-disclosure agreements in reducing the leakage of a firm's technology is very patchy. Blatant violation of these measures is apparent in some cases, but legal action uses up valuable financial and technical resources. In practice, it appears that some smaller firms, in particular, decide not to pursue legal action and accept the situation as a fact of life.
- Cross-licensing of technology between firms is seen as being increasingly important, and was cited as one method of avoiding the threat of protracted legal disputes. Even for two firms in competition with one another, it can still be preferable to exchange technologies and compete with each other on some other basis.
- In a similar vein, strategic relationships and collaborations can significantly reduce development times and open up new commercial possibilities. Numerous examples were quoted of collaborations with firms in other industries, direct competitors, academic institutions and customers. A move away from in-house component manufacture towards greater external procurement can also reduce the time and uncertainty of new developments.
- Formalized scanning of the wider technological environment is also rather patchy. In general, it seems to be undertaken at a fairly high corporate level, rather that at subsidiary level where the 'front-line' engineers and managers are working. Acquisition of other companies as a means of accessing their technology would also be handled at corporate level.

Organizational Issues

There was strong agreement during the interviews about the importance of a cross-functional approach to new developments, in line with frequent advice in the academic literature. It seems that all firms use interdisciplinary teams in which personnel from R&D, manufacturing, marketing and finance are formally involved early in the development process. In particular, the R&D and marketing departments are most intimately involved at the beginning, in support of the market-driven philosophy to innovation, closely followed by manufacturing. Some firms split the development into separate stages of concept and feasibility, definition, prototype manufacture and full-scale manufacture. At each new stage, where the commercial worth of the development becomes more apparent, additional human and financial resources are allocated to the project. In one company, the approach includes the generation of a formal business plan for each new technology. The plan is assessed by senior managers and automatically addresses cross-functional issues such as marketability, manufacturing requirements, project financing, etc.

Some interviewees referred to periods in the past, when the R&D unit alone decided on the suitability of technology developments. At a certain stage, the project would be 'thrown over the wall' to manufacturing, who at some later point, would 'throw it over the wall' to marketing. This phase has most definitely been consigned to the past. The new approach has also meant that technology managers have gained an increased awareness of wider business issues, often through formal training.

The increased importance of exchanging information across departmental boundaries is matched by the need for increased communication across the corporate network as a whole. For all except the Strategic Independents, there is a strong requirement to integrate and coordinate activities with other plants. For MNCs with various Miniature Replica plants, the question of which subsidiary is best suited to undertake a particular development is a crucial one, to avoid expensive and wasteful duplication of efforts.

The proposition that a flexible and 'organic' environment is more conducive to the process of innovation was generally accepted by interviewees. However, only two firms appear to have made any real attempt to create a separate working environment for R&D. Both seem to have produced favourable results. It is interesting that these two firms are amongst the smallest in the study and both were classed as Strategic Independents. Also, they were the only two where it was felt the firm was stronger in the process of innovation than in the implementation of new developments into commercial products. This connection between environment/cultural heterogeneity and strength in innovation is in keeping with Gresov's (1984) observations.

In most firms, the requirement for a more rigid and controlled environment for manufacturing seemed to dominate, and their strength lay more towards implementation. (Dedicated corporate research laboratories were said to be quite different.) There firms are larger and tend to have a more obviously homogenous corporate culture, strongly allied towards the parent company. This could be sensed almost immediately on entering the plant. As might be expected, the effect tends to be less pronounced in Strategic Independents. Lack of information about the organizational structure meant that it was difficult to assess the second of Gresov's innovation/implementation relationships.

In practice, the boundary between R&D and manufacturing may not be clear. Often, the same individual performs a role in both innovation and implementation activities. In such cases, the recruitment of personnel was said to become more critical. Separate from any question of technical competence, it was thought vital to identify people that had the temperament to switch comfortably and efficiently between the two roles in a balanced way.

CONCLUSIONS

Some weaknesses in the research methodology need to be acknowledged as a precaution to facile generalization of the above conclusions. First, though the sample included all the major players in the Scottish electronics industry, the number included in the fieldwork was small. Substantial variation occurred over these nine firms on many of the strategic dimensions used, and the inclusion of the five other major firms carrying out substantial non-defence R&D (who declined to participate in the research) may well have added additional perspectives and/or enriched the interpretation of archetypes. Second, the sample comprised seven US-owned and two European-owned affiliates. There is much evidence in the field of subsidiary strategy that ownership is an important variable (for example, Young *et al.*, 1988; Taggart, 1996b), though there is also implication that ownership may not be critical in every case (for example, Birkinshaw and Morrison, 1995). Other than the observation that the only product mandate strategy in the sample was followed by a European-owned affiliate, Table 7.1 does not really indicate any ownership-related variances. It is likely that the research method used here may not have been sufficiently sensitive to isolate such diversity. Third, while at least two technical officers were interviewed in each firm, this subsequently appeared insufficient in large and complex affiliates. In these cases a better approach would be to interview the senior technical officer in the subsidiary, together with those responsible for full-cycle development projects completed within the last five years. Fourth, though respondents were asked to focus on such projects (and repeatedly reminded of this requirment during the interview process), it was readily apparent that many were prone to using current projects as ready examples to illustrate conceptual discussions. It is impossible to assess, however, the extent to which respondents actually followed the prompting, and this may have introduced some measurement error. Finally, it should be noted that this research specifically does not focus on individual products or attempt to establish differences or similarities in processes and issues involved on the basis of a product-to-product comparison. Such an evaluation would be of great interest, but is beyond the scope of this project.

This exploratory study has considered some of the key issues involved in the management of innovation and technology in the Scottish electronics industry. The basis of the empirical investigation was a series of personal interviews with senior technology managers in nine large electronics manufacturing subsidiaries. Based on the data, the main conclusions of the study are:

- Some of the approaches to innovation and new technology development in the firms have changed considerably in the last ten years or so. This has been prompted by strong commercial pressures brought about by general environment trends such as the shortening of product life-cycles, increased global competition, and in particular, the need to introduce new products to the market quickly and frequently. This has resulted in an increased emphasis on:

- careful development project selection,
- strategic relationships with customers and competitors,
- cross-licensing agreements and greater external procurement,
- greater coordination and integration of information and resources with other plants in the corporate network.

- In selecting technological developments in the past, most companies appeared to place too much emphasis on technology for its own sake. This has now been balanced by a much clearer emphasis on a market-driven approach. The pressure to maintain a constant stream of profitable developments from limited technical and financial resources means that technology developments must be managed much more strategically than before.

- According to academic classifications of general subsidiary strategy and R&D role in particular, there is a great diversity of types within the sample of firms. Typically, the role of the R&D unit changes in support of general changes in the overall subsidiary strategy. Many plants were originally established as Miniature Replicas of the parent company or of other subsidiaries, and were supported by a R&D group that was basically a Transfer Technology Unit. As the plant developed a 'higher status' role over time, the R&D function would be upgraded to an Indigenous or Global Technology Unit. Three plants were classified as being Strategic Independents, which is the most complex level in White and Poynter's classification. These were all supported by Global Technology Units, with the highest proportion of development staff; two of the units were considerably older than the sample average, though one was notably younger.

- Most firms have used a range of strategies to manage their innovations, even though they rarely think of them in terms of the idealized strategies presented here. In general, the aggregate approach is slanted towards one of the early-to-market strategies, in line with the increasing emphasis on reducing the time to market. After the introduction of a new product, process technologies are often developed as part of a cost minimization strategy, before the next generation of products is introduced.

- Each of the firms employ a formal, cross-functional team approach to technology development. In support of the market-driven philosophy, R&D and marketing work closely together at the start of the development, closely followed by manufacturing and finance.

- Most interviewees considered their plant to be stronger in the implementation of technological developments, rather than the basic innovation process. This is probably due to the manufacturing bias of the firms. The two plants that were stronger in innovation were much smaller than average, they were both Strategic Independents, and they had a noticeably more flexible and heterogeneous working environment.

Generalizing these conclusions is difficult owing to the industry-specific nature of the study and to the small sample size. However, on the basis of the companies studied here, it appears that Scottish subsidiaries of electronics MNCs are well aware of the strategic importance of technology management. However, defence-oriented firms, affiliates owned by Asian parents, R&D intensive firms outside the electronics industry, and all R&D intensive subsidiaries in core economic areas (as opposed to peripheral Scotland) may well pose a variety of different issues. First, defence firms are much more likely to be technology driven, and also more likely to pursue a market segmentation strategy, than the firms evaluated here. Second, it may be speculated that national culture and its impact on corporate culture may yield an important additional dimension when subsidiaries of Asian firms are included; in particular, Gresov's matrix may be unable to differentiate sufficiently between such affiliates, in that observation suggests an initial concentration on implementation only, followed (10 or more years later) by a focus on both innovation and implementation. Third, it may be expected that non-electronics firms that are technology intensive will be affected by much the same processes and issues as have been discussed here but, where the industry is less technology intensive, the traditional approach to subsidiary strategy is likely to outweigh the significance of an integrated technology strategy as explored in this chapter. Fourth, with regard to MNC subsidiaries located in core economic areas (for example, Europe's 'golden triangle'), it is to be expected that the integration of technology strategy with overall business strategy would be a much more significant dimension and that, generally, the R&D intensity of the representative subsidiary would be substantially higher than that of the average MNC affiliate in Scotland. While these four sets of alternative issues represent a tempting research agenda, the next step in this study will be to widen the investigation to include some less technology-intensive industries to assess whether the linkages between strategic management and technology strategy are in any way attenuated.

References

Adler, P.S., D.W. McDonald and F. McDonald (1992) 'Strategic management of technical function', *Sloan Management Review*, 33(3), pp. 19–37.

Ansoff, I. and J.M. Stewart (1967) 'Strategies for a technology based business', *Harvard Business Review*, 45(6), pp. 71–83.

Behrman, J.N. and W.A. Fischer (1979) 'The co-ordination of foreign R&D activities by transnational corporations', *Journal of International Business Studies*, 10(3), pp. 29–35.

Berry, M.M.J. and James H. Taggart (1993) 'The technology-strategy interface', *Strathclyde International Business Unit*, Working Paper 93/9, University of Strathclyde.

Berry, M.M.J. and James H. Taggart (1994) 'Managing technology and innovation: a review', *R&D Management*, 24(4), pp. 341–53.

Birkinshaw, Julian M. and Allen J. Morrison (1995) 'Configurations of strategy and structure in subsidiaries of multinational corporations', *Journal of International Business Studies*, 26(4), pp. 729–54.

Dodgson, M. (1991) 'Managing corporate technology strategy', *International Journal of Technology Management*, Special publication on the role of technology in corporate policy, pp. 95–102.

Erickson, T.J., J.F. Magee, P.A. Roussel and K.N. Saad (1990) 'Managing technology as a business strategy', *Sloan Management Review*, 31(3), pp. 73–8.

Freeman, C. (1982) *The Economics of Industrial Innovation*, 2nd edn (London: Frances Pinter).

Goodridge, M., J. Harrington and B. Twiss (1988) *Management of Technology: Technology, Management and Change* (London: Manpower Services Commission).

Gresov, C. (1984) 'Designing organisation to innovate and implement: using two dilemmas to create a solution', *Columbia Journal of World Business*, 19(4), pp. 63–7.

Hedlund, Gunnar (1981) 'Autonomy of subsidiaries and formalization of headquarters–subsidiary relationships in Swedish MNCs', in Lars Otterbeck (ed.), *The Management of Headquarters–Subsidiary Relationships in Multinational Corporations* (Aldershot, Hants: Gower).

Jarillo, J. Carlos and Jon I. Martinez (1990) 'Different roles for subsidiaries: the case of multinational corporations in Spain', *Strategic Management Journal*, 11, pp. 501–12.

Kantrow, A.M. (1980) 'The strategy-technology connection', *Harvard Business Review*, 58(4), pp. 6–21.

Kodama, F. (1992) 'Technology fusion and the new R&D', *Harvard Business Review*, 70(4), pp. 70–78.

Levitt, T. (1965) 'Marketing myopia', *Harvard Business Review*, 38(4), pp. 45–56.

Maidique, M.A. and P. Patch (1989) 'Corporate strategy and technological policy', in M.L. Tushman and W.L. Moore (eds), *Readings in the Management of Innovation*, 2nd edn (Cambridge, Massachusetts: Ballinger Publishing Company).

McGee, J. and H. Thomas (1989) 'Technology and strategic management: progress and future directions', *R&D Management*, 19(3), pp. 205–13.

Merrifield, D.B. (1991) 'Value-added: the dominant factor in industrial competitiveness', *International Journal of Technology Management*, Special publication on the role of technology in corporate policy, pp. 226–35.

OECD (1977) *Import of Multinational Enterprises on National Scientific and Technological Capacities: Pharmaceutical Industry* (Paris: Organisation for Economic Co-operation and Development).

Pavitt, K. (1990) 'What we know about the strategic management of technology', *California Management Review*, Spring, pp. 17–26.

Perrino, A.C. and J.W. Tipping (1989) 'Global management of technology', *Research-Technology Management*, 32(3), pp. 12–19.

Porter, M.E. (1980) *Competitive Advantage* (New York: Free Press).

Porter, M.E. (1983) 'The technological dimension of competitive strategy', in R.S. Rosenbloom (ed.), *Research on Technological Innovation, Management and Policy*, vol. 1 (Greenwich, CT: JAI Press) pp. 1–33.

Porter, M.E. (1985) *Competitive Advantage* (New York: Free Press).

Prahalad C.K. and Y.L. Doz (1987) *The Multinational Mission* (New York: The Free Press).

Ronstadt, R.C. (1978) 'International R&D: the establishment and evolution of research and development abroad by seven US multinationals', *Journal of International Business Studies*, 9(1), pp. 7–24.

Roth, Kendall and Allen J. Morrison (1990) 'An empirical analysis of the integration-responsiveness framework in global industries', *Journal of International Business Studies*, 21(4), pp. 541–64.

Scottish Enterprise (1995) *Electronics and Support Companies in Scotland* (Glasgow: Scottish Enterprise).

Sethi, N.K. (1985) 'Can technology be managed strategically?', *Long Range Planning*, 18(4), pp. 89–99.

Taggart, James H. (1989) 'The pharmaceutical industry: sending R&D abroad', *Multinational Business*, Spring, pp. 10–15.

Taggart, James H. (1992) 'Multinational subsidiaries in Scotland', *Multinational Business*, (Summer), pp. 6–15.

Taggart, James H. (1996a) 'Evolution of multinational strategy: evidence from Scottish manufacturing subsidiaries', *Journal of Marketing Management*, 12(6), pp. 533–49.

Taggart, James H. (1996b) 'Multinational manufacturing subsidiaries in Scotland: strategic role and economic impact', *International Business Review*, 5(5), pp. 447–68.

Taggart, James H. and M.C. McDermott (1993) *The Essence of International Business* (London: Prentice Hall).

Terpstra, V. (1977) 'International product policy: the role of foreign R&D', *Columbia Journal of World Business*, (Winter), pp. 24–32.

Wheelwright, S.C. and K.B. Clark (1992) 'Creating project plans to focus product development', *Harvard Business Review*, 70(2), pp. 70–82.

White, R.E. and T.A. Poynter (1984) 'Strategies for foreign-owned subsidiaries in Canada', *Business Quarterly*, (Summer), pp. 59–69.

Wilson, I. (1986) 'The strategic management of technology: corporate fad or strategic necessity?', *Long Range Planning*, 19(2), pp. 21–2.

Young, S., N. Hood and S. Dunlop (1988) 'Global strategies, multinational subsidiary roles and economic impact in Scotland', *Regional Studies*, 22(6), pp. 487–97.

8 Human Resource Management in the Multinational Enterprise: Styles, Modes, Institutions and Ideologies

Mark Casson, Ray Loveridge and Satwinder Singh

In their pioneering text *Human Resource Management in the Multinational Company*, Robert Desatnick and Margo Bennett (1977) advise that 'If the right man is hired and properly trained to manage the foreign subsidiary, the corporate parent need not worry; but periodic audits are always advisable. His training should be concentrated at the operating company level, within US or Europe' (p. 114). Even twenty years ago the wording of this prescription might have seemed a little archaic. Yet even if the authors had substituted Japan or Korea as the subjects of their own ethnically and sexually biased discourse they would, perhaps, have not been far from an accurate description of human resource management (HRM) practice in parent enterprises today.

Clearly many examples can be drawn from HRM practice across corporations having roots in a variety of national cultures that might well have been described by Perlmutter (1969) as ethnocentric. Indeed, as late as 1993 Dunning summed up recent research as suggesting a steadily increasing centralization of decision making within the parent locations of multinational enterprise (MNE). However his own classification of the different functional activities performed by overseas affiliates of MNEs, as well as that of Young, Hood and Hamill (1985), suggested that of all functional activities those concerning HRM were most likely to be modified by regional context.

Against a background of marxiant criticism over the 1980s this finding might seem surprising. The English translation of Fröbel, Heinrichs and Kreye's book *The New International Division of Labour* (NIDL), in 1980, stimulated a revival of the dual-labour market thesis over that decade. According to this perspective, developing countries, particularly those of

158

South East Asia, were seen to provide reservoirs of 'surplus labour' for MNEs based in the developed economies of Japan, USA and Europe. Essentially foreign direct investment (FDI) from these latter countries was regarded by NIDL theorists as driven by the ability of MNEs to fragment and to de-skill tasks and thus to enable the exploitation of labour markets in the Pacific Rim countries. While evidently true of some companies in some sectors, like most world-view pronouncements the NIDL thesis can be, and, indeed, had already been, refuted as an all-embracing explanation of FDI by evidence of firm-specific and location-specific advantages enjoyed by MNEs (Dunning, 1980). Similarly the pessimism displayed by some 'New Geographers' on the future 'hollowing-out' of developing regions as 'branch economies' of MNEs has been matched by evidence of the success of proactive regional policies pursued by governments or trade associations (Okimoto, 1989; Hood and Young, 1980).

The nature of HRM both formally and informally is likely to be affected by the manner in which state agencies within the host country regards its citizens, as well as by the manner in which the values and beliefs prevalent within the country affect the attitudes and commitment held by local employees. The styles and modes of control which the parent company seek to utilize in managing a local enterprise are likely to be modified through their translation and interpretation in day-to-day behaviour within a different institutional and ideational context (Hickson and Pugh, 1995). Nevertheless the decision to invest has evidently been prompted by a desire to exploit the locational advantage of producing in the region or of competing in local markets through facilities owned partially or wholly by the parent. We would therefore anticipate that the HRM policies pursued by the local affiliate will reflect this strategy. Indeed, accepting the findings of Purcell and Ahlstrand (1994) we could hypothesize that modes and styles of HRM adopted within large multi-divisional firms will be a down-the-line *derivative* of the global product market strategy pursued by corporate management. This need not, of course, be pursued in the unremitting and unmodified forms postulated by Fröbel *et al.* (1980). It could, however, be the driving force behind the manner in which the MNE shapes its responses to local conditions.

In reviewing this debate we draw from a questionnaire survey of two hundred affiliates and fifty parent MNEs and of forty-seven firms in which interviews were carried out with either or both senior HRM executives and chief executives over the period 1993 to 1995.

HRM IN PERSPECTIVE

The term HRM has been in widespread use among large US firms since the 1960s. It derived from the work of economists such as Becker (1964) and

Schultz (1967) and from the emergence of strategic planning within the large multi-divisional firm over that period. At that time it indicated the rising significance of the personnel function in the estimation of many executive boards of North American corporations. In particular it placed a new emphasis upon the long-term development of a management cadre and on the planning of career structures, selection and appraisal procedures and rewards systems. Subsequently, and most particularly over the last decade, the term has acquired a different connotation. In Europe in particular it has come to be associated with fundamental changes in workplace relations towards the adoption of modes of organization modelled on those of Japanese companies (Storey, 1992). These, together with other forms of organizational re-modelling, such as the 'de-layering' of management hier-archies and 'single-status' employment contracts, are seen to have provided the personnel function with greater executive authority and influence in the *design* of corporate strategy.

In some respects then, the different usages of the term HRM reflect a temporal and somewhat contradictory movement in personnel practice. In its earlier use it reflected the importance of long-term planning and career stability for management of the MNE, in its later use the growing need for operational flexibility both in task-related skills and in numbers employed on a given task or project. For some observers (see Loveridge, 1982) this contradiction was seen to be resolved through a segmentation of the inter-nal labour market of the large firms (see Figure 8.1). Whether consciously or not the firm learns to treat different groups of employees in distinctive ways on the basis of their knowledge input and of the analyzability (meterability) of their output. This may be argued on the basis of the transaction costs of management in the way hypothesized by Williamson (1981) or of the attempted appropriation of the added-value of employee inputs by the employer (Loveridge and Mok, 1979). In either case employee groups may be assumed to be equally concerned with the establishment and protection of the value of their proprietorship over their knowledge and skills. Thus boundaries between segments may be subject to complex social and economic negotiation, as well as to the forces of technical and organi-zational change coming from outside the firm.

Either way it is assumed that the employer will seek to reduce his or her uncertainty and exposure to the risks of dependency on the employee through the adoption of an appropriate mode of internal governance. This is indicated by the modal titles in each quadrant. These are largely based on the relational modes described by Williamson. Over the last decade of the 1980s much of the HRM rhetoric placed emphasis on the need for execu-tives to 'change the culture' of their corporation. This usually implied the fostering of normative commitment among indispensable senior manage-ment treated as members of a corporate 'clan', and among their dependant

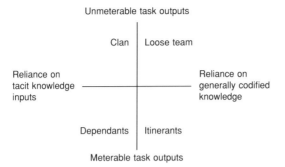

Figure 8.1   Principal factors determining the internal segmentation of the firm's labour market

Source: adapted from Loveridge (1982).

supervisees in the workplace. At the same time, commitment among professional employees in the top right segment should be focused upon short-term loyalty to 'projects'. Temporary workers should be encouraged to gain transferable skills in order to reach a new status of 'employability' (Marchington, 1997). These are of course, skills that must, in the first instance, be of value within the production process of the employing firm. Hence flexibility within the work organization could be seen to complement the employee's need for later marketability.

The use of cultural control presents a particular problem for HRM within the MNE. To the tensions that exist between the desire of employees for autonomy in task performance and control over task knowledge is added that between the HQ's desire to control and coordinate the global activities of the MNE in its various locations. This implies a need to adapt to a multiplicity of differentiated cultural contexts in which the parent body operates abroad. Furthermore, as Morgan (1986) argues, international HRM often involves the procurement, allocation and utilization of expatriates from a number of different countries and their relocation in settings that are equally foreign for the parent firm. Detailed attempts at 'matching' cultural propensities have been attempted in recent analysis of international HRM such as that of Florkowski (1997). These usually incorporate the use of Hofstede's (1980) measures of nationally unique values, as well as taxonomies of national systems of employment law. However as Perlmutter (1969) suggested it is likely that the encultured orientation of the parent company will help shape the formal policies and procedures of overseas affiliates. This may well be polycentric in allowing or even encouraging local autonomy in orientation and structuring of activities, or be based on a global or geocentric view of the MNE's operations.

PARENT AFFILIATE RELATIONS

Bartlett and Ghoshal (1989) have promoted the notion that overseas affiliates (subsidiaries and joint ventures) can be seen as achieving varying levels of self-governing mandates within MNC management, on the basis of a centrally shaped corporate strategy. On the other hand Hedlund (1986) sees the status of overseas affiliates as deriving from locally determined contexts, both market and political. Evidently from the view point of the host nation the question is an extremely significant one. From the perspective of the MNE the basis for devolving mandatory authority to local affiliates is likely to be a corporate judgement on the relative benefits derived from FDI in the affiliate when balanced against the net cost of locating production in a given overseas location. Some writers distinguish between the contribution made by the affiliate plant at the local level and that at the global level (Gupta and Govindarajan, 1991). Others separate the affiliate's contribution in knowledge or *know-how* from the value of *operational* contributions whether at local or global level. Thus we may place local affiliates in relation to these two dimensions. Adopting a similar neo-rational approach to that described above, Loveridge (1997) has suggested that relations between parents and affiliates might well accord with the taxonomy set out in Figure 8.2.

(i) According to this scheme we would expect affiliates supplying the global value chain serviced by the MNE to be more incorporated into a so-called clannish form of governance to the extent that the local operation contributes to new designs. (ii) If it simply produces outputs designed elsewhere in the MNE, or to bought-in designs, it is likely to be subject to central authority. (iii) On the other hand, if servicing a local market, say a

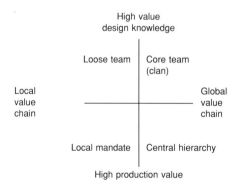

Figure 8.2   Likely mode of local governance to be adopted within MNEs

Source: adapted from Loveridge (1997).

regional supply chain, it will be more likely to hold a local mandate. (iv) If designing its own products for the local supply chain it is even more likely to be regarded as an important team player or member of the *federal* governance of the MNE (for example in a joint-venture or strategic alliance with a local firm).

However such a model is both static and close ended. Loveridge (1997) suggests that national and regional governments have their own developmental strategies designed to promote a clock-wise evolution around the quadrants illustrated in Figure 8.1. A local affiliate might, for example, move from being a supplier of commodity production for a central MNE hierarchy, through the establishment of a regionally based supply chain, to the creation of their own nationally based research centre contributing to the design of global best-practice within the MNE and beyond. For example Ferdows (1997) traces the manner in which Hewlett-Packard was able to upgrade the strategic role of its affiliate in Singapore. The process is seen by Ferdows to entail movement through the status of off-shore factory to global design leader by way of four intermediate roles within the company. Kummerle (1997) demonstrates how Eli Lilly has networked developmental laboratories in Singapore, Malaysia and Japan working in a loose team. However the findings of Pearce and Singh (1992) suggest that few large firms invest in the R&D carried out by their affiliates. Much of this activity is likely to be carried out in the form of product development within regionally based supply chains. This can involve learning about the needs of a customer, such as an original equipment supplier, within its own domestic market in order to solicit its custom within another regional market. Such transfers of technology seem more likely to occur by way of a mobile cadre of global management, than in interchanges between geographically dispersed operational units.

THE STUDY

The purpose of the study was to explore the relationship between the practice of human resource management within the MNC and stances adopted by senior management towards other strategic issues, most importantly allowing for differences between parent or head office views and those held in overseas subsidiaries or affiliates. The survey has been described in detail elsewhere (Casson, Loveridge and Singh, 1996a) and only a brief account will be given here. The final sample included thirteen parent countries in which firms were headquartered, together with twelve host countries in which they operated. Some two hundred affiliates and fifty parents responded to our postal questionnaire and a total of forty-seven firms were subsequently interviewed *in situ* using semi-structured approaches. Some countries such as France are represented by parents

Table 8.1   Countries and industrial categories participating in the survey

(a) *Countries participating in the survey*	
Parent locations	Host locations (affiliates)
Canada	Canada
Finland	Brazil
France	India
Germany	Italy
Japan	Japan
Netherlands	Other European
Other European	Switzerland
Sweden	Taiwan
Switzerland	UK
UK	USA
USA	

(b) *Industrial categories used in placing respondents*
Aircraft and electrical engineering
Chemicals
Coal and petroleum
Food and drink
Mechanical engineering
Motor vehicles
Metal manufacturing
Non-metal manufacturing
Office equipment
Pharmaceuticals
Paper and related products (used as control)
Other manufacturing

only, while others, such as Brazil, are represented as host countries (see Table 8.1).

A separate questionnaire was sent to parents and affiliates, but considerable commonality was maintained in the substance of the questions to allow responses of parents and affiliates to be compared. The format for both consisted of five sections. In the first we attempted to ascertain the formal objectives of the organization and the strategies adopted in their pursuit. The second part focused on the organization and responsibilities of the personnel function including the director or senior executive. This concern extended to the third section which explored the company's policies and attitudes to recruitment, training and retention of staff. Part four addressed issues concerning the rewards, incentives and motivation of company employees, while the final section refocused on corporate culture and relations between parent and affiliate.

It is evident from the responses to the questions about the organization of HRM that the size of the affiliate is an important factor, and to allow for this factor the size of the affiliate has been incorporated as an explanatory variable in all the regressions. The results are to be reported in a separate paper. All the regressions were estimated by ordinary least squares (OLS) and, where appropriate, by tobit and logit regressions. The different methods appear to make hardly any difference to the results. Non-responses were often within smaller firms and those that appeared to be most heavily affected by current concerns with the process of managerial delayering, restructuring, or the effects of recent acquisition and merger. In telephonic follow-up interviews with non-respondents it became clear that many personnel managers were involved in large scale de-staffing exercises which they found professionally demoralizing. In this context the subject of our enquiry took on added significance and provoked a disbelief in its random nature. The overall response of 17 per cent is therefore reflective of the current preoccupations of the senior personnel executives to whom it was addressed.

In this paper the main source of supportive evidence will be drawn from the replies received in semi-structured interviews with senior HRM executives and, in some cases, with chief executive officers. The nature of this evidence does not allow us to claim anything other than it provided insight and depth of meaning to the replies received to the questionnaire schedule. It also enabled the authors to grasp the idiosyncratic nature of corporate responses to apparently similar operational contingencies. However it also enabled the compilation of the following ideal types of strategic response and their complementing HRM systems.

STRATEGIC STYLES AND HRM IDEOLOGIES

Individual multinationals appeared to display their own strategic characteristics that did not necessarily accord with a national stereotype. We seem to be able to group these in three categories:

1. There is the *enterprising traditionalist* with a longstanding record of steady if unexciting innovation. The culture is often implicit rather than articulated in formal rhetoric. Its origins can be traced back at least to the 1930s and is often identified with a heroification of the founder. The firm tends to grow organically or through friendly acquisition. Top management are concerned to retain corporate reputation in the operational field rather than in the stock exchange.
2. We identify a second type as being appropriately labelled as the *postmodernist*. The typical postmodernist is the product of 1980s' restructuring through acquisition and merger. Its rhetoric is 'designer labelled' and emphasizes the importance of collaboration at all levels of the company in transactions with other firms. In practice its short-term changes in direction create fear and uncertainty for employees, suppliers

and customers, as well as to long-term equity holders. It is often under-resourced for the tasks that it has set itself in the global market place and higher gearing can only be obtained at substantial cost.

3. The *conservative firm* relies on conventionally bureaucratic modes to solve problems and to create opportunities. It generally uses the most professionally endorsed management systems including matrix management and multi-disciplinary teams, and frequently occupies a dominant position in a mature market and possesses a large stock of intellectual capital. It is often treated by the national government as its champion in the field.

Needless to say the conservative firm is often to be found in markets that have been relatively stable or growing and that continued to grow, though at a reduced rate, even during the depressions of the early 1980s and early 1990s. They are most likely to be found in relatively cohesive business systems such as are provided in Germany and Japan or in some sectors in the USA like aerospace. Such firms are now experiencing changes in their environment from which they have been relatively protected in the past. In terms of Goold and Campbell's (1987) typology of management styles (see Figure 8.3) they tend to be planner-coordinators attempting to shape both inputs and outputs from affiliates. These MNEs often have most difficulty in communicating between parent and affiliates since the parents see themselves as striving for geocentricity, while affiliates regard them as entirely ethnocentric. For instance Western affiliates of Japanese MNEs universally described their expatriate Japanese managers as 'detail-addicts' or entirely concerned with operational standards rather than 'the big picture'. On the other hand, Japanese executives expressed greatest difficulty in adapting to local operating conditions, whilst at the same time being most concerned to do so. By contrast US parents tended to be seen by their affiliates as being unwilling to adapt their procedures, believing their standards to be the benchmark against which local performance should be judged. To this may be added the attempted control of professional expertise brought by expatriate technicians and technologists. Most difficulty in communication among US parents was expressed by a multinational aerospace firm.

Postmodern styles were most likely to be found in British, US and Canadian MNE's. The reason for their immediate focus on the design of devolved structures and processes related to recent experiences of financial crises, often in turn, related to market failure. They suffer from the fact that their constituent affiliates were not very good to begin with and may have been acquired for reasons other than the quality of their operating performance. The focus of the postmodern firm's strategy is upon the devolution of responsibility for performance to operational units, the introduction of 'lean-production' methods and upon 'spinning off' non-core activity. However the new rhetoric seems to often to lack conviction and to carry

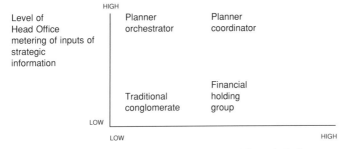

Figure 8.3   A typology of strategic style

Source: adapted from Goold and Campbell (1987).

an underlying cost-related focus reminiscent of a financial holding group. Success in bringing about the restructuring and reorientation of affiliates is patchy. This may be related to an underlying lack of trust among employees in business units at home and abroad, and among customers who lack confidence in the long-term viability of such suppliers.

The enterprising traditionalist can be found across a number of national environments and has, so far, been able to use a record of trustful mutuality in its transactions to bring about incremental changes that have enabled it to catch up with spaced-out change such as, for instance, the forty years it has taken for microelectronics to become a generic technology. Again the markets served by such firms tend to be relatively stable and their position relatively strong. However there is evidence in the histories of such companies of their ability to act upon their environment to ensure their continued survival through late acquisitions in emerging markets. At present our interview data suggest an awareness of the need to form strong strategic alliances and joint ventures in order to appropriate new knowledge and positions in nascent markets. Nevertheless an underlying unease was expressed by respondents in, for example, German, Dutch and Swedish MNEs. This feeling related to the future instability of their national labour markets and of the institutions that have assured their continued structure. It also related to the mimetic pressures of the practices within postmodern competitors and of their rhetoric in professional management education and discourse.

HRM AND CORPORATE STRATEGY

The model of the internal segmentation of the labour force appeared most strongly articulated in our interviews with postmodern firms. Yet it might be said to be more institutionally ingrained in countries like Germany and Japan where the internal structures of enterprising traditionalists were buttressed by overtly bifurcated external labour markets over much of their post Second World War period of rapid growth. Taken in the wider sense, however, most corporations from the latter countries seemed to possess a coherent HRM approach which resulted from the traditional relationships within and towards their affiliations, or strategic business units, and the general style of their senior executives. One might note that customers, suppliers and equity shareholders ranked more highly as stakeholders than employee interests across the whole of this sample of personnel directors (with national interest last, see Casson *et al.*, 1996b). However in the social- ization of new management staff, the inculcation of corporate values of respectability ranked more highly than a work ethic or other ethical standards across all informants. The provision of stable career structures for such a core of long-term employees was relatively confined to enterpris- ing traditionalists among MNEs, of whom net the most prominent were Japanese.

In a more explicit sense senior personnel staff appeared to have little direct influence on corporate strategy in spite of their claim to prioritize organizational design over all other activities (Casson *et al.*, 1996b). Their technical input into the design of recruitment, appraisal and records systems and structures was clearly significant especially in larger conservative bureaucracies. However even here the use of a specialist subordinate (usually female) and external consultants in preparing advice to the board appeared normal. In their responses to the questionnaire, personnel directors in both parent and subsidiary firms were generally inclined to give most weight to a traditional strategic division of responsibil- ity. However, outside of North American MNEs it was difficult to find any evidence of the close monitoring of the local application of HRM pro- cedures by HQ staff. Polycentricism seemed universal but of two distinctly different kinds. In the passive form it appeared as a laissez-faire holding group approach. In its more active form, such as that operating in some British and Japanese MNEs, it was more of an exploratory learning process largely carried on through expatriate secondees who could transfer their experience from one overseas location to another at different stages of their career.

Evidence of differences in the governance styles adopted by a single parent towards different affiliates was difficult to validate within the rela- tively narrow focus of our survey. However, it seemed that claims to au- tonomy were more likely in affiliates operating in one major Tryiad region relative to a parent in another. In other words, where the affiliate was playing a major role in orchestrating operations or in appropriating new knowledge within a significant regional market outside that of the parent, it might be seen to attribute its achievement to the effectiveness of its own strategies and the local management know-how on which they were based.

CONCLUSIONS

In this chapter we have put forward the view that international HRM might be approached from the perspective of the problematical nature of control and coordination over a variety of national and occupational cultural boundaries. Two tentative models incorporating corporate perspectives on the nature of organizational dependencies on the inputs and outputs of labour services and of local affiliates have been presented, together with Goold and Campbell's (1987) taxonomy of corporate responses to these dependencies. This latter puts its analytical emphasis on ideological and stylistic differences between interventionist governance styles and non-interventionist financial monitoring. We have taken this cultural emphasis further in tentatively suggesting the existence of three orientation sets among the replies given by corporate executives interviewed in 47 MNE's and in the questionnaire survey undertaken across 250 parent and affiliate organizations. We have found it difficult to attribute strategic significance to the formal carrying out of the HRM function. In the less explicit sense suggested by our typologies of segmented relations within the MNE, there seems much more explanatory value to be explored. The manner in which such HRM configurations emerge from executive decisions made in respect to other stake-holders perceived to have more strategic value would make an appropriate subject for future research.

References

Bartlett, C. and S. Ghoshal (1989) *Managing Across Borders* (Boston, MA: Harvard Business School Press).
Bartlett, C.A. and S. Ghoshal (1990) 'Managing innovation in the transnational corporation', in C.A. Bartlett, Y. Doz and G. Hedlund (eds), *Managing the Global Firm* (London: Routledge), pp. 215–55.
Becker, G. (1964) *Human Capital* (New York: Columbia University Press).
Casson, M., R. Loveridge and S. Singh (1996a) 'The ethical significance of corporate culture in large multinational enterprises', in F.N. Brady (ed.), *Ethics in International Business* (Berlin: Springer Verlag).
Casson, M., R. Loveridge and S. Singh (1996b) 'Corporate culture in Europe, Asia and North America: implications for global competition', in A.M. Rugman and G. Boyd (eds), *Europe Pacific Investment and Trade* (Cheltenham, UK: Edward Elgar).
Chakravarthy, B.S. and H.V. Perlmutter (1985) 'Strategic planning for a global business', *Columbia Journal of World Business*, 20, pp. 3–10.
Desatnick, R. and M. Bennett (1977) *Human Resource Management in the Multinational Company* (Aldershot, UK: Gower).

Dunning, J.H. (1980) 'Towards an eclectic theory of international production: some empirical tests', *Journal of International Business Studies*, 11, pp. 9–31.

Dunning. J.H. (1993) *Multinational Enterprises and the Global Economy* (Wokingham, UK: Addison-Wesley).

Ferdows, K. (1997) 'Making the most of foreign factories', *Harvard Business Review*, March-April, pp. 73–88.

Florkowski, G.W. (1997) 'Managing diversity within multi-national firms for competitive advantage', in E.E. Kossek and S.A. Lobel (eds), *Managing Diversity* (Oxford: Blackwell), pp. 337–64.

Fröbel, F., J. Heinrichs and O. Kreye (1980 trans.) *The New International Division of Labour* (Cambridge: Cambridge University Press).

Goold, M. and A. Campbell (1987) *Strategies and Styles* (Oxford: Basil Blackwell).

Gupta, A.K. and V. Govindarajan (1991) 'Knowledge flows and the structure of control within multinational corporations', *Academy of Management Review*, 16(4), pp. 768–92.

Hedlund, G. (1986) 'The hypermodern MNC: a heterarchy?', *Human Resource Management*, 25, pp. 9–36.

Hickson, D.J. and D.S. Pugh (1995) *Management Worldwide* (London: Penguin).

Hofestede, G. (1980) *Culture's Conrequemes* (Beverly Hills, CA: Sage).

Hofestede, G. (1993) 'Cultural dimensions in people management', in V. Puick, N.M. Tichy and C.K. Barnett (eds), *Globalizing Management* (New York: Wiley).

Hood, N. and S. Young (1980) *European Development Strategies of US owned Manufacturing Companies located in Scotland* (Edinburgh: HMSO).

Kummerle, W. (1997) 'Building effective R&D capabilities abroad', *Harvard Business Review*, March-April, pp. 61–70.

Loveridge, R. (1983) 'Behavioural approaches to manpower planning – introduction'; 'Contingency control and risk – the utility of manpower planning in a risky environment'; 'Labour market segmentation and the firm', all in J. Edwards *et al.*, *Manpower Planning: Strategy and Techniques in an Organizational Context* (Chichester: John Wiley & Sons).

Loveridge, R. (1997) 'The role of ASEAN affiliates in respect to European parents', Aston Business School Working Paper (forthcoming).

Loveridge, R. and A.L. Mok (1976) *Theories of a Labour Market Segmentation* (Berlin: de Gruyter).

Marchington, M. (1997) *Core Human Resource Management* (London: Prentice-Hall).

Morgan, P.V. (1986) 'International human resource management: fact or fiction', *Personnel Administrator*, 31(9), pp. 43–7.

Okimoto, D.I. (1989) *Between MITI and the Market* (Stanford: Stanford University Press).

Pearce, R.D. and S. Singh (1992) 'Internationalisation of R&D: organisation and motivation', in O. Granstrand, L. Håkanson and S. Sjölander (eds), *Technology and Management in International Business* (Chichester, UK: Wiley), pp. 137–62.

Perlmutter, H.V. (1969) 'The tortuous evolution of the multi-national enterprise', *Columbia Journal of World Business*, 4(1), pp. 9–18.

Purcell, J. and B. Ahlstrand (1994) *Human Resource Management in the Multi-Divisional Company* (Aldershot: Dartmouth).

Schultz, A. (1967) *The Phenomenology of the Social World* (Evanston North Western University Press: Evanston).

Storey, J. (1992) *Developments in the Management of Human Resources* (Oxford: Blackwell).

Williamson, O.E. (1981) 'The economics of organisation: the transaction cost approach', *American Journal of Sociology*, 87 (November), pp. 548–77.

Young, S., N. Hood and J. Hamill (1985) 'Decision making in foreign owned multinational subsidiaries in the UK', *ILO Working Paper No 35* (Geneva: ILO).

Part Three

International Business in
Developing Markets

Introduction to Part Three
Graham Hooley

The first sections of this book concentrated on the internationalization process and the context in which competitive advantage is created. This final section goes on to explore international business in developing markets. In particular, the markets of Central and Eastern Europe (CEE) are considered.

In Chapter 9, Hooley, Cox, Beracs, Fonfara and Snoj draw on data from a large-scale study of enterprises (2699 in total) in CEE to examine the changes taking place in those markets since the collapse of the Berlin Wall in 1989. The study shows that businesses in the region face many of the same challenges that businesses elsewhere face – increasingly demanding customers, increased competition, pressure to keep costs and prices down, more rapid technological change and more rapid new product introduction. In addition, however, businesses in transition economies face a number of problems or challenges arising out of the transition process itself. In CEE the business infrastructure is often not conducive to enterprise, because of political instability, high levels of bureaucracy, poor legal and financial frameworks and the existence of significant 'black' or 'grey' economies.

In order to accelerate the development of market-led economies, governments in the region have pursued various policies of privatization (through the sale of state-owned enterprises and/or the encouragement of the development of the 'organic' private sector). Foreign direct investment (FDI), as an agent for change, has been pursued with differing levels of vigour, and with differing consequences across the region. FDI has been most substantial in Hungary but slow to take off in Poland, not actively encouraged in Slovenia and positively discouraged in Bulgaria. Where it has taken place FDI has generally had a positive effect, introducing much needed investment capital and encouraging the development of new enterprises with the skills and resources to meet the challenges of the new market economies.

In Chapter 10, Ali and Mirza discuss foreign direct investment from the perspective of the investor. They focus their attention on British investments in Hungary and Poland. A sample of 67 British firms investing in Hungary and Poland were surveyed concerning their entry mode decisions and their subsequent performance, in sales volume and market share terms. The most popular forms of market entry in both Hungary and Poland were exporting (34 per cent and 30 per cent of entrants to each market respectively) followed by the use of agencies and wholly owned subsidiaries (22 per cent and 24 per cent respectively). The authors suggest that the longer reform period of the Hungarian market allowed more firms to learn through exporting while the agency type modes were employed because of uncertainty and to reduce risk.

Ali and Mirza conclude that the majority of British firms entered these international markets with low-risk methods such as exporting, use of agents and minority joint ventures, but once they had gained experience they often made deeper commitments to the country by forming majority joint ventures and setting up wholly owned subsidiaries. The mode of operations changed rapidly for many firms, indicating rapid learning in the new markets. This pattern of investment is broadly in line with internationalization theory as propounded by the Uppsala School, but with the important additional finding that, in rapidly changing markets such as CEE, operational modes can also change more rapidly than that theory would suggest.

Brouthers, Brouthers and Nakos (Chapter 11) also examine the activities of foreign investors in CEE. In this case, however, the focus is on comparison of the experiences and approaches of US, Dutch and German investors. Central to their explanation of alternative entry modes are differences in risk perception and culture between the three investing countries. Comparisons are made between published results for 122 US firms and fresh empirical work conducted with 43 Dutch and 39 German companies, again using mailed questionnaires. The authors conclude that US firms have been less willing to commit resources to CEE than have Dutch or German firms. US firms have typically more often employed low resource commitment methods for manufacturing, sales and marketing and R&D, while Dutch and German firms have been more likely to establish wholly owned subsidiaries in CEE. To explain these differences the authors suggest differences in risk assessment, related in part to choice of markets (US firms operating in Russia, Dutch firms in the Czech Republic, Hungary and Poland, and German firms across the whole region but particularly in Poland, Russia, the Czech Republic and Hungary).

In Chapter 12, Selassie and Hill take the discussion of international business to different developing markets, those of sub-Saharan Africa in general and Zimbabwe in particular. The focus of this study is international joint-venture formation (IJV). A total of 32 Zimbabwe-based organizations were researched through face-to-face interviews and case studies. Unlike the countries of CEE discussed above, a major plank of government policy in Zimbabwe following independence in 1981 was the reduction of foreign domination of the economy. At the same time there was some evidence that government was actually increasing (rather than decreasing) its stake in business through the 'localization' process. The authors present a model of the international joint-venture relationships suggesting the need for a '4th link', a non-profit-making organization sponsored by the host government, international donor organizations, and/or private organizations, which can facilitate IJV formation and early operation.

The final chapter in this section, indeed in the book, returns to Europe, in this case the Baltic states of Poland, Latvia, Estonia and Lithuania. Carr discusses the functions of German Chambers of Commerce and their extensive networking capabilities. The role of the Kiel Chamber in promoting trade in the entire Baltic region is discussed in detail, culminating in the formation of the Baltic Sea Chambers of Commerce Association in July 1992. The discussion demonstrates the effectiveness of networking in rapidly encouraging business development.

Taken together, the chapters in this section show the role that foreign firms and agencies can play in aiding economic development and the transition to market-led economies. The conclusions to emerge are that foreign investment and aid are generally positive factors in encouraging and speeding transition. In particular, investors bring with them both capital and human (skills and attitudes) resources that can be deployed to the mutual advantage of investor and host company or country.

9 The Role of Foreign Direct Investment in the Transition Process in Central and Eastern Europe[1]

Graham Hooley, Tony Cox, Jozsef Beracs, Krzysztof Fonfara and Boris Snoj

INTRODUCTION

The economies of Central and Eastern Europe (CEE) have seen substantial changes in the last decade, as they have, with varying levels of success, sought the transition from centrally planned to market-led economics (Fingleton *et al.*, 1996).

Two major planks of government strategy have emerged. First, the privatization of state-owned corporations (Glowacki, 1991). This has been undertaken for a number of reasons, chief amongst them a belief that ownership in the private sector, without state subsidy, will be a major spur to ensuring that production of goods and services is matched more closely to the requirements of customers (business and consumer). Governments have also, of course, sought to minimize the drain on their limited resources that many of the state-owned firms posed.

Second, governments have, to varying degrees across the region, encouraged foreign direct investment (FDI) by way of greenfield investment, joint venture with local companies, or the purchase of equity stakes in existing ventures. These have been pursued as a means of injecting capital, technology and managerial know-how (Artisien, Matija and Svetlicic, 1992; McDonald, 1993; Williams, 1993; Buckley and Ghauri, 1994; Tovias, 1994; Tesar, 1994; Buckley, 1996).

Often, however, the impacts of these two policies at the micro, or firm, level have not been fully appreciated. Indeed, in some countries the policies of privatization and encouragement of FDI seem almost to have been conducted in competition with each other, or as alternative means of encouraging the transition. In Hungary, FDI has been seen as a major potential boost to transition, while in Poland transition has been pursued to date primarily through the encouragement of 'organic privatization', or the domestic private sector.

176

Research in the field of economics has concentrated primarily on macro-economic changes, relating percentages of GDP accounted for by the private sector or emphasizing success in attracting foreign investment (see, for example, PlanEcon, 1993, and Table 9.1). There has been relatively little research attention paid to how recently privatized firms, or those with foreign participation, differ in their activities, approaches and performance from state-owned firms. The research project on which this chapter draws (Hooley, 1997) sought to examine the effects of privatization and FDI on the marketing activities of firms in the region. This chapter focuses on the changes taking place in the business environment in CEE and the impacts of privatization and FDI on the resources and capabilities of firms in the region.

FOREIGN DIRECT INVESTMENT IN CEE

The inflow of FDI to emerging economies in general increased from 5 per cent of exports in 1990 to 9 per cent in 1995 (*The Economist*, 1996b). In CEE specifically there has been a substantial volume of foreign direct investment since the commencement of the wide-scale transition at the end of the 1980s. The European Bank for Reconstruction and Development estimates that in the last seven years £30.7bn of foreign direct investment flowed into CEE. Table 9.1 below shows the extent of FDI to date.

In the region Hungary has been the major recipient of that foreign investment (EBRD, 1994; Cook and Kirkpatrick, 1996). In 1990 Hungary received 54 per cent of all foreign investment into Central Europe, and again in 1991, 1992 and 1993 received the largest single share. Of a total foreign inflow of US$3.5bn in 1993 two-thirds (US$2.5bn) was into Hungary. By 1995 the total stock of FDI in Hungary had reached nearly

Table 9.1   Foreign direct investment ($m)

	FDI 1994	FDI 1995	FDI 1996 (est.)	Cum FDI 1989–96	89–96 FDI per capita	1996 FDI per capita	Ratio FDI to GDP 1995
Bulgaria	105	98	150	450	54	18	0.8%
Croatia	98	81	300	584	118	63	0.5%
Czech Rep.	750	2525	1200	6606	642	117	5.6%
Hungary	1146	4453	1900	13266	1288	184	10.2%
Poland	542	1134	2300	4957	128	60	0.9%
Romania	341	367	555	1434	63	24	1.0%
Slovakia	181	180	150	767	144	28	1.1%
Slovenia	128	176	160	731	366	80	1.0%

Source: European Bank for Reconstruction and Development.

US$10bn, twice that of the next biggest recipient, the Czech Republic (Lengyel, 1995). By the end of 1996 the total stock of foreign investment in Hungary was US$15bn (Privatization Research Institute, 1997). An indication of the importance of FDI to the Hungarian economy can be seen from the fact that 60 per cent of Hungarian exports are now generated by firms with some foreign participation.

International joint venture agreements in Hungary totalled 21500 in 1993, around 25 per cent of those in the region as a whole (ECE, 1994). By the end of 1996 there were 32000 enterprises with foreign investment in a total of around 150000 enterprises. In addition a substantial proportion of the FDI into Hungary has come in the form of 'greenfield' investments where foreign companies have set up their own operations without domestic partners. Between 1992 and 1995 around $2.5bn of investment was of this type (World Bank, 1996). Those investments were made by a total of 190 companies with just 6 companies accounting for half the investment value.

The Hungarian government continues to be encouraging to foreign investment. New foreign exchange laws became operative in January 1996 allowing foreign partners in international joint ventures (IJVs) to hold and use foreign currency profits more liberally than before. Measures to reduce import duties on manufacturing equipment were introduced in January 1997. Laws to help avoid the double payment of tax, laws for the protection of investment, and tax concessions for firms investing for the long term have also been introduced to induce foreign investors.

Foreign investment into Hungary has come primarily from Western Europe. At the end of 1996 the biggest investors were German (28 per cent of total investment to date), American (26 per cent), Austrian (11 per cent), French (10 per cent), Dutch (5 per cent) and Italian (4 per cent) with other nationalities accounting for the remainder. Investments have been primarily in manufacturing industry (49 per cent), telecommunications (14 per cent), energy production and distribution (12 per cent), trade (10 per cent) and financial services (7 per cent) (Privatization Research Institute, 1997).

The FDI investments have had a major impact on the structure of Hungarian industry. In several sectors foreign investors have begun to dominate the local market. In the sugar industry, for example, all the main players but one are now foreign. The tobacco industry is dominated by four large foreign multinationals – Philip Morris, BAT, Resma and R.J. Reynolds. In automobiles, Opel, Suzuki, Audi and Ford dominate. The IJV between General Electric and Tungsram now leads the lighting equipment industry, and the refrigerator industry is dominated by Electrolux (Lengyel, 1995). By December 1996 two-thirds (67 per cent) of the largest 200 Hungarian firms included foreign participation and 120 were majority foreign-owned (Privatization Research Institute, 1997).

Foreign investment in other countries of the region has been less substantial to date but there are signs that the potential of the Polish market in particular is coming under increasing foreign attention. Indeed, in 1996 it was estimated that FDI inflow to Poland would exceed that to Hungary for the first time.

Motivations for Foreign Investment

The potential gains from FDI for foreign investors have been discussed extensively in the international business and marketing literature. They include access to new markets, exploitation of relatively cheap factor inputs and the acquisition of exploitable strategic assets (Quelch, Joachimsthaler and Nueno, 1991; Benito and Welch, 1994; Culpan and Kumar, 1994; Healey, 1994; Tietz, 1994; Haiss and Fink, 1995). For governments in the region, foreign investment offers the potential for hard currency cash generation to fund national debt repayment and other government spending together with the encouragement of competition to create market-led economies (Bishop, Kay and Mayer, 1994; *The Economist*, 1996a; Culpan, 1995). Individual host firms may seek inward investment as a means of achieving domestic competitive advantage through the acquisition of assets and capabilities in short domestic supply (Hooley *et al.*, 1996).

Although there are inherent attractions and government incentives for foreign investment, international joint ventures (IJVs), as one common form of FDI, are known to involve potential problems, including difficulties of managerial and operational integration, mistrust and conflict between partners (Lecraw, 1984; Gomes-Casseres, 1989, 1990; Hill, Hwang and Kim, 1990; Blodgett, 1991; Gray and Yan, 1992). In addition, in CEE, economic and political instability together with often complex privatization practices make IJVs particularly challenging to manage (Geringer and Herbert, 1989; Cavusgil and Ghauri, 1990; Lyles and Baird, 1994; Szanyi, 1994). It is by no means assured, therefore, that performance expectations of foreign partners in CEE will be realized. Nor is it assured that the objectives of the host governments and domestic partners will be met through the establishment of IJVs.

The objectives of this chapter are to review the current market conditions in CEE, and to assess the impact of the privatization programmes and foreign investment activities on businesses in the region.

METHODOLOGY

The research reported below was undertaken over a two-year period from March 1995 to March 1997. Fieldwork was carried out by a multinational team of researchers from four countries in the region (Hungary, Poland, Bulgaria and Slovenia) under the coordination of colleagues from the UK and Ireland.

Fieldwork was undertaken in three phases. First, in-depth case studies were conducted in each country with companies who had gone through, or were in the process of, privatization or the formation of joint ventures with foreign investors. Between 10 and 15 cases were undertaken in each of the four countries under study. The purpose of the cases was to explore issues relating to the privatization and foreign investment processes and to identify the potential benefits and problems experienced by the firms. In addition a number of interviews were conducted with government officials responsible for the privatization process or for attracting or regulating foreign investment. For a detailed discussion of the case study research in Bulgaria, see Marinova *et al.* (1997).

The second phase involved the creation of a structured questionnaire exploring issues arising from the case studies. Topics identified included: the changes taking place in the business environments of the countries studied; the changes in firm resources and capabilities following privatization and/or foreign investment; market orientation; marketing strategy; marketing implementation; and company performance. The questionnaire was then pilot tested in each country and refined for use in subsequent mail surveys.

The third phase involved mailed surveys and personal interviews in the four countries of CEE studied. In Hungary and Bulgaria a mailing list of 3000 enterprises was constructed, in Poland and Slovenia the mailing list was 2000 enterprises. In all cases the lists were created to be representative of all industrial sectors and ownership structures. These mailing lists included state-owned enterprises, privatized firms, wholly foreign-owned and international joint ventures. Questionnaires were despatched, addressed to chief executives, in three waves during autumn 1996. In addition, due to low response rates to previous mailed surveys in Bulgaria, substantial personal interviewing was undertaken by researchers in that country. By the cut-off date for replies (November 1996) a total of 2699 replies had been received (27 per cent response rate overall). Response rates varied from country to country, the personal interviews in Bulgaria resulting in the highest response of 1080 firms (36 per cent), while the wholly mailed survey method resulted in 629 (31 per cent) in Slovenia, 589 (20 per cent) in Hungary and 401 (20 per cent) in Poland. Tests for non-response bias showed no systematic differences by industry category. There was, however, a tendency for marginally better response from larger firms than from small operators. Results are therefore marginally biased towards the opinions of managers in larger companies. This does, however, reflect their greater significance to economic performance.

THE CHANGING BUSINESS ENVIRONMENT IN CEE

In the surveys, respondents were shown a number of statements, derived from both the literature on change in the region and the in-depth case studies conducted in Phase I of the research. They were asked to indicate whether they agreed with each statement, and the extent of the impact of the factor on their business.

Table 9.2 shows responses to a series of questions concerning customers and their expectations. The changes noted come as little surprise, since they affected markets throughout the world in the 1990s. Particularly noticeable, however, is the strength of agreement on two key pressures on business: first, that customers are becoming increasingly demanding in the quality and reliability they expect from the goods and services they buy (96 per cent of respondents); second, that customers are becoming increasingly price sensitive (94 per cent of respondents). Indeed, it is the balancing of demands for improvements in quality with lower prices that is the critical issue facing managers in developed and developing markets alike across the world.

Central to these pressures has been the increase in choice available to many customers (94 per cent) as markets have become deregulated and competition encouraged. While there is still some way to go in the encouragement of free markets (see below) the changes brought about since the early 1990s have served to heighten competition and this in turn has increased choice for customers and encouraged a general raising of their expectations levels.

It was also interesting to note the increasing number of firms reporting customers becoming more sensitive to the environmental impact of business (60 per cent). This was especially marked in Hungary but significant across the region as a whole. Again, this concern beyond purely personal satisfaction signifies rising expectations of the role of business in society.

While there was a high level of agreement with the above statements the impact of the factors on the specific businesses surveyed was, predictably, less marked.

Across the sample as whole the factor having the greatest impact was the increasing price sensitivity of customers (79 per cent) followed by demand for better quality (63 per cent) and the effects of greater customer choice (62 per cent). These factors have affected all four countries in the study but some differences are worth highlighting. It is interesting, for example, to note the very high proportion (89 per cent) of Bulgarian firms citing the impact of increasing price sensitivity compared with the relatively smaller number (66 per cent) of Polish firms. This difference is directly related to the market conditions prevailing in Bulgaria at the time of the study, with high levels of inflation and a great deal of economic uncertainty.[2]

Table 9.2 Changing customer expectations

Which of the following statements would you agree with? Which factors have had a big impact on your business?	Total (n = 2672)	Hungary (n = 585)	Poland (n = 386)	Bulgaria (n = 1080)	Slovenia (n = 621)
Customers are increasingly demanding better quality and reliability	96% (63%)	93% (53%)	98% (73%)	96% (63%)	98% (65%)
Customers are becoming increasingly price sensitive	94% (79%)	95% (75%)	89% (66%)	94% (89%)	94% (72%)
There is increasing customer choice	94% (62%)	94% (59%)	98% (62%)	92% (68%)	97% (52%)
New market segments are emerging with different needs and expectations	85% (42%)	81% (34%)	77% (32%)	90% (55%)	86% (35%)
Customers are becoming increasingly sensitive to the environmental impact of business	60% (21%)	79% (53%)	38% (18%)	65% (13%)	59% (26%)

Note: First figures show percent of respondents from each country agreeing with the statement. Figures in brackets show percent of respondents from each country reporting a big impact of the factor on their business. All above differences statistically significant at 0.001 level.

While nearly two-thirds (60 per cent) of respondents agreed that customers were becoming increasingly concerned about the impact of business on the environment, only one-third of these (21 per cent) reported a significant impact on their own firm. The figure was significantly higher in Hungary (53 per cent). The impact in Bulgaria was the lowest, where, again, economic pressures and uncertainty may be delaying the impact of environmental concerns on business.

In addition to changes in customer requirements and expectations a number of other pressures on business evident in Western markets were also present in the CEE countries studied. Table 9.3 shows three of the most significant.

Again, as in Western businesses, a dominant pressure is to keep costs in check (93 per cent). This was especially important during the recessions of the early 1990s and reflects directly back to the concerns of customers over pricing levels. Keeping business costs down is important to firms in all four countries studied, but the impact has been particularly strong in Bulgaria and Slovenia. Across the region attempts to keep costs down have often been translated into 'downsizing' and the reduction of employment opportunities, resulting in unemployment levels significantly higher than those seen in previous decades.

Technological change also affects firms in all countries and CEE is no exception. Rapid technological change is attended by new products and services coming to market more quickly than in the past, heightening the need for marketing skills to ensure their success.

Table 9.4 shows managers' views on the progress that each of the four economies has made to date on the road towards creating market-led economies. It is immediately clear that progress varies dramatically across the region.

Bulgaria stands out from the other three economies as significantly less advanced on the road to a market-led economy. Only 5 per cent of Bulgarian respondents agreed with the first statement in Table 9.4. Perhaps surprising was that not more of the Slovenian, Hungarian and Polish managers agreed with this statement, indicating that their perceptions of progress are somewhat behind the popular image presented by politicians. But the consensus across all four countries was that the movement towards market-led economies is irreversible, despite the slow progress to date in some quarters.

The role of FDI in helping that transition is also shown in the table. As discussed above, Hungary has been a major beneficiary of much of the foreign investment into the region and this is shown in the high level of agreement in Hungary with the third statement. In Bulgaria, however, FDI has been relatively sparse, and recent economic uncertainty is adversely affecting even these flows.

Table 9.3 Pressures on business

Which of the following statements would you agree with? Which factors have had a big impact on your business?	Total (n = 2672)	Hungary (n = 585)	Poland (n = 386)	Bulgaria (n = 1080)	Slovenia (n = 621)
There is increased pressure to keep business costs down	93% (75%)	93% (63%)	89% (66%)	90% (83%)	99% (76%)
New products and services are coming to market more quickly than in the past	85% (55%)	86% (50%)	94% (56%)	77% (60%)	93% (52%)
Technology is changing rapidly	66% (37%)	73% (44%)	73% (41%)	49% (26%)	86% (49%)

Note: First figures show percent of respondents from each country agreeing with the statement. Figures in brackets show percent of respondents from each country reporting a big impact of the factor on their business. All above differences statistically significant at 0.001 level.

Table 9.4 Progress towards market-led economies

Which of the following statements would you agree with? Which factors have had a big impact on your business?	Total (n = 2672)	Hungary (n = 585)	Poland (n = 386)	Bulgaria (n = 1080)	Slovenia (n = 621)
The country is well advanced on the road towards a market-led economy	34% (46%)	60% (41%)	53% (43%)	5% (54%)	50% (37%)
The move towards a market-led economy is irreversible	79% (40%)	85% (55%)	88% (62%)	75% (25%)	75% (41%)
Foreign investment has been a major boost to creating a market-led economy	30% (28%)	71% (55%)	31% (30%)	15% (20%)	19% (18%)

Note: First figures show percent of respondents from each country agreeing with the statement. Figures in brackets show percent of respondents from each country reporting a big impact of the factor on their business.
All above differences statistically significant at 0.001 level.

Table 9.5 The infrastructure for business

Which of the following statements would you agree with? Which factors have had a big impact on your business?	Total (n = 2672)	Hungary (n = 585)	Poland (n = 386)	Bulgaria (n = 1080)	Slovenia (n = 621)
Over-taxation on enterprises is reducing the funds available for re-investment	96% (82%)	94% (82%)	92% (78%)	99% (97%)	96% (76%)
The level of official bureaucracy is a deterrent to foreign investment	72% (42%)	63% (43%)	58% (35%)	90% (45%)	60% (39%)
There is a high level of business uncertainty in the market	71% (63%)	62% (49%)	50% (37%)	89% (88%)	59% (45%)
The 'black market' is a deterrent to trade and legitimate enterprise	65% (40%)	75% (57%)	39% (28%)	71% (33%)	63% (42%)
The political situation in the country is conducive to business activity (disagree)	63% (47%)	52% (34%)	49% (28%)	86% (69%)	42% (30%)
The legal framework in the country is conducive to business activity (disagree)	75% (48%)	61% (32%)	60% (43%)	88% (60%)	75% (46%)
The financial infrastructure is conducive to business activity (disagree)	80% (59%)	63% (34%)	63% (42%)	98% (84%)	77% (49%)

Note: First figures show percent of respondents from each country agreeing with the statement. Figures in brackets show percent of respondents from each country reporting a big impact of the factor on their business.
All above differences statistically significant at 0.001 level.

Table 9.5 shows responses to a series of statements concerning the infrastructure for business. It can be seen that managers share a number of significant concerns over the business infrastructure in which they operate. Across the region there is a managerially held belief that high levels of taxation on business are hindering reinvestment and hence limiting the potential for growth. With regard to encouraging foreign investment there is a view that high levels of bureaucracy deter investment (especially in Bulgaria) and that there is a high level of uncertainty in the market in general (again especially in Bulgaria).

A number of specific areas emerged that warrant attention from policy-makers in the region. The 'black' or 'grey' market is believed by many managers to be hindering business development. This is particularly so in Hungary, but less of a problem in Poland. In Hungary over half of respondents report that the black market has had a big impact on their businesses.

The political, legal and financial infrastructure in which businesses operate also gives cause for concern. Here the proportions of respondents disagreeing that these aspects of the infrastructure were conducive to business were high (very high in Bulgaria) so that the impact figures show the impact of an unconducive infrastructure. Of greatest concern across the region in this regard has been the financial infrastructure and the availability of investment funding. In Bulgaria this is cited as having a big impact in 84 per cent of firms. While the Bulgarian figure is significantly higher than elsewhere in the other countries, between a third and a half of firms reported similar concerns.

In summary, the Polish and Hungarian business infrastructures (with the exception of the concerns over the black market in the latter) appear the most conducive to business, followed by Slovenia. The business environment in Bulgaria can best be characterized as 'hostile'.

It is clear that businesses in the region face many of the same problems (and opportunities) faced by businesses in Western and other developed markets. These include increasing customer expectations in terms of better quality and reliability while at the same time demanding competitive prices. These pressures have been fuelled by the increased levels of competition across the region and firms are being forced to respond through cost-cutting, development of new market offerings and innovations in the ways they operate.

In addition to these global pressures, however, firms in the region also have to cope, to a greater or lesser extent, with an infrastructure not as conducive as it might be to business. High levels of taxation, the existence of the black market and poor financial, legal and political infrastructures all make the jobs of managers in the region increasingly demanding. While management can deal with the general business pressures, it requires policy-makers and governments to address the infrastructure issues to provide an environment where a market-led economy can flourish.

THE EFFECTS OF PRIVATIZATION ON BUSINESS RESOURCES AND CAPABILITIES

Privatization programmes have been pursued with varying levels of vigour, through various approaches and with various levels of success throughout the region. Across the sample as a whole there was a strongly held opinion, however, that governments were officially encouraging privatization but in reality doing little to implement it, or were even discouraging it through excessive bureaucracy (see Table 9.6). Privatization was thought to be most strongly encouraged in Hungary and least encouraged in Slovenia.

Just as concerning were responses from organic private firms indicating their views that governments in all four countries are doing very little in practice to encourage the development of the private sector (see Table 9.7). Indeed the view again prevailed that government words and deeds did not match up and that while the official policy was to encourage the development of the private sector the reality discourages it.

Privatization has taken different forms in each country. In Hungary, previously state-owned enterprises have been sold into private ownership, sometimes foreign ownership. In Poland, privatization of state assets has been slow but the growth of the 'organic' private sector has been rapid. According to the views of respondents from Poland, however, the rapid development of the organic private sector has been despite, not because of, government policies and attitudes.

Where privatization has occurred managers were asked to identify the changes to their companies that had arisen (Table 9.8). Differences between countries did emerge, relating in part to the types of privatization pursued and in part to the wider business environment. The table shows the percentage of managers in each enterprise listing asset and competence changes.

The most significant effects of privatization vary by country. In Hungary, for example, the most significant factors are the improvement of relations with customers, and access to greater entrepreneurial and marketing skills. In Poland, the most significant factors are enhancement of company reputation, better credibility with financiers, and greater credibility with customers. In Bulgaria, the prime impact has been access to financial resources (in sharp contrast to other countries), credibility with financiers and relationships with distributors. Finally, in Slovenia, the most significant changes have been enhancement of company reputation, credibility with financiers and relationships with customers.

Also striking in Table 9.8 is that the effects of privatization overall appear far less marked in Slovenia than in the other countries.

Table 9.6 Government attitudes to privatization

Opinions of managers of state-owned enterprises (SOEs): How strongly is the government pursuing the privatization of your industry?	Total (n = 983)	Hungary (n = 39)	Poland (n = 90)	Bulgaria (n = 750)	Slovenia (n = 104)
Very strongly in both stated intentions and deeds	16%	23%	9%	18%	6%
The official policy is to encourage privatization but the reality discourages	65%	33%	71%	67%	59%
The goverment makes no attempt to pursue privatization	20%	44%	20%	16%	36%

Opinions of managers of former SOEs that have now been privatized through domestic investment: How strongly is the government pursuing the privatization of your industry?	Total (n = 525)	Hungary (n = 103)	Poland (n = 88)	Bulgaria (n = 89)	Slovenia (n = 245)
Very strongly in both stated intentions and deeds	19%	27%	26%	30%	8%
The official policy is to encourage privatization but the reality discourages	64%	55%	66%	61%	67%
The goverment makes no attempt to pursue privatization	18%	18%	8%	9%	25%

Differences statistically significant at 0.001 level.

Table 9.7 Government attitudes to the private sector

Opinions of managers of domestic firms that have arisen organically: How strongly is the government encouraging the development of the private sector in your industry?	Total (n = 521)	Hungary (n = 183)	Poland (n = 24)	Bulgaria (n = 200)	Slovenia (n = 114)
Very strongly in both stated intentions and deeds	2%	3%	4%	2%	1%
The official policy is to encourage the private sector but the reality discourages	50%	62%	50%	30%	66%
The government makes no attempt to encourage the private sector	48%	36%	46%	68%	33%

Differences statistically significant at 0.001 level.

Table 9.8 Changes brought about by privatization

Opinions of managers of former SOEs, now privatized companies: How have your company's assets and capabilities changed since the introduction of private domestic investment?	Total (n = 536)	Hungary (n = 112)	Poland (n = 90)	Bulgaria (n = 89)	Slovenia (n = 245)
Our relationships with customers is enhanced***	45%	71%	48%	64%	24%
Our company reputation has been enhanced***	41%	50%	56%	38%	32%
We now have greater credibility with our financiers***	39%	30%	54%	74%	24%
We now have greater credibility with our customers***	38%	47%	52%	62%	19%
Our relationships with suppliers is enhanced***	36%	43%	43%	66%	20%
We now access to greater financial resources***	33%	36%	38%	84%	12%
Our ability to research and understand the market is enhanced***	32%	49%	34%	65%	11%
Our production and operations capability is enhanced***	31%	35%	48%	53%	14%
We have access to marketing skills that we didn't have previously***	28%	59%	21%	55%	6%
We have access to entrepreneurial skills that we didn't have previously***	28%	65%	21%	47%	7%
Our new product development capability is enhanced***	23%	27%	36%	39%	10%
Our relationships with distributors is enhanced***	23%	17%	21%	69%	9%
Our relationships with other related companies is enhanced***	18%	30%	20%	21%	11%
We have access to new brands that we can exploit domestically***	11%	17%	16%	19%	3%
There has been no real change***	27%	17%	13%	1%	47%

*** Significant at 0.001 level, ** significant at 0.01 level, * significant at 0.05 level.

THE EFFECTS OF FOREIGN INVESTMENT

FDI is most strongly encouraged, in both words and deeds, in Hungary (see Table 9.9). A major reason advanced for this relative success in attracting foreign investment to Hungary has been that the country is seen as the one in the region with the greatest financial sophistication and the greatest degree of legal protection to investors. Poland has been slow to privatize and has not yet attracted significant levels of FDI. Following the re-scheduling of national debt in 1994, however, and the upturn in the economy, foreign investment has increased significantly year on year. It is believed that relatively low production costs, coupled with the sizeable domestic market, are the main draws to investment in Poland.[3]

Across the sample as a whole the prevailing view was that while governments officially espouse the encouragement of FDI the reality of their actions and the levels of bureaucracy engendered actually discourage investment. This was the view of two-thirds of managers of companies with FDI experience in Poland, Bulgaria and Slovenia.

Table 9.10 shows the motives of foreign investors, as judged by the local managers of firms with foreign investment in them. The most significant factor across the sample was the opportunity to build a long-term position in the domestic market. Only in Slovenia was access to skilled labour seen as more significant than the attraction of the local market. This is explained by the relatively small size (around two million people) of the domestic market. Note, however, that labour costs in Slovenia are around three times those of Central Europe as a whole, hence the relatively smaller percentage citing low labour costs, rather than skilled labour, as an investment motivator.

As predicted, relatively low labour costs (of skilled labour) in Poland were considered almost as important as access to the local market. The opportunity to make good short-term profits was relatively low in all countries except Bulgaria, suggesting that FDI in general is concerned with long-term market and production opportunities rather than short-term financial expediency.

Despite the attitudes of governments a number of significant benefits of FDI were listed by the respondents. These are presented in Table 9.11. The magnitude of the effects varies significantly by country. This is related in part to the types of FDI (greenfield, IJV with state, IJV with local partner, outright purchase of assets, etc.) and in part to the business and economic climate in each country.

In Hungary, the most significant benefit of FDI was the injection of greater financial resources, followed by an improvement in both company reputation and operations capability. In Poland, where FDI to date has been significantly lower but is now gaining momentum, the effects were similar but the order of the top two was reversed. In Bulgaria, where FDI

Table 9.9 Government attitudes towards foreign direct investment

Opinions of managers of companies with foreign investment (including greenfield investments and joint ventures with domestic firms): How actively does the government encourage foreign investment into the country?	Total (n = 234)	Hungary (n = 86)	Poland (n = 77)	Bulgaria (n = 41)	Slovenia (n = 30)
Very strongly in both stated intentions and deeds	24%	50%	12%	2%	7%
The official policy is to encourage investment but the reality discourages	61%	44%	73%	71%	67%
The government makes no attempt to encourage foreign investment	15%	6%	16%	27%	27%

Differences statistically significant at 0.001 level.

Table 9.10 Foreign investor reasons for investing in a country

Opinions of managers of companies with foreign investment (including greenfield investments and joint ventures with domestic firms): How important are the following to foreign investors when deciding to invest in Hungary/Poland/Bulgaria/Slovenia?	Total (n = 232)	Hungary (n = 90)	Poland (n = 71)	Bulgaria (n = 41)	Slovenia (n = 30)
The opportunity to built a long-term position in the market***	82%	79%	89%	100%	50%
Access to the local market***	65%	52%	86%	81%	33%
To take advantage of low labour costs***	61%	67%	76%	34%	43%
To take advantage of a skilled labout force*	59%	53%	68%	56%	60%
Using the local market as a gateway to the region**	42%	40%	57%	24%	37%
The opportunity to make good short-term profits***	31%	22%	33%	56%	20%
To take advantage of government grants or tax concessions***	27%	31%	46%	0%	10%
To take advantage of raw material sources***	16%	21%	26%	2%	0%

*** Significant at 0.001 level, ** significant at 0.01 level, * significant at 0.05 level.

Table 9.11 Changes brought about by foreign investment

Opinions of managers of firms with foreign investment: How have your company's assets and capabilities changed since the introduction of foreign investment?	Total (n = 253)	Hungary (n = 91)	Poland (n = 88)	Bulgaria (n = 41)	Slovenia (n = 33)
We now have access to greater financial resources***	55%	62%	44%	85%	23%
Our company reputation has been enhanced*	50%	45%	46%	73%	43%
We have greater credibility with our customers***	45%	42%	41%	73%	27%
We have greater credibility with our financiers***	44%	36%	40%	83%	27%
Our relationships with customers is enhanced***	41%	44%	25%	73%	30%
Our production and operations capability is enhanced	40%	45%	41%	34%	33%
We have access to marketing skills that we didn't have previously***	39%	42%	26%	76%	13%
Our ability to research and understand the market is enhanced***	35%	33%	23%	68%	30%
Our relationships with suppliers is enhanced	29%	25%	33%	20%	43%
Our new product development capability is enhanced	28%	21%	34%	27%	33%
We have access to new brands that we can exploit domestically*	26%	34%	22%	10%	37%
We have access to entrepreneurial skills that we didn't have previously*	22%	25%	23%	5%	30%
Our relationships with distributors is enhanced*	20%	12%	26%	32%	10%
Our relationships with other related companies is enhanced	19%	17%	13%	32%	20%
There has been no real change	7%	11%	3%	10%	3%

*** Significant at 0.001 level, ** significant at 0.01 level, * significant at 0.05 level.

has been small and there are little signs of improvement, the most significant benefits were financial – the injection of greater capital resources, improvement of credibility with financiers and access to marketing skills. In Slovenia, where again there has been little FDI in absolute terms but per capita FDI exceeds Poland, the most significant factor was the enhancement of reputation followed by improved relationships with suppliers and enhanced new product development capability.

These effects of FDI are somewhat different from the effects of privatization across the whole sample, but inevitably vary by country as privatization practices and FDI patterns vary. The most striking difference in effects is the injection of much needed capital to enterprises in the region. While privatization can encourage more market-focused activity and generate greater credibility with customers and financiers alike, foreign direct investment can provide the capital needed, together with greater boosts to the firms' reputations, and improvement of operations, marketing and research capabilities.

Figure 9.1 compares the impacts of privatization and FDI graphically. It is interesting to note that nearly all the effects of privatization are provided also by FDI, whereas the specific effects of FDI related to enhanced

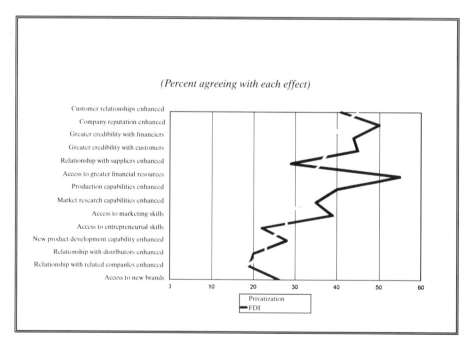

Figure 9.1   The effects of privatization and foreign direct investment

financial resources and marketing capabilities are less evident from privatization.

CONCLUSIONS

The developing market environments of Central and Eastern Europe share many of the characteristics of developed and developing markets elsewhere around the globe. Customers are becoming increasingly demanding in the products and services they buy, but at the same time they are becoming increasingly price sensitive, leading to intense pressure to keep costs down. Increased choice brought about by higher levels of competition, more rapid technological change, new products and services coming to market and the emergence of new market segments with different requirements means that marketing expertise is a vital ingredient for business success.

In addition to these global pressures, however, businesses in CEE face a number of problems arising out of the transition process. While each country is at a different stage in that transition there was a high level of agreement that the environments were not conducive to business. Specific problems emerged with regard to the financial infrastructure, the legal framework, political instability, levels of bureaucracy and the presence of the 'black' or 'grey' market. Most striking, however, was the very high proportion of respondents (overall, nineteen out of twenty) reporting that high levels of taxation were deterring re-investment. These macroeconomic and political issues cannot be tackled by individual businesses but should be the concern of governments across the region.

Managers' views on the level of encouragement that governments have given to privatization varied across countries and depending on the type of business managed. Few, however, felt that government words and deeds matched up, with two-thirds of all respondents reporting that, in their experience, the official policy of encouraging and facilitating privatization was not reflected in the reality. Similarly, very few respondents managing firms that had started up organically believed that their government strongly encouraged the development of private sector economy.

Foreign direct investment has been most substantial in Hungary and was seen as a major stimulus to the development of a market-led economy. In Poland, FDI has been slow to take off but is now accelerating rapidly. In Slovenia it has not been actively encouraged, and in Bulgaria the realities have tended to discourage investment. Where foreign investment has taken place it is generally accompanied by long-term aspirations in the domestic market coupled with taking advantage of relatively low skilled labour costs (Poland and Hungary). FDI has had a generally positive effect where encouraged and facilitated, producing new enterprises with the skills and resources to meet the challenges of the new market economies. Their levels of success will encourage, if not force, their domestic rivals to improve their operations to compete.

Where privatization has occurred, the main benefits enjoyed are improvements in relationships with customers, reputation enhancement and financial credibility. The most significant benefits of foreign investment, however, centre around the injection of much needed capital for investment purposes. FDI also serves to improve company and brand reputation and establish greater credibility with customers and financiers.

The extent to which these findings are transferable to other transition economies is a fruitful area for further research.

Notes

1. The research reported in this chapter was funded by the European Union under its ACE94 initiative. The contributions of Professors David Shipley, John Fahy, Irma Agardi, Marin Marinov, Svetla Marinova, and Vladimir Gabrijan to the wider four country study are gratefully acknowledged.
2. During 1996, GDP in Bulgaria fell by 10 per cent, monthly inflation was in double digits, the value of the currency dropped from US$1 = 80 Leva in early 1996 to 1600 Leva in early 1997, and unemployment rose to 14 per cent of the workforce (*The Economist*, 12 April 1997).
3. A survey conducted by the Polish Agency for Foreign Investment (PAIZ) in October 1995 showed that 61 per cent of foreign investors put low labour costs as very important in their decision to set up in Poland, followed by 49 per cent rating the size of the Polish market (*source*: *Foreign Investment in Poland: Private and Public Attitudes*, PAIZ, 1996).

References

Artisien, P., R. Matija and M. Svetlicic (eds) (1992) *Foreign Direct Investment in Central and Eastern Europe* (London: Macmillan).

Benito, Gabriel R.G. and Lawrence S. Welch (1994) 'Foreign market servicing: beyond choice of entry mode', *Journal of International Marketing*, 2(2), pp. 7–27.

Bishop, M., J. Kay and C. Mayer (eds) (1994) *Privatization and Economic Performance* (Oxford: Oxford University Press).

Blodgett, L.L. (1991) 'Partner contributions as predictors of equity share in international joint ventures', *Journal of International Business Studies*, 21(1), pp. 63–73.

Buckley, P.J. (1996) 'Regional and global issues in international business', in Burton, Yamin and Young (eds), *International Business and Europe in Transition* (London: Macmillan Business), pp. 253–6.

Buckley, P.J. and P. N. Ghauri (eds) (1994) *The Economics of Change in East and Central Europe* (London: Academic Press).

Cavusgil, S.T. and P.N. Ghauri (1990) *Doing Business in Developing Countries: Entry and Negotiation Strategies* (London: Routledge).

Cook, P. and C. Kirkpatrick (1996) 'Privatization in transitional economies – East and Central European experience', in Burton, Yamin and Young (eds), *International Business and Europe in Transition* (London: Macmillan Business), pp. 168–83.

Culpan, R. (1995) 'Transforming enterprises in post-communist countries', in Culpan and Kumar (eds), *Transformation Management in Post-Communist Countries: Organisational Requirements for a Market Economy* (Westport, CT: Quorum Books), pp. 1–13.

Culpan, R. and N. Kumar (1994) 'Co-operative ventures of Western firms in Eastern Europe: the case of German companies', in Buckley and Ghauri (eds), *The Economics of Change in East and Central Europe* (London: Academic Press).

EBRD (1994) *Transition Report*, European Bank for Reconstruction and Development, October.

Economic Commission for Europe (ECE) (1994) *Economic Survey of Europe in 1993– 1994* (New York and Geneva: United Nations).

Economist The, (1996a) 'Sofia's choice', *The Economist*, 339(7964), p. 45.

Economist The, (1996b) 'Emerging market indicators', *The Economist*, 339(7968), p. 102.

Fingleton, J., E. Fox, D. Neven and P. Seabright (1996) *Competition Policy and the Transformation of Central Europe* (London: Centre for Economic Policy Research).

Geringer, J.M. and L. Herbert (1989) 'Control and performance of international joint ventures', *Journal of International Business Studies*, 20(3), pp. 235–54.

Glowacki, R. (1991) 'State of the market structure and its implications', *International Studies of Management and Organisation*, 21, pp. 39–58.

Gomes-Casseres, B. (1989) 'Ownership structures of foreign subsidiaries: theory and evidence', *Journal of Economic Behaviour and Organisation*, 11, pp. 1–25.

Gomes-Casseres, B. (1990) 'Firm ownership preferences and host government restrictions: an integrated approach', *Journal of International Business Studies*, 23(1), pp. 33– 50.

Gray, B. and A. Yan (1992) 'A negotiations model of joint venture formation, structure and performance: implications for global management', *Advances in International Comparative Management*, 7, pp. 41–75.

Haiss, P. and G. Fink (1995) 'Western strategies in Central Europe', *Journal of East-West Business*, 1(3), pp. 37–46.

Healey, N. (1994) 'The transition economies of Central and Eastern Europe: a political, economic, social and technological analysis', *Columbia Journal of World Business*, 29(1), pp. 62–70.

Hill, C.W., P. Hwang and W.C. Kim (1990) 'An eclectic theory of the choice of international entry mode', *Strategic Management Journal*, 2, pp. 117–28.

Hooley, G.J. (ed.) (1997) *The Effects of Privatization and Foreign Direct Investment on the Marketing Approaches, Strategies and Performance of Firms in Central and Eastern Europe*, Final Report to ACE94, May, 350 pages.

Hooley, G.J., D. Shipley, J. Fahy, A.J. Cox, J. Beracs and K. Kolos (1996) 'Foreign direct investment in Hungary: resource acquisition and domestic competitive advantage', *Journal of International Business Studies*, 27(4), pp. 683–709.

Lecraw, D.J. (1984) 'Bargaining power, ownership and profitability of subsidiaries of transnational corporations in developing countries', *Journal of International Business Studies*, 15(1), pp. 27–43.

Lengyel, L. (1995) 'Towards a new model', *The Hungarian Economy*, 14.

Lyles, M. and S. Baird (1994) 'Performance of international joint ventures in two Eastern European countries: the case of Hungary and Poland, *Management International Review*, 34(4), pp. 313–29.

McDonald, K. (1993) 'Why privatization is not enough', *Harvard Business Review*, May– June, pp. 49–59.

Marinova, S., G.J. Hooley, M. Marinov and A.J. Cox (1997) 'Host and investor marketing related motives, promises and actions in explaining the success and failure of privatization through foreign direct investment in Bulgaria', 26th Annual Conference, *Marketing: Progress, Prospects and Perspectives*, Warwick, UK, May, pp. 824–42.

PlanEcon (1993) *Business Report*, vol 3.

Privatization Research Institute (1997) *Foreign Direct Investments in Hungary at the End of 1996*, Research paper of the Privatization Research Institute, February.

Quelch, J.A., E. Joachimsthaler and J.L. Nueno (1991) 'After the wall: marketing guidelines for Eastern Europe', *Sloan Management Review*, Winter, pp. 82–93.

Szanyi, M. (1994) *Experiences with foreign direct investment in Hungary*, Institute for World Economics, Hungarian Academy of Sciences, Working Paper No 32, April.

Tesar, G. (1994) 'Assessment of mutually beneficial technology: East–West perspective', *R&D Management*, 24(3), 199–205.

Tietz, B. (1994) 'The opening up of Eastern Europe: the implications for West European Business', in *The Economics of Change in East and Central Europe*, eds Buckley and Ghauri (London: Academic Press) pp. 55–89.

Tovias, A. (1994) 'Modernising Hungary's industrial infrastructure: the contribution of the EC', in *The Economics of Change in East and Central Europe*, eds Buckley and Ghauri (London: Academic Press) pp. 131–47.

Williams, K. (1993) 'Can Western investments in Eastern Europe succeed?', *Management Accounting*, 74(8), p. 17.

World Bank (1996) 'Hungary's greenfield FDI soars', *East European Markets*, 16, pp. 6–12.

10 Entry Mode and Performance in Hungary and Poland: The Case of British Firms

Shaukat Ali and Hafiz Mirza

INTRODUCTION AND GENERAL OVERVIEW

The collapse of communism in the late 1980s undoubtedly stands out as the most important global political phenomenon since the Second World War. Economically, the transition from a centralised system to a market economy on such a vast scale, covering the entire Central and Eastern European region, constitutes a unique and unprecedented situation. Central and Eastern Europe has opened up previously undreamed of opportunities for Western firms, permitting access to markets hitherto accessible only to a very limited extent. For most Western companies, relatively little local competition (especially following the steady withdrawal of government subsidies to state-owned enterprises), coupled with the liberalization of prices for almost all products and services, has further increased the scope for profitable operations in these markets (Buckley and Ghauri, 1994; Hooley *et al.*, 1996).

However, the euphoria which initially gripped the West following this dramatic turn of events has given way to a more sombre assessment of business prospects in the region. Firms have realized that along with opportunities come increased costs and complexities of doing business; and rather than instant profits, success in the region will clearly come from establishing a long-term presence in the market (Paliwoda, 1995; Rojec and Jermakowiz, 1995).

Problems in the region are common across most countries. East European economies remain characterized by heavy overmanning and have been starved of investment for years, if not decades. This has resulted in growing, unsatisfied needs for a wide range of consumer and industrial goods (Kornai, 1980; Kot *et al.*, 1995). Having to deal with these problems is difficult enough, but on top of this the countries of the region are going through political traumas associated with the jettisoning of the communist system and the move to Western-style democracies. Given such a background, it is not surprising that thoughts of instant profits have evaporated.

Having said this, the progress being made by many of the region's countries is encouraging. Three countries in particular, the Czech Republic, Hungary and Poland, are moving forward and may become the 'motor economies' of the region. Poland and the Czech Republic were the first to climb out of the region's deep post-communist recession. Polish output began rising from mid-1992 with Czech recovery following a year later. In 1993 the Polish economy grew by some 3.0–4.0 per cent, with the Czechs achieving 0.5–1.0 per cent growth. The effects of a severe drought on farming in Hungary, coupled with export disappointments, held the country back, but industrial output began to recover in the spring of 1993. All three countries have established the basic framework of commercial law necessary to a market economy, including bankruptcy legislation to stiffen the financial discipline of both state and private sectors. High priority is being given to re-creating a market-based banking system and all three of these countries have liberalized foreign trade and achieved current account convertibility of their national currencies.

In order to achieve macroeconomic stability and a microeconomic, technological and financial transformation of these countries, foreign direct investment (FDI), which brings with it much-needed management skills and technical know-how, is expected to play a vital role (Vanous, 1992; Bagó and Kulcsár, 1990). Furthermore, foreign direct investment is viewed as a linchpin in integrating these economies with the industrialized countries, particularly in Western Europe (Junz, 1991). While foreign direct investment in Eastern Europe is not entirely a post-Cold War phenomenon, its economic importance cannot be separated from global concerns about the political stability of the region. Given the enormity of the task and the destabilizing effects of authority abuse and 'frontier capitalism', FDI is seen to be critical in efforts to achieve an orderly, equitable and economically efficient transition from central planning to market-based economies (Buckley and Ghauri, 1994).

Despite the economic and political stakes involved, it is clear that FDI activity by British firms is relatively low and unbalanced across the region. The source country share of FDI in the three countries mentioned above is, 27 per cent for the USA, 24 per cent for Germany, 13 per cent for Austria (13.4 per cent), and 7 per cent for France; the UK brings up the rear with just 5 per cent.[1] An improved understanding of FDI in Central and Eastern Europe is therefore of broad-based concern for UK firms with global aspirations, British public policy-makers interested in political and economic stability, and researchers from the fields of international relations, international economics and international business.

Nevertheless, British firms, although slow in getting started, have responded to the challenge and invested in most countries of Central and

Eastern Europe. This chapter, part of a larger research project exploring British and German firms' investment strategies in the Czech Republic, Hungary and Poland, looks at the British experience in Hungary and Poland. In particular the chapter focuses on the type of entry strategies utilized by British investors in these countries, as well as their performance. Before explaining the methodology and presenting the preliminary findings, the chapter examines foreign entry strategies in Central and Eastern Europe, as well as the economic background within which the investment is occurring.

FOREIGN DIRECT INVESTMENT IN CENTRAL AND EASTERN EUROPE

Since the transition to a free market economy, substantial foreign direct investment (FDI) has occurred in Central and Eastern Europe, both demand and supply led (Artisien *et al.*, 1992; Buckley and Ghauri, 1994; Engholm, 1993; Howell, 1994; Johnson and Loveman, 1995; Paliwoda, 1995; Shama, 1995; Williams, 1993). Governments and local firms have been eager to benefit from transfers in capital, technology and managerial skills, while foreign firms, led by transnational corporations (TNCs), have been eager to pursue new growth opportunities (Egan *et al.*, 1995; Shama, 1995).

Companies seeking to expand into foreign markets have a choice of entry modes, including exporting, licensing, franchising, management contracts, joint ventures, strategic alliances, and wholly owned subsidiaries, among others. The choice of entry strategy is determined by the scale of investment and the risk–return on investment calculus (Cateora, 1993; Czinkota *et al.*, 1993; Daniels and Radebaugh, 1993; Paliwoda, 1993; Young *et al.*, 1989). Existing studies on the internationalization process of firms suggest that firms proceed in a consistent stepwise fashion along some continuum as they develop their international activities (Daniels and Radebaugh, 1993; Kim and Hwang, 1992; Kogut, 1983; Root, 1987; Turnbull, 1987; Strandsov, 1986; Welch and Luostarinen, 1988; Young *et al.*, 1989). This incremental movement through various stages of learning and commitment, has received substantial attention (Buckley and Casson, 1981; Cavusgil, 1980; Johanson and Wiedersheim-Paul, 1975; Kaynak, 1988; Falbe and Dandridge, 1992; Root, 1987; Tookey, 1969; and Wind *et al.*, 1973).

Most of the above studies are based on firms entering developed country markets over relatively long periods of time. This is in marked contrast to the sequence of entry into the new markets in Central and Eastern Europe, where markets opened up almost overnight, providing unpredicted opportunities for which competitive pressures required rapid market entry through FDI. Given this, to what extent do these theories explain investment in the region (Healey, 1994)? While knowledge of the appropriate entry strategies by transnational corporations (large and SMEs) into industrialized markets and many parts of the developing world is well established, this is not the case in Central and Eastern Europe. Indeed, because significant foreign investment into this region is occurring for the first time in the post-war era, much can be learned about the 'primary' mechanisms, motives, etc. of TNCs. Hence while previous studies on the internationalization process were developed and tested in familiar markets, Central and Eastern Europe, with its unique characteristics, offers unique opportunities to explore changing patterns of investment.

What sort of characteristics might be expected of foreign investors in the region? First, it hardly needs reiteration that the region offers huge opportunities. One should therefore expect a very wide variety of firms by industry and size; FDI in services can be expected to be as important as that in manufacturing, perhaps more so. Although the entry process is normally gradual, one would expect quite rapid entry because of the need to seize advantages under competitive circumstances. A key factor in determining the entry mode is the availability of competent local managers and skilled workers. Given the lack of previous experience one might also expect many variations in initial entry modes and, possibly, rapid subsequent changes in modes.

The initial entry will usually be cautious with regard to the level of commitment. Affiliates will tend to be small and joint ventures quite frequent. The latter, however, might not be stable because of the limited number of suitable partners and this might lead rapidly to the establishment of wholly owned subsidiaries. Similarly, the use of low-equity modes will be limited.

ECONOMIC DEVELOPMENTS IN HUNGARY AND POLAND

Hungary was East and Central Europe's pioneer in adopting democratic and pro-market reforms (Hare, 1993). Indeed, it began its reform process during the 1970s, continued gradually throughout the early 1980s, and more forcefully from 1986 onwards, well before the collapse of communism; and its example is thought to have hastened reforms in neighbouring countries. By 1990, Hungary was reckoned to be well ahead of other countries in re-establishing the groundwork for the transition to a competitive market economy and pluralistic society. The apparatus of state control and central planning had been dismantled. Prices and trade had been freed. Private ownership and private businesses had been allowed. Competition had been restored. A framework of commercial laws and institutions had been re-instituted, privatization initiated and a banking system and a capital market had been re-created. As a result, in the early years the country attracted as much foreign direct investment as the rest of the region put together. Legislation on the rules, procedures and financial/fiscal conditions for joint ventures opened the way for a dramatic increase in joint ventures. By 1991, as a result of the favourable market environment and stable political situation, practically half the joint ventures in Central and Eastern Europe were established in Hungary. By 1995 FDI in Hungary amounted to 31 per cent of the total stock of foreign direct investment throughout Central and Eastern Europe (UNCTAD, 1996), a very high proportion given the relative size of the country. Many of its neighbours received almost no foreign investment. Hungary is an attractive market for foreign investors for many reasons, not least because of its perceived political stability, the good education and reliable work habits of the workforce, and its proximity to Western markets, as well as its potential to provide a springboard for entry into other eastern markets (Hare, 1993).

The Polish economy, after a period of crisis, has been growing rapidly over the last few years. While output fell dramatically during the first two years of rapid macroeconomic stabilization, it began to improve from late 1992 onwards and inflation has fallen. The measure of success in restructuring the economy is evidenced by the spectacular growth in the private sector, which grew by some 40–50 per cent in 1991 and again in 1992 and is now estimated to account for more than 60 per cent of GDP. Much of the improvement in the economy has been export led. FDI in Poland in 1995 was 23 per cent of the total regional stock, second only to Hungary (UNCTAD, 1996).

RESEARCH METHODOLOGY

The research instrument was a seven-part mail questionnaire, developed after an extensive literature review. It was piloted in three stages, initially on five academic staff and four researchers experienced in cross-cultural surveys, and subsequently mailed to ten companies in the UK, chosen randomly from the sample. Suggestions were duly incorporated into a modified questionnaire and tested again in person with three executives during the CEETEX 1994 exhibition held at Earls Court in London. This resulted in very minor changes, and the revised questionnaire, containing 54 open and closed ended questions was mailed to named individuals, in the UK, Hungary and Poland. The companies involved were of different sizes, ranging from small to major TNCs, spread across many industry sectors.

The original database contained over 450 British firms with investments in Hungary (207 firms) and Poland (250) respectively. Various sources were used for the sample, including the commercial sections of British embassies in Hungary and Poland, the Polish and Hungarian embassies in London, the East European Trade Council (EETC), The Polish Agency for Foreign

Investment (PAIZ) and various publications: *East European Markets, Acquisitions Monthly, Business Central Europe, Business Eastern Europe, Central European Economic Review,* etc. Given the various sources, the authors were confident that the data base gave a fair and comprehensive representation of UK firm activity in the two countries.

The next step involved identifying shelf companies, investment by UK-based (though non-UK) registered TNCs, firms having relocated, closed down, etc. which were subsequently removed from the list. To save costs on mailing, and printing of questionnaires, and to avoid reminders, as well as to improve the response rate, a letter was sent, enclosing a pre-addressed fax form, to each company in the host countries, explaining the purpose of the research and asking for a contact name in the UK, Hungary or Poland, as appropriate, who could assist.

Following the fax responses, 82 firms refused to cooperate for reasons of confidentiality, lack of time or staff or inappropriateness of their firm to the study. A further 29 letters were returned unopened, indicating the firms had closed down or relocated. Questionnaires were sent to the remaining 301 firms in January 1995. A reminder was sent towards the end of February, and a second wave of questionnaire sent in late March. A final reminder was sent in early June. In total, 73 questionnaires were returned, of which 67 were usable, representing a response rate of 22.2 per cent, which is acceptable given the length and complexity of the questionnaire (Hart, 1987), in comparison with response rates obtained in the region by Hooley *et al.* (1993, 1995), using native researcher collaboration. Comparing the unique codes showed that there was a slight responses bias towards manufacturing firms, but other than that, firm size and other indicators were similar. The returned questionnaires were coded on SPSS for windows.

ANALYSIS OF RESPONSES

Profile of the Sample

The overall research sought to ascertain the characteristics and experiences of UK investing firms in Central Europe, focusing on senior managers. Table 10.1 shows the functional positions of the respondents. In total, 17 functions were represented, but the categories have been grouped under five broad functions. As the table shows, for Hungary the majority of the respondents were Chief Executive Officers, 43.1 per cent (14.3 per cent for Poland), whereas for Poland the predominant category was marketing staff, 45.3 per cent (34.1 per cent for Poland). Together these two categories accounted for 77.2 per cent and 59.6 per cent of all respondents for Hungary and Poland respectively.

While marketing manager/directors were targeted, it is an interesting fact

Table 10.1   Functional positions of respondents

Position of the respondents	Countries			
	Poland		Hungary	
	Frequency	%	Frequency	%
CEO/MD	6	14.3	19	43.1
Marketing/sales/commercial function	19	45.3	15	34.1
Finance function	6	14.3	3	6.8
Partner	4	9.5	1	2.3
Regional/country/business manager	7	16.7	6	13.7
Total	42	100.0	44	100.0

that a relatively large number of CEOs chose to answer the questionnaire personally, indicating that not only are strategic investment decisions being made at the highest levels, as one would expect, but also, perhaps unexpectedly, that top management is personally monitoring the investment outcome and has direct knowledge of the business. Another significant factor is the comparatively wide diversity of positions occupied by the respondents, adding richness and depth to the survey as well as providing a diverse perspective of the investment climate in Hungary and Poland.

In examining British direct investment in Hungary and Poland, a deliberate attempt was made to obtain a manifold perspective by ascertaining the views of a variety of companies. As a result, firms responding to the survey included banks, publishers, manufacturing and construction firms, business and management consultants, insurance and financial services; in all, over 30 separate business industries were represented. These have been grouped under 6 categories as shown in Table 10.2. The business category most represented is manufacturing (over 38 per cent, for both countries), followed by services (25.8 per cent for Hungary and 31.2 per cent for Poland) and the financial sector (15.8 per cent and 14.3 per cent). 'Miscellaneous', which includes such industries as transportation, communications and public utilities, is the next largest category (13.6 per cent for Hungary and 4.8 per cent for Poland).

Developing the profile of respondents further, Table 10.3 gives an indication of the size of the UK firms participating in the survey, in terms of the number of employees. The largest single categories of firms were those with employees greater than 30000. Clearly these were major TNCs, with considerable international business experience. The significance of this experience will become apparent later, when the market entry strategies are looked at. The remaining employee sizes are widely dispersed, with small and medium sized firms well represented. Grouping the firms into SMEs and large sizes gives a more informative picture.[2] In total, 45 firms in the

Table 10.2 Business activities of sample firms

Business categories	Countries			
	Hungary		Poland	
	Frequency	%	Frequency	%
Manufacturing	18	38.8	16	38.1
Services	10	25.8	13	31.2
Finance	7	15.8	6	14.3
Miscellaneous	6	13.6	2	4.8
Construction	2	4.6	2	4.8
Wholesale/retail	1	2.3	2	4.8
Natural resources	–	–	1	2.4
Total	44	100	42	100

Table 10.3 Size of UK firms (grouped)

Business categories	Countries			
	Hungary		Poland	
	Frequency	%	Frequency	%
SMEs	25	56.8	20	47.6
Large	19	43.2	22	52.4
Total	44	100	42	100

Table 10.4 Number of employees in host affiliates

Number of employees	Countries			
	Hungary		Poland	
	Frequency	%	Frequency	%
0–99	29	65.9	32	76.2
100–149	2	4.5	1	2.3
200–399	2	4.5	1	2.3
400–499	2	4.5	3	7.1
500–599	2	4.5	1	2.3
600–699	–		2	4.8
800–999	1	2.2	1	2.3
1000–3499	4	9.0	1	2.3
	2	missing	–	–
Total	44	100	42	100

sample were SMEs, while 41 were large. For individual countries, Hungary had more SMEs than large firms, whereas for Poland it was the reverse.

Table 10.4 shows the corresponding size of the affiliates in the two Visegrád countries. As the table shows, the vast majority of affiliates, more than 76 per cent in Poland and 65 per cent in Hungary, have less than 99 employees; a further 20 per cent of firms have between 100 and 999 employees. Only 5 firms (four in Hungary and one in Poland) have more than 1000 employees. The latter are the result of acquisitions, resulting from the privatization process. Many of the small affiliates, particularly those under ten employees, are often nothing more than sales and marketing operations. Most of these are staffed by one or two expatriates, with the remainder of the staff being local. The purpose of the offices is not just for marketing activities, but also to gain first-hand knowledge of the country and scan for suitable opportunities, partners, etc.

Entry Modes

Figure 10.1 shows the various years in which initial market entry took place. Three companies either had some business relationship or were exporting to Hungary prior to 1970 (one in Poland). Significantly, in the case of Hungary, just over 37 per cent of the sample companies had a presence or business dealings in the country before the collapse of communism in late 1989 (31 per cent for Poland). This clearly shows that investors, in the case of Hungary, were encouraged by its reforms in the 1970s and 1980s and had considered it an attractive market with potential. Furthermore, the evidence suggests that, at least during the 1980s, investors had similar, favourable, expectations of Poland. However, and perhaps given their

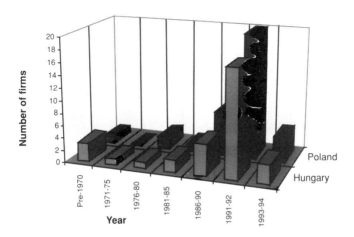

Figure 10.1 Year of entry

cautious nature, the vast majority of the sample firms entered the Hungarian and Polish markets (53.1 per cent and 57.1 per cent respectively) during 1991–2, some two years after the fall of communism in the region. This shows that many UK firms were perhaps too cautious in entering the market, to their competitive disadvantage in terms of first-mover advantage.

Figures 10.2 and 10.3 show the entry methods used by the firms when investing in Hungary and Poland respectively. The figures indicate the dynamics of various strategies as the firms developed their operations. In Hungary, as a first step strategy, 34.4 per cent of the firms used exporting, with agency and wholly owned subsidiary both being used by 21.9 per cent of the firms. Majority and minority joint ventures were used as a first step entry by 9.4 per cent and 6.3 per cent of firms respectively, while licensing, turnkey and franchising were used, significantly, in only 3.1 per cent of the cases. Management contracts were used in 6.3 per cent of the cases. The implication here is that for an equity stake, firms prefer to have ownership control. This is further shown by the fact that in steps two and three (that is, following later reorganization) the number of wholly owned subsidiaries increased at each step, so that by the third step more than 60 per cent of the firms had wholly owned subsidiaries (WOSs).

The picture is a little different in the case of Poland. In comparison to Hungary, slightly less (30.3 per cent) of the firms used exporting as a first entry, while slightly more (24.2 per cent) used agency and wholly owned subsidiaries. (Clearly, given Hungary's longer reform process, more firms used exporting to develop business relationships and gain market knowl-

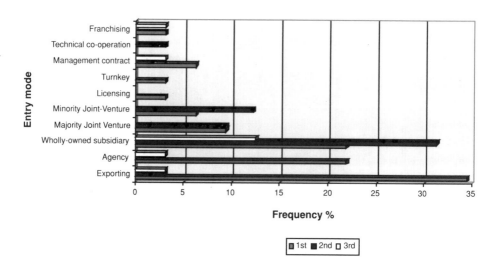

Figure 10.2   First three entry modes used in Hungary

edge over a longer period.) In addition firms in Poland used more agency type modes initially because of uncertainty and in order to reduce risk, a view which seems contradictory, since they also used WOSs in equal numbers. The most likely explanation is that in the case of Poland, firms that entered in the early years (pre-1989) used agency modes, while later entrants, driven by industry-specific and other competitive pressures, chose WOSs (Ali and Mirza, 1997a). This view is further supported by the fact that by the third step, over 60 per cent of the firms were WOSs.

With regard to joint ventures (JVs), the picture is much more dynamic in the case of Poland than in that of Hungary. Majority JVs were used much more often as a first, second and third step, whereas in Hungary they were only used as a second step. Minority JVs on the other hand were less used, both at the initial and subsequent stages. It would appear that firms perceiving risk and uncertainty in Poland were unwilling to *initially* commit large resources in the form of WOSs and instead chose the JV route while keeping equity control.

Another interesting point in Figures 10.2 and 10.3 is the scant use of both licensing and turnkey entry strategies. The few occasions in which these were used appear to be during the 1970s and 1980s. Licensing requires a local partner capable of using the technology, which may not always be possible, especially given chaotic local conditions; moreover local regimes are keen on encouraging equity investment as part of a bid to increase familiarity with the market system. The use of turnkey operations is very much dependent on large-scale infrastructure projects, which for the

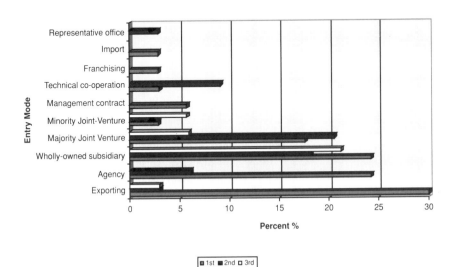

Figure 10.3 First three entry modes used in Poland

present do not appear to be planned, particularly in the case of Poland. Similarly, franchising has not been used to any significant extent, although it has to be stated that many of the retailing businesses conducive to franchising declined to respond to initial contacts, and therefore the picture regarding this may not be accurately portrayed.

Performance

The respondents were asked to assess the performance of their Hungarian and Polish affiliates in terms of sales volume and market share, both relative to their original objectives. The results are shown in Figures 10.4 and 10.5. Firms have had mixed results in the two countries, for while almost 47 per cent of the Polish sample thought their sales volume was 'as expected', only 9 per cent of the Hungarian sample thought so. The picture is completely reversed when the sales volume is 'better than expected', with almost 47 per cent for the Hungarian sample and only just over 14 per cent for the Polish. The responses for the other three categories ('much better than expected', 'worse than expected' and 'much worse than expected') were broadly similar in both countries. These results suggest that firms had realistic sales volume expectations for the Polish operations but perhaps were too pessimistic in the Hungarian case. Taken as a whole, with regard to sales volume, more than 75 per cent of the Hungarian respondents assessed their performance as expected or better. A total of 66 per cent of firms were doing 'better' or 'much better than expected' (mean score 3.72). Only 20 per cent thought their sales volume was worse or much worse than expected. For Polish affiliates, more than 77 per cent had sales volume as expected or above. A total of 31 per cent of the firms were doing better or much better than expected (mean score 3.31). Only 20 per cent thought their sales volume was worse or much worse than expected. This shows that in general UK firms are successful in getting business in both countries.

For market share, 47 per cent of the Hungarian and 20 per cent of the Polish investments were thought to be performing 'better than expected'. Similar to the case for sales volume, the Polish businesses were broadly in line with expectations with regard to market share (40 per cent), while in the case of the Hungarian affiliates only 20 per cent of the respondents had achieved expected market share. In contrast to sales volume, firms in Poland had a 'much better than expected' market share in comparison with Hungarian businesses, although as Figure 10.5 shows, a large number of the Polish firms also did 'much worse than expected' (15 per cent). UK firms also appear to be quite successful in gaining market share, since in the Hungarian case an overwhelming 81 per cent of them were doing either 'as expected' or above. An encouraging 62 per cent of them said their market share was either 'better' or 'much better than expected' (mean score 3.81). For the Polish subsidiaries, 83 per cent of them were doing either as expected or above, with 43 per cent having market share better or much better than expected (mean score 3.6).

The mean scores for these variables and three other performance measures (return on assets, return on investment, and cash flow) are shown in Table 10.5. Broadly the results show a positive picture, with all performance measures being perceived as at least 'as expected' or 'better than expected', with a significant number performing 'much better than expected'. Bearing in mind the respondents were asked to judge these measures in comparison with their original objectives and hence the figures are not absolute, this type of performance can be explained in one of two ways. Either firms are genuinely performing well, or perhaps their response indicates that they were initially too pessimistic and set low targets for their local operations.

The above discussion implies that UK firms have generally had realistic expectations and are aware that in many areas success will need to be

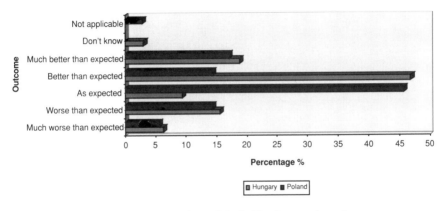

Figure 10.4 Performance compared to original objectives – sales volume

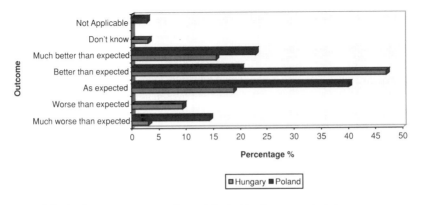

Figure 10.5 Performance compared to original objectives – market share

Table 10.5 Performance relative to original objectives

Factors	Hungary*		Poland**	
	Mean score	S.D.	Mean score	S.D.
Sales volume	3.72	1.40	3.31	1.18
Market share	3.81 (n = 34)	1.25	3.60	1.09
Return on assets	3.33 (n = 34)	1.30	3.42 (n = 33)	1.54
Return on investment	3.10 (n = 34)	1.45	3.38	1.58
Cash flow	3.25	1.32	3.06	1.31

Scale: 1 = Much worse than expected, 2 = Worse than expected, 3 = As expected, 4 = Better than expected, 5 = Much better than expected. *n = 32 unless otherwise stated. **n = 35 unless otherwise stated.

Table 10.6 Overall assessment of the investment

Factors	Hungary (%)	Poland (%)
Highly exceeded expectations	9.7	11.8
Exceeded expectations	25.8	17.6
Met expectation	38.7	47.1
Failed expectations	22.6	14.7
Don't know	3.2	
Too early to judge	–	8.6
Mean score	3.35	3.53
N	31	34

Scale: 1 = Completely failed expectations, 2 = Failed expectations, 3 = Met expectations, 4 = Exceeded expectations, 5 = Highly exceeded expectations, 6 = Too early to judge performance.

measured over many years. Respondents were asked to rate the overall performance of their investment. Their responses are shown in Figure 10.6 and Table 10.6.

In the case of Hungarian subsidiaries, just over 38 per cent (47 per cent for Polish subsidiaries) of the investments appear to have met the firms' expectations, with a further 25.8 per cent and 9.7 per cent having exceeding their expectations and highly exceeded their expectations respectively (17.6 per cent and 11.8 per cent for Poland). This of course does not necessarily equate with profitability or other measures thought to signify success. Different firms had different expectations. For some it was to establish a local presence before setting up a wholly owned subsidiary; thus, although the venture lost money, it met their expectations. While a significant number stated that the venture had failed their expectations (22.6 per cent), quali-

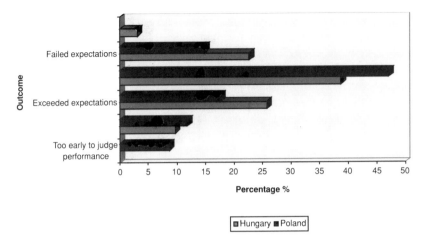

Figure 10.6 Overall assessment of the investment

tative insights from the respondents indicate that these were due to conflicts between joint venture partners.

DISCUSSION OF FINDINGS

British TNCs are taking the Hungarian and Polish markets very seriously, as is evinced by the fact that our respondents are frequently CEOs and top-level executives. The findings show that it is market opportunities and the changing political-economic environment that dictates the scale and mode of entry to these markets. The early British reticence in entering Central and East European markets was mainly due to concern about the levels of risk and uncertainty, not a lack of familiarity or cultural proximity. When the situation was judged appropriate British TNCs became dynamic players in Hungary and Poland, albeit not to the same extent as some other countries.

As anticipated, British FDI in Hungary and Poland is sectorally diversified and small and medium-sized TNCs are very well represented, possibly because SMEs are generally more entrepreneurial and opportunistic than larger firms. From the year of entry, UK firms appear to have adopted a cautious approach following the collapse of communism, and as a result have possibly forgone first-mover advantages. Most of them entered the region between 1991 and 1992. In terms of different entry strategies, many firms chose low-risk methods such as exporting, use of agents, and joint ventures, apparently confirming international market entry theory. However, once experience had been gained, they re-evaluated their options and reassessed the risk/rewards potential of their business and made deeper commitment to the country by forming majority joint ventures and setting up wholly owned subsidiaries. The significant factor is that change of mode occurred within a narrow time-frame, much shorter than predicted by established market entry theory.

The mode of local operations changed rapidly for many firms, sometimes a number of times. If one compares the dynamics of these market entry strategies with the internationalization process proposed by the Uppsala School (Johanson and Weidersheim-Paul, 1975; Johanson and Vahlne, 1990; Vahlne and Nordstrom, 1988), it is clear that there are significant differences between their establishment chain and the behaviour of firms in Hungary and Poland (allowing for an adaptation of the Uppsala model in order to analyze entry into markets rather than internationalization *per se*). The Uppsala Model argues that internationalization is reflected in the increasing degree of involvement by firms in foreign markets, with implications for both the size of resource commitment and the acquisition of market information. In the case of Hungary, over 30 per cent of the firms used majority equity modes as an initial entry method (40 per cent in Poland), while those employing exporting and agency representation quickly changed their modes within a year or so in the light of their experience. Of course, this does not mean that the motives and conditions determining choices relating to mode of entry and operation in Eastern Europe differ from those prevalent in other markets. However this chapter is a first step in throwing some light on the contingencies involved.

While UK firms perceive abundant market opportunities in Hungary and Poland, market entry to these countries and other countries in the region is not without risk. As a result firms have made risk-potential assessments, giving due regard not only to different types of risks but also to the different levels of risk in their strategies towards these and other Central and East European markets. The analysis of performance does, however, suggest that British TNCs were perhaps initially a little too pessimistic in their assessment of the local situation. On the other hand, the vast majority of the investments had met firms' expectations and companies were sufficiently optimistic to the extent that many planned to increase their holdings, as well as move into other countries in the region.

CONCLUSIONS

This chapter has analyzed the entry mode and performance of British TNCs with operations in Hungary and Poland. Although latecomers, they have taken advantage of the many market opportunities available. As a result, their operations are highly diversified and, as their familiarity with the local economies increases, there has been a rapid 'speciation' whereby their mode of local operation has changed rapidly in an evolving political-economic environment. Normally the tendency has been towards high equity modes (i.e. majority joint ventures and wholly owned subsidiaries). This has certain implications for theory, especially those which stress a gradualistic approach to internationalization or market penetration.

Notes

1. *Accountancy*, August 1995.
2. In this chapter, small and medium sized *parent* firms are those with employees in the range 1 to 499, while those with 500 and over are classed as being large sized.

References

Ali, S. and H. Mirza (1997a) 'Market entry strategies in Poland: a preliminary report', *Journal of East-West Business*, 3(1).
Ali, S. and H. Mirza (1997b) 'Market entry, motives and performance in Central Europe: the case of British firms', *Journal of East-West Business*, 3(2).
Ali, S. and H. Mirza (1998) 'Investing in the Czech Republic: a British firm's perspective', *Journal for East European Management Studies*, forthcoming.
Artisien, P., M. Rojec and M. Svetlicic (eds) (1992) *Foreign Direct Investment in Central and Eastern Europe* (London: Macmillan).
Bagó, J. and S. Kulcsár (1990) 'Experience with the establishment and operation of industrial joint ventures', in *Foreign Direct Investment and Joint Ventures in Hungary: Experience and Prospects* (Hungarian Scientific Council for World Economy, ed. Budapest).
Beamish, P.W. and J.C. Banks (1987) 'Equity joint ventures and the theory of the multinational enterprise', *Journal of International Business Studies*, Summer.
Brewer, T. (1993) 'Government policies, market imperfections and foreign direct investment', *Journal of International Business Studies*, 24(1).
Buckley, P.J. (1989) 'Foreign direct investment by small- and medium-sized enterprises', *Small Business Economics*, 1.
Buckley, P.J. and M. Casson (1976) *The Future of the Multinational Enterprise* (London: Macmillan).
Buckley, P.J. and M. Casson (1981) 'The optimal timing of a foreign direct investment', *Economic Journal*, 92.
Buckley, P.J. and P.N. Ghauri (eds) (1994) *The Economics of Change in Central and Eastern Europe* (London: Academic Press).
Casson, M.C. (1987) *The Firm and the Market* (Oxford: Basil Blackwell).
Cateora, R.P. (1993) *International Marketing* (Boston, MA: Urwin).
Cavusgil, S.T. (1980) 'On the internationalisation process of firms', *European Research*, 8.
Czinkota, M.R., P. Rivoli and I.A. Ronkainen (1993) *International Business* (London: The Dryden Press).
Daniels, J.D. and L.H. Radebaugh (1993) *International Business: Environments and Operations* (Reading, Massachusetts: Addison-Wesley).
Dunning, J.H. (1981) *International Production and the Multinational Enterprise* (London: George Allen & Unwin).

Dunning, J.H. (1988) *Explaining International Production* (London: Unwin Hyman).

Dunning, J.H. and A.M. Rugman (1985) 'The influence of Hymer's dissertation on the theory of foreign direct investment', *American Economic Review*, 75(May).

Egan, C., D. Shipley, W. Neal, G. Hooley and J. Danko (1995) 'Joint ventures in Hungary: expectations and experience', *Proceedings of the MEG Conference*, University of Bradford.

Engholm, C. (1993) *The Other Europe* (New York: McGraw-Hill).

Falbe, C.M. and T.C. Dandridge (1992) 'Franchising as a strategic partnership: issues of co-operation and conflict in a global market', *International Small Business Journal*, 10(3).

Hare, P. (1993) 'Economic prospects in Hungary: the rise of the private sector', *Business Strategy Review*, 4(2).

Harrigan, K.R. (1986) *Managing for Joint Venture Success* (Lexington, Mass.: Lexington Books).

Hart, S. (1987) 'The use of the mail survey in industrial market research', *Journal of Marketing Management*, 3.

Healey, N. (1994) 'The transition economies of Central and Eastern Europe: a political, economic, social and technological analysis', *Columbia Journal of World Business*, 29(1).

Hennart, J.F. (1988) 'A transaction cost theory of equity joint ventures', *Strategic Management Journal*, 9(4).

Hennart, J.F. (1991a) 'The transaction cost theory of joint ventures: an empirical study of Japanese subsidiaries in the United States', *Management Science*, 37(4).

Hennart, J.F. (1991b) 'Control in multinational firms: the role of price and hierarchy', *Management International Review*, Special Issue.

Hooley, G.J., A.J. Cox, D. Shipley, J. Fahy, J. Beracs and K. Kolos (1996) 'Foreign direct investment in Hungary: resource acquisition and domestic competitive advantage' *Journal of International Business Studies*, 27(4), pp. 683–709.

Hooley, G.J., D. Shipley, J. Beracs and K. Kolos (1995) 'Investing in cherries and resurrecting the dead: foreign direct investment in Hungary', *Proceedings of the MEG Conference*, 1995.

Howell, J. (1994) *Understanding Eastern Europe* (London: Kogan Page).

Johanson, J. and F. Wiedersheim-Paul (1975) 'The internationalization of the firm – four Swedish cases', *Journal of Management Studies*, 12, pp. 305–22.

Johanson, J. and J.E. Vahine (1990) 'The mechanism of Internationalization', *International Marketing Review*, 6(4), pp. 11–24.

Johnson, S. and G.W. Loveman (1995) *Starting Over in Eastern Europe* (Lexington, Mass.: Harvard Business School Press).

Junz, H.B. (1991) 'Integration of Eastern Europe into the world trading system', *American Economic Review*, 81(2) (May).

Kaynak, E. (ed.) (1988) 'Global franchising: European and North American perspectives', *Transnational Retailing* (Berlin: de Gruyter).

Kim, W.C. and P. Hwang (1992) 'Global strategy and multinationals' entry mode choice', *Strategic Management Journal*, 11, pp. 123–8.

Kogut, B. (1983) 'Foreign direct investment as a sequential process', in C.P. Kindleburger and D. Audretsch (eds), *Multinational Corporations in the 1980s* (Cambridge, Mass.: MIT Press).

Kornai, J. (1980) *The Economics of Shortage*, vols 1 and 2 (Amsterdam: North-Holland).

Kot, J., M. Dziura, E. Piasecka, J. Hardy and A. Rainnie (1995) 'The flexible firm goes East?', *Proceedings of the 21st EIBA Conference*, Urbino, Italy.

Lecraw, D.J. (1992) 'Multinational enterprises in developing countries', in P.J. Buckley (ed.), *New Directions in International Business: Research Priorities for the 1990s* (London: Edward Elgar).

Paliwoda, S. (1993) *International Marketing* (Oxford: Butterworth Heinemann).

Paliwoda, S. (1995) *Investing in Eastern Europe: Capitalizing on Emerging Markets* (Reading, Massachusetts: Addison Wesley).

Rojec, M. and W. Jermakowiz (1995) 'Management versus state in foreign privatizations in Central European countries in transition', *Proceedings of the 21st EIBA Conference, Urbino, Italy*.

Root, F.R. (1987) *Entry Strategies for International Markets* (Lexington, Mass: Lexington Books/D.C. Heath & Co.)

Rugman, A.J. and A. Verbeke (1992) 'A note on the transnational solution and the transaction cost theory of multinational strategic management', *Journal of International Business*, 23(4).

Rugman, A.J., D.J. Lecraw and L.D. Booth (1985) *International Business: Firm and Environment* (New York: McGraw-Hill).

Shama, A. (1995) 'Entry strategies of US firms to the newly independent states, Baltic states, and the Eastern European countries', *California Management Review*, 37(3) (Spring).

Strandsov. J. (1986) 'Towards a new approach for studying the internationalization process of firms', *Working Paper 4*, Copenhagen School of Economics, 1986.

Terpstra, V. and C.M. Yu (1988) 'Determinants of foreign investment of CPS advertising agencies', *Journal of International Business Studies*, 19(1).

Tookey, D. (1969) 'International business and political geography', *British Journal of Marketing*, 3.

Turnbull, P.W. (1987) 'A challenge to the stages theory of the internationalization process', in P.J. Rossen and S.D. Reed (eds), *Managing Export Entry and Expansion* (New York: Praeger).

UNCTAD (1996) *World Investment Report 1996: Investment, Trade and International Policy Arrangements* (United Nations).

Vahlne, J-E. and K. Nordstrom (1988) 'Choice of marketing channel in a strategic perspective', in N. Hood and J-E. Vahlne (eds), *Strategies in Global Competition* (London: Croom Helm).

Vanous, J. (1992) 'Economic recovery of Eastern Europe', *PlanEcon Report*, 8(47).

Welch, L.S. and R. Luostarinen (1988) 'Internationalization: Evoustion of a concept', *Journal of General Management*, 14(2).

Williams, K. (1993) 'Can Western investments in Eastern Europe succeed?', *Management Accounting*, 74(8), p. 17.

Wind, Y., S.P. Douglas and H.V. Perlmutter (1973) 'Guidelines for developing international marketing strategies', *Journal of Marketing*, 37, pp. 14–23.

Young, S., J. Hamill, C. Wheeler and J.R. Davies (1989) *International Market Entry and Development: Strategies and Management* (London: Prentice-Hall).

11 Central and Eastern Europe Investments: A Comparison of US, Dutch and German Firm Activities[1]

Keith D. Brouthers, Lance E. Brouthers and George Nakos

INTRODUCTION

As the previous chapters in this book have pointed out, rapid changes have occurred in Central and Eastern Europe (CEE) since 1989. These changes have affected the lives of millions of people living in CEE, as well as having an impact on people outside the region. For businesses, the changes that have occurred have meant hardship, disappointment, opportunity, and growth. One of the most dramatic changes to affect businesses both within and outside the region has been the change from centrally planned economies to free-market economies. This has meant that CEE-based firms are now free to compete among themselves. Free-market economics also has meant that foreign firms are welcome to compete within the formerly closed markets of CEE. Western firms have responded to these changes in a number of ways. For the majority of Western firms the economic, political, and social uncertainties in CEE have made them hesitant to begin doing business in the region. For other firms, the economic and social reforms have signalled a new, unexplored, potentially large market for their goods and services. This second group of firms have begun entering the CEE markets using various forms of operation, depending on their attitude toward future prospects in the region.

In this chapter we explore the investment activities of Western firms in the newly developed CEE market. Specifically we compare and contrast the activities of US firms with those of Dutch and German firms. Hofstede (1989) and others (Erramilli, 1996; Agarwal, 1994; Shane, 1994) have suggested that firms from different parts of the world may react differently to opportunities in foreign countries because of differences in their national cultures. Other scholars (Brouthers, 1995; Agarwal and Ramaswami, 1992) have found that risk perceptions appear to have a strong influence on foreign mode choice. Because of cultural, geographic, political and historic differences there is a strong possibility that US, German, and Dutch firms will react differently to the changes occurring in CEE. By identifying these differences in culture and risk perception, and their subsequent impact on entry mode choice, we hope to be able to expand theory in this area and offer improved practical solutions to firms entering these new international markets.

In the first part of this chapter we examine the general trends in foreign investment in Central and Eastern Europe. Then we discuss the theory behind our study, including a discussion of entry mode options, national cultural attributes, and risk perceptions that may create differences in the investment approaches to CEE. Following that, we compare and contrast the activities of German and Dutch firms, through two samples of Dutch and German companies, with the activities of US firms, through a sample of US companies. Finally we conclude with recommendations to management on investment strategies for firms desiring to participate in the dynamic CEE region.

FOREIGN INVESTMENT IN CEE

An explosive growth of foreign investment in Central and Eastern Europe was expected after the dismantling of the Iron Curtain in 1989. However, this expectation has proved to be overly optimistic. Although most countries in the region have adopted fairly open foreign direct investment (FDI) regimes, the flow of FDI into CEE remains quite small in volume and is disproportionately concentrated in a few relatively small areas (EBRD, 1994). Several reasons for this slower than expected pace of investment can be identified (KPMG, 1994). First, the actual political, legal and social transition from central planning towards an open-market economy is proceeding much slower than expected by most experts. Second, at the same time several other areas of the world have emerged as potential investment candidates, for example Mexico and Southeast Asia specifically China. These areas are attracting investments that may have otherwise gone into CEE. Third, Western countries experienced a recession during 1993 and 1994, thus overall investment decreased. Finally, for Germany the addition of the eastern region has cost far more than expected, thus decreasing the capital available for foreign investment.

Despite the slower pace, annual FDI inflows to CEE rose ten-fold between 1990 and 1993. However, in 1993 for example FDI inflows to CEE represented only approximately 10 per cent of total FDI flows into developing countries. In fact, '[b]y the end of 1993 cumulative paid-in investment in the region was approximately $9 billion, which is less than a third of the amount invested in China in 1993 alone' (Rolfe and Doupnik, 1996, p. 1). In addition, these investments appear to be concentrated in a few countries, with the Czech Republic, Hungary and the Slovak Republic attracting about two-thirds of the total. The rest of the region, with 91 per cent of the population, received only 32 per cent of cumulative inflows (EBRD, 1994).

Until 1991 most countries in CEE did not allow foreign companies to have a majority interest in a local firm, therefore minority joint ventures were the most popular form of FDI (KPMG, 1994). Since 1991 full ownership by foreign firms has been legal in most CEE countries. As a consequence, the percentage of wholly owned subsidiaries has increased and the percentage of joint ventures decreased (KPMG, 1994).

While the information is still not complete, there are some indications as to the size of investments being made by foreign entities in CEE. Rolfe and Doupnik (1996) examined the number of Western investments (wholly owned or joint venture only) in CEE (including only the six main markets: Hungary, Czech Republic, Bulgaria, Poland, Romania, and Slovakia). They found that US investors have made the largest number of investments in the region with a total of 448, German investors made the second most investments at about 380, and the Netherlands ranked tenth with only 45 investments. However, using a more extensive data-base, based on the size (dollar value) of their investments in CEE, Meyer (1995) suggests that German investors are the largest group of investors, with the US ranked third or fourth, and the Dutch trailing behind.

As is the case with the US, most Dutch and German investment is done by large multinationals and other large companies (KPMG, 1994). German investments tend to be spread throughout the region, while Dutch investment has concentrated in the six main CEE markets. US investments appear to be more widely spread than the Dutch, but more concentrated than the Germans (Meyer, 1995).

THEORETICAL BACKGROUND

Entry Mode Options

The investment options open to Western firms in CEE may be determined by a combination of need for control and aversion to risk. Much of the present literature on entry mode selection assumes that Western firms prefer highly integrated forms of entry, that is wholly owned subsidiaries. This preference is based on the fact that coordinating the activities of a wholly owned subsidiary is much easier then controlling a cooperative venture or independent operation. Strong coordination is especially important for multinational corporations pursuing a global strategy. However, wholly owned operations are not always the best solution. For example, investment risk may be so high that investing firms are not willing to commit the substantial resources needed to gain total control (Hill, Hwang and Kim, 1990; Dunning, 1988).

In addition to highly integrated modes, three alternative forms of entry exist. First, cooperative ventures (joint ventures, consortia, strategic alliances) can be used in all CEE countries and have traditionally been the host government's preferred method. These ventures allow the Western firm a large measure of control, but also reduce the risks of operation by reducing asset exposure and increasing local commitment. Second, firms can use independent modes, such as licensing or franchising. These forms greatly reduce the control of the Western partner but also reduce the financial risk of the Western firm. Finally, exporting can be used as a method of providing goods and services to a CEE country without much investment and without sharing the operation with another, CEE firm (Hill *et al.*, 1990).

Risk Perception

Previous research (Brouthers, 1995) has shown that risk perception has a significant impact on the entry structure choice. We believe that differences in CEE mode selection will stem, at least in part, from different perceptions of risk between US, Dutch, and German firms.[2] Differences in risk perception can be caused by differences in historic ties to an area, social, political, and economic exchange experience, knowledge of and experience in a specific region or in international business as a whole. This study does not concentrate on the causes of differing risk perceptions, but simply proposes the relationship between risk and mode choice.

Two types of risk have been identified in the literature: investment and contractual risk. Investment risk is caused by changes in political, economic, and social behaviour in a country. Firms facing high investment risk will tend to use more independent entry modes, to try and minimize the impact of these changes (Agarwal and Ramaswami, 1992). Contractual risk is related to the concept of internalization (Dunning, 1988). Contractual risk is the risk of working with other parties in a foreign country. Firms perceiving high contractual risks will tend to use more integrated entry modes, to minimize the impact of third party behaviour (Agarwal and Ramaswami, 1992). This leads us to the first two propositions of this study:

Proposition 1   Firms perceiving low levels of investment risk will use more integrated entry modes than firms perceiving high levels.

Proposition 2   Firms perceiving high levels of contractual risk will utilize more integrated entry modes than firms perceiving lower levels.

Cultural Differences

Recently, international business scholars have suggested that national cultural differences may influence a firm's strategic decisions and in particular their foreign entry mode decisions. There are a number of studies in the area of strategic management that have provided evidence of national culture influencing strategic decisions (Schneider, 1989; Buzzell and Gale, 1987). These studies have shown that national cultural attributes have a direct impact on the strategic decisions made. A number of entry mode studies (Brouthers, Brouthers and Werner, 1996; Agarwal and Ramaswami, 1992) have included national culture as one of a group of variables that influence entry mode choice. Kogut and Singh (1988), Shane (1994), and Agarwal (1994) examined national culture as the main influence on firms' entry mode decision and found that national culture was an important determinant. More recently, Erramilli (1996) and Pan (1996) explored national cultural influences on entry mode selection by examining equity ownership percentages. Pan (1996) found that national cultural differences influenced the percentage ownership in equity joint ventures in China. Erramilli (1996) found that two attributes of national culture appear to be especially important in influencing the entry mode decision. These two attributes are a nation's attitude toward uncertainty avoidance and power distance. Finally, Hofstede (1989) suggests that the uncertainty avoidance measure of national culture may be the more important force behind foreign market organizational structure decisions; however, he provides no empirical support.

Hofstede's (1980) overall measure of national culture shows that the US measure of culture (59.75) and the German measure of culture (58.25) are quite similar, while the Dutch measure (46.25) is far lower. For the two individual national cultural attributes that have been suggested to have the most influence on entry mode choice (power distance and uncertainty avoidance) this relationship does not hold. The US has a power distance measure of 40 and an uncertainty avoidance measure of 46. The Netherlands has a power distance measure of 38 and an uncertainty avoidance measure of 53. Germany has a power distance measure of 35 and uncertainty avoidance measure of 65. It therefore appears that based on average national cultural measures US and German firms would make similar organizational structure decisions, but that Dutch firms would be different. However, based on the more accurate measures of power distance and uncertainty avoidance, it appears that US structural decisions would be different from German or Dutch decisions.

These differences in national culture should, according to previously developed theory and limited empirical results, mean that the mode choices made by Dutch, German, and US managers will be different. Power distance is a measure of how power is distributed throughout an organization

(Hofstede, 1980). In high power distance societies power is concentrated with those at the top of the organization, while in low power distance countries power tends to be distributed throughout the business organizations. Erramilli (1996) suggests that in high power distance cultures firms will utilize more integrated modes of entry to maintain their highly centralized power structures. He suggests that in firms from low power distance cultures, more independent entry modes are acceptable. Based on the power distance measures of the three countries in our sample, we would expect that US firms would utilize more integrated (wholly owned) entry modes than Dutch and German firms and that Dutch firms would utilize more integrated entry modes than German firms.

Proposition 3   US (high power distance) firms will prefer highly integrated entry modes, German (low power distance) firms will use less integrated modes and Dutch firms will fall between these two, based on their level of power distance.

Uncertainty avoidance reflects a society's attitude toward risk (Hofstede, 1980, 1989). In high uncertainty avoiding cultures, managers will be risk averse and attempt to minimize internationalization risks by controlling foreign operations (Erramilli, 1996; Hofstede, 1989). In less uncertainty avoiding countries, managers feel more comfortable dealing with individuals from other cultures and will therefore find more independent entry modes acceptable (Erramilli, 1996). Based on the uncertainty avoidance measure, we would expect German firms to use more integrated entry modes than the Dutch or US and the Dutch would use more integrated modes than the US.

Proposition 4   German (high uncertainty avoidance) firms will use highly integrated entry modes, US (low uncertainty avoidance) firms will use less integrated modes and Dutch firms will fall between these two, based on their level of uncertainty avoidance.

METHODOLOGY

In order to explore the activities of western firms in CEE, and to test our propositions, we had to obtain a number of samples of Western companies doing business in the region. First, a sample of Dutch companies was drawn from firms in the Netherlands who indicated they did business in Central and Eastern Europe. Using the REACH CD-rom data-base, a total of 122 firms were identified as doing business in CEE. Second, a sample of German firms was drawn from the AMADEUS CD-rom data-base. It was not possible to identify those German firms active in CEE, therefore the largest (based on turnover) 204 German companies were selected to receive the questionnaire. Third, the US sample came from a previously published study by Shama (1995), and consisted of 125 US multinational companies that had investments in CEE.

The Dutch and German data were collected through a questionnaire which was mailed to each firm, along with a return envelope. The questionnaire contained closed-end questions which could be scored on a seven-point Likert scale and open-ended questions that could be completed with a few words or numbers. It included questions such as 'How many years have you been doing business in CEE? In which markets in the CEE do you do business? and How would you rate the risk of entry compared to your domestic market?' Each firm was requested to indicate their most recent entry into CEE and provide details on the mode used, perceived levels of investment and contractual risks, perceived level of performance to date, and function of the operation established in the specific CEE country.

For the Dutch and German firms we addressed the issue of risk perception directly. As part of the questionnaire completed by the Dutch and German companies we included three questions relating to investment risk and three questions relating to contractual risk. These questions were taken from the study of Agarwal and Ramaswami (1992). In this way we attempt to measure directly managers' perceptions of risk in the CEE countries in which they invest.

Data collection in Germany and the Netherlands took place in 1995. Questionnaires were mailed directly to the manager of CEE operations at the corporate headquarters of each company, not to the CEE location managers. This was done to assure that the information obtained related to corporate-level decision-makers, not subsidiary manager perceptions. In an attempt to increase response size, there were three separate mailings of the questionnaires. In addition, the Dutch and German questionnaires were translated and back-translated into the appropriate language to assure consistency with the original English language version.

According to Shama (1995), data for the US sample were obtained by questionnaire and telephone interviews. For the US sample, data appear to have been collected on all CEE operations for each company.

FINDINGS

Respondents

Of the 122 Dutch firms, a total of 63 firms responded providing 43 completed questionnaires. For the 204 German firms, a total of 82 questionnaires were returned of which 39 were usable. Most of the non-usable responses were a result of the firms not doing business in CEE. Because we did not have a reliable listing of firms doing business in CEE for either Germany or the Netherlands, we could not look for response bias.

Respondents to the Dutch questionnaire came from both manufacturing (56 per cent) and service (44 per cent) industries. Specific industry segments included (1) Food and beverages (17 per cent), (2) chemical (14 per cent), (3) agricultural (10 per cent), (4) electronics (7 per cent), (5) metallurgical (7 per cent), (6) insurance (7 per cent), and (7) miscellaneous industries such as consultancy, paper & packaging, banking, etc. For German respondents, 21 (54 per cent) companies considered themselves manufacturers, and 18 (46 per cent) considered themselves service-providers. The types of business represented in the German sample included; (1) chemical industry (22 per cent), (2) wholesale & trade industry (16 per cent), (3) pharmaceutical industry (11 per cent), (4) food & beverage industry (8 per cent), (5) metallurgical industry (5 per cent), (6) energy & electricity industry (5 per cent), and other industries like car & truck manufacturing, real estate industry, personal care industry, leasing industry, tourist industry and financial brokerage companies. For the US sample no breakdown is given by industry type, but a review of the list of responding US firms appears to reflect a similar make-up of firms, about evenly split between manufacturing and service providers.

The participating Dutch firms ranged in size from 106 to 315000 employees. The average number of employees was 19802. German firms ranged in employment from 160 to 207000. The average number of employees was 28827. Average worldwide sales of the responding Dutch firms was about $3.9 billion. On average, 65.7 per cent of the worldwide sales were made outside the Netherlands, with sales in CEE amounting to 16.1 per cent. For German firms, average worldwide sales were DM 11.92 billion. On average, 44.1 per cent of these sales were made outside Germany, with 12.7 per cent of total worldwide sales taking place in CEE.

The responding Dutch companies indicated that on average they did business in 50 countries outside the Netherlands and that, on average, they had 42 years of international business experience. The responding German companies indicated that on average they did business in 45 countries outside Germany and that they had 42 years of international experience. The Dutch respondents did business in 7 CEE countries on average and had been present in CEE for an average of 13 years. German firms averaged 9 Central and Eastern European countries and had on average been in CEE for 27 years. It appears from these figures that the sample of both Dutch and German firms included large, internationally experienced firms.

Unfortunately no comparable firm size and international experience figures were available for the US sample.

Activities in Central and Eastern Europe

Table 11.1 reveals the number and percentage of entries made by the US, Dutch and German firms into CEE. It appears that US firms are mostly setting up sales and marketing related activities in CEE and have only made minor entries for manufacturing, and research and development purposes. The Dutch and German firms appear also to be establishing the majority of their operations as sales and marketing outlets. However, in contrast to the US, Dutch and German firms appear to be setting up a far greater portion of manufacturing operations in CEE. Explanations for these differences in investment philosophy may be explained by differences in the perceptions of risk, and the cultural acceptance of risk. Manufacturing investments require far greater financial commitments, and puts the investing firm at far greater economic risk than a sales and marketing investment. Manufacturing investment also reflects a firm's greater confidence in and ability to manage the foreign operation. Sales and marketing operations, in contrast, are much more mobile and can be reduced or eliminated very quickly, management control needs are far less and the introduction of one investing country national can suffice to manage the sales and marketing effort. Manufacturing operations require various levels of expertise which can either be obtained locally or imported from the investing country. It takes a large number of managers to set up and operate a manufacturing operation, thus a greater investment of management time is required for this type investment. The information in Table 11.1 would therefore indicate that Dutch and German investors are more willing to take risks than are US investors.

Second, differences in types of operation may reflect differing time horizons and evaluation of long-term prospects. Sales and marketing operations generate profits much faster than do manufacturing operations. Additionally, sales and marketing operations take advantage of short-term opportunities while manufacturing operations reflect much longer-term investment commitments. Thus, differences in the type of operation established in CEE may reflect different time perspectives, differences in investment philosophy, and differences in managerial expertise. All these differences are influenced by the risk perceptions of firm managers.

Location Preferences

Table 11.2 shows the CEE location of each entry. For US firms, Russia appears to be the most popular CEE investment location, followed by the Czech Republic, Hungary, Poland and the Ukraine. Dutch firms have a preference for investing in Poland, the Czech Republic and Hungary, with Russia and the Ukraine being less popular. German firms, like the Dutch, tend to prefer Poland as the main target; Russia and the Czech Republic

Table 11.1 CEE activities of US, Dutch and German firms

Activity	Number of US entries	Percentage of US entries	Number of Dutch entries	Percentage of Dutch entries	Number of German entries	Percentage of German entries
Sales & Marketing[1]	279	63%	39	54%	34	53%
Manufacturing[2]	90	20%	25	35%	19	30%
R&D	63	14%	8	11%	9	14%
Other	10	3%	0	0%	2	3%
Total	442 (n = 122)	100%	72 (n = 43)	100%	64 (n = 39)	100%

[1] Includes sales and marketing, service and support, retailing, consulting, and administration and finance.
[2] Includes manufacturing, refining, and assembly.

Table 11.2 Number of CEE entries by country

Country	Number of US entries	Percentage of US entries	Number of Dutch entries	Percentage of Dutch entries	Number of German entries	Percentage of German entries
Russia	87	32%	9	13%	10	16%
Czech Rep.	49	18%	14	20%	10	16%
Hungary	40	15%	13	19%	8	12%
Poland	39	15%	20	29%	17	26%
Ukraine	15	6%	5	7%	2	3%
Other	39	14%	9	12%	17	27%
Total	442 (n = 122)	100%	72 (n = 43)	100%	64 (n = 39)	100%

follow with Hungary a bit behind. German firms tend to have a low number of investments in the Ukraine, but a large number of investments in other parts of CEE. These differences in location preference appear to be related to the historic ties of the investing countries. The US has historically had strong, albeit tense, political and economic ties with the former Soviet Union, and in particular the Russians. Thus, as opportunities for investment opened in CEE the political ties were used to ease entry into the economic sector. US ties with the Czech Republic, Hungary and Poland were much less intense, especially in the period immediately preceding the change in economic and political attitudes. In the 1970–90 period the US treated the Czech Republic, Poland and Hungary as satellite states of the former Soviet Union and thus economic and political ties were routed through Moscow.

Contrary to the US position, both the Netherlands and Germany have had strong economic ties with the Czech Republic, Hungary and Poland for many years. Even during the Soviet domination, economic ties were maintained with these countries. Thus, as the investment climate in CEE began to change, Dutch and German managers took advantage of already established economic ties in the region and increased their investments in the neighbouring states. In addition, Germany's tie to the former Soviet Union, through Eastern Germany, has created opportunities to expand investments in that area. Finally, German investment in a broad range of CEE countries appears to be related to the historic ties between Germany and these CEE countries as well as Germany's proximity to the region.

Entry Structures

Table 11.3 presents the entry strategy by country. As can be seen, for the Dutch and German samples of firms the most often used entry strategies are the wholly owned subsidiary and cooperative ventures. Licensing and exporting were used by few Dutch or German firms. The integrated (wholly owned subsidiary) mode appears to be the preferred method of structuring entry into the Czech Republic, representing 79 per cent of the Dutch and 70 per cent of the German entry structures used in that country. For Russia and Poland the wholly owned subsidiary structure also appears to be the dominant mode. In Hungary the cooperative entry mode appears to dominate. German and Dutch firms tend to differ in their structural choice in the Ukraine. For German firms wholly owned subsidiaries dominate; for Dutch firms cooperative modes are preferred. In general, Dutch and German firms tend to avoid using low control modes such as licensing and exporting. This high use of high control modes may reflect the high level of uncertainty avoidance found in German and Dutch national cultures.

US firms appear to favour much less integrated and therefore less resource-intensive entry modes in CEE. For example, in Russia, Hungary, the Czech Republic and Poland, US firms prefer to use cooperative entry

Table 11.3 Entry strategy by country (in percentage)

Country	Exporting			Licensing			Cooperative[1]			Wholly owned		
	US	Dutch	German	US	Dutch	German	US	Dutch	German	US	Dutch	German
Russia	33%	11%	0%	5%	0%	13%	53%	11%	25%	9%	79%	63%
Ukraine	56%	0%	0%	11%	11%	0%	33%	80%	0%	0%	20%	100%
Hungary	21%	0%	0%	12%	0%	14%	42%	54%	57%	21%	46%	29%
Czech R.	21%	0%	0%	15%	7%	0%	43%	14%	30%	19%	79%	70%
Poland	18%	5%	0%	6%	5%	0%	41%	40%	18%	29%	50%	82%

[1] Cooperative ventures include joint ventures, strategic alliances and consortia.

Table 11.4 Entry strategy by activity (in percentage)

Country	Exporting			Licensing			Cooperative[1]			Wholly owned		
	US	Dutch	German	US	Dutch	German	US	Dutch	German	US	Dutch	German
Sales and Marketing[2]	26%	10%	6%	13%	10%	3%	46%	28%	24%	15%	52%	67%
Manufacturing[3]	39%	0%	0%	6%	4%	0%	43%	48%	50%	12%	48%	50%
R&D	29%	0%	0%	13%	0%	22%	45%	38%	44%	13%	62%	33%

[1] Cooperative ventures include joint ventures, strategic alliances and consortia.
[2] Includes sales and marketing, service and support, retailing, consulting, and administration and finance.
[3] Includes manufacturing, refining, and assembly.

modes. In the Ukraine, US firms tend to favour exporting. In addition, US firms use independent entry modes, such as licensing and export entry, to a far greater extent than do Dutch or German firms. Over one-third of all US entries tend to be through licensing and exporting modes. Thus US firms appear to be more willing to utilize less integrated entry modes, possibly based on the lower level of uncertainty avoidance in US national culture.

Table 11.4 shows the entry structures based on the business activity undertaken by US, Dutch and German firms in CEE. As we saw from Table 11.1, US firms prefer sales and marketing operations in CEE. Table 11.4 shows that these operations are set up as cooperative ventures 46 per cent of the time, export operations 26 per cent of the time, and wholly owned or licensing 15 and 13 per cent of the time respectively. By contrast, Dutch and German firms mostly use wholly owned sales and marketing subsidiaries in CEE (52 and 67 per cent of the time respectively). Cooperative ventures are also used (28 and 24 per cent of the time respectively), but Dutch and German managers tend to minimize the use of licensing and exporting (10 and 3 per cent of the time for licensing respectively, and 10 and 6 per cent of the time for exporting respectively) for sales and marketing operations. Once again, the difference in investment intensity appears to be driven by differences in risk perception and the cultural feature, uncertainty avoidance.

Table 11.4 also shows that US firms setting up manufacturing operations tend to use cooperative (43 per cent of the time) and export (39 per cent of the time) modes most often. These two modes represent 72 per cent of US firm manufacturing activities in CEE. Wholly owned manufacturing operations are only a small, 10 per cent of the US investments in CEE, and licensing represents a minor 6 per cent. Dutch and German firms, however, seem to prefer wholly owned and cooperative manufacturing ventures. These two structures represent 96 per cent of Dutch manufacturing operations and 100 per cent of German manufacturing operations in CEE. Again, both Dutch and German managers appear to prefer entry structures that require far greater financial commitment and show a greater degree of faith in the future economic developments in CEE than do the US firms. In addition, these differences in manufacturing firm mode choice may be a result of the higher level of uncertainty avoidance in Dutch and German culture, as compared with the US.

Finally, for research and development operations US firms prefer co-operative modes (45 per cent of the time). This is followed by exporting (29 per cent), wholly owned subsidiaries (13 per cent) and licensing (13 per cent). Dutch firms on the other hand prefer wholly owned research operations (62 per cent of the time) or as a minimum share in the development effort by establishing cooperative structures (38 per cent of the time). There were no uses of export or licensed research and development operations for the Dutch firms in our sample. Finally, German firms tended to use cooperative modes (44 per cent of the time) or wholly owned subsidiaries (33 per cent of the time) for research and development activity. Licensing was also popular among the German firms, accounting for 22 per cent of research and development activity. Like the Dutch, German firms did not use exporting for their research needs.

Perceptions of Risk

Shama (1995) tried to address the issue of risk perception of US firms in CEE by exploring the change in entry mode patterns over a six-year time period. According to Shama, as risk perception decreased, firms would tend to use more wholly owned subsidiaries. Thus, by following the pattern of entry structure since 1989, he hoped to identify US firm changes in risk perception. Unfortunately, Shama found no difference in the entry growth rates between CEE countries, despite differences in the stage and success of market reforms in the countries. Looking at changes in the type of entry structure used over the six-year period, Shama suggested that the use of wholly owned subsidiaries increased at a faster rate than the use of exporting or cooperative ventures. Additionally, he suggested that the use of licensing went down during the period. However, by examining the entry types as a percentage of total entry by year, instead of in nominal terms, a different picture develops. As a percentage of the number of annual investments, exporting and licensing grew the fastest, wholly owned subsidiaries grew, but at a slower rate, and cooperative ventures dropped by about the same percentage as the increase in wholly owned subsidiaries. However, the overall shift in percentages was not large, thus no significant changes were noted. Shama also noted that US firms' risk perception appears to be lower in Hungary, the Czech Republic, and Poland than in Russia. However, his same data indicate that US firms prefer to invest in Russia. Thus, his argument that US firm investments in the CEE are risk-driven does not appear to be validated by his data. Finally, Shama stated that there is a change in the type of activity US firms are establishing in CEE. He suggested that US firms have recently increased their entry into manufacturing, and research and development, again responding to lower risk perceptions.

We believe that the reason that Shama (1995) could not find a relationship between risk perception and entry activity for the US firms is that Shama's method of measuring risk was flawed. In fact, changes in investment patterns may reflect changes in laws and regulations that open up new investment opportunities. Changes in investment patterns may also reflect the availability of potential investment opportunities (i.e., privatization of state-owned companies) and changes in competitor and customer behaviour. Investment risk attitudes may not change but firms may be pulled into differing or more intense investments due to these outside influences. Risk perceptions need to be measured more directly.

Based on the responses to our questionnaires, we found that Dutch firms' investment risk perceptions in the Czech Republic had the lowest ratings at 2.3 (out of a possible 7.0), followed closely by Hungary and Poland at 2.6 each. Dutch firms tended to perceive investment risk in the Ukraine as high at 3.9, and in Russia this risk was perceived as very high at 4.7. For German firms, the Czech Republic also had the lowest investment risk rating at 1.9, followed by Poland at 3.3 and Hungary at 3.5. German firms tended to perceive investment risk in Russia as high at 3.7, and in the Ukraine this risk was perceived even higher at 4.3.

For contractual risk, we found that Dutch firms perceived Hungary as having the lowest level of risk at 3.1, followed by the Czech Republic at 3.5 and Poland at 3.6. Both the Ukraine and Russia were perceived by Dutch managers as having higher contractual risk – 4.4 and 5.0 respectively. German managers ranked the contractual risk in the Czech Republic as being lowest at 2.4, followed by Hungary at 3.3 and Poland at 3.5. Like the Dutch, the German managers perceived contractual risk in Russia and the Ukraine as high, at 4.0 and 4.3 respectively.

CONCLUSIONS AND RECOMMENDATIONS

This study set out to explore the differences and similarities of Western firm investment activity in Central and Eastern Europe. Previous studies of foreign market entry strategy have noted that country level (investment) and interorganizational (contractual) risks impact mode choice. In addition, some recent research has suggested that national culture may play a larger role in mode choice than was previously considered. We explored the investment activities of US, Dutch, and German firms in CEE and examined the impact of investment and contractual risk, and national culture on entry mode choice.

In general, it appears that US firms have been less willing to commit resources to CEE than have Dutch or German firms. This has resulted in US firms utilizing low resource commitment, and low management control entry modes for manufacturing, sales and marketing, and research and development. Both Dutch and German firms have been much more inclined to make the resource commitments needed to establish wholly owned subsidiaries in CEE.

One factor behind these differences in willingness to commit resources may be differences in risk perception. US firms are primarily investing in Russia. Russian economic reforms have been slow and are developing in spurts. There still is a large block of political pressure intent on slowing or reversing the economic reforms that have been made in Russia. In addition, recent press accounts have highlighted the strong impact and control of organized crime in the Russian economy. All these factors would provide persuasive arguments for minimizing present financial commitments to the region. This finding appears to support proposition 1, which states that firms perceiving high investment risk would use more independent entry modes. It may also provide some support for proposition 4; since US culture has lower levels of uncertainty avoidance, less integrated entry modes are possible.

The Dutch have invested primarily in the Czech Republic, Poland, and Hungary. These three countries, while substantially smaller than Russia, are much more advanced in their economic reform programmes. Investment risk in these three countries is much less because political and social pressures are for the most part in support of the economic reforms. Dutch investments in these three countries have tended to include large resource commitment modes providing higher control for Dutch firms to take advantage of the quickly developing economic boom in the region. This tends to support two of the propositions. First, proposition 4 states that because the Netherlands has a high uncertainty avoidance culture, they will prefer more integrated entry modes. Second, proposition 1 states that perceptions of low levels of investment risk will also result in highly integrated entry modes. However, propositions 2 and 3 do not appear to be supported. Lower level of power distance in Dutch culture did not result in less integrated entry modes, nor did lower levels of contractual risk in these markets.

German firms have spread their investments in CEE over a larger number of countries. Poland appears to have the greatest level of German investment, followed by Russia, the Czech Republic and Hungary. With the exception of Russia, German investments, like those of the Dutch, tend to be in lower investment risk countries. German mode choice also is similar to the Dutch, preferring highly integrated modes in most cases. The preliminary findings for German firms also tend to support propositions 1 and 4. German firms use highly integrated entry modes, possibly due to high levels of uncertainty avoidance in their culture and or low perceptions of investment risks in the target markets (excluding Russia). As with the Dutch sample, propositions 2 and 3 do not appear to be supported. Power distance does not appear to influence mode choice in CEE, nor does level of contractual risk.

Thus, there appear to be a number of important implications for future theoretical development in the area of entry mode selection. First, the data in this study tends to indicate that uncertainty avoidance is a critical cultural factor in determining entry mode. Future studies should concentrate on establishing a more direct link between this cultural attribute and mode choice. Second, investment risk appears to be more important than contractual risk in mode selection decisions in CEE. Additional studies of these two important risk factors may help determine if this relationship is true for areas outside CEE and for firms from countries other than the Netherlands and Germany. Finally, it would be interesting to examine the impact of both investment risk and uncertainty avoidance on mode choice. Studies with differing cultures, and similar risk perceptions, will help establish the strength of both measures in decisions relating to entry mode choice.

Recommendations to Management

While this study suffers from a number of important limitations, including the lack of information on the US sample and the small sample size for the German and Dutch samples, there are a number of important managerial observations that can be made. First, if national cultural attributes such as uncertainty avoidance are driving the entry mode choice, instead of objective managerial assessment of individual situations, firms may be choosing sub-optimal entry modes. Since entry modes are difficult to change once established, managers must be more diligent to assure that mode choice is made based on rational/objective evaluation of each situation, and not influenced by cultural based biases such as aversion to risk. Second, managers may want to take a closer look at market selection issues. There appear to be obvious differences in the targeted CEE market between Dutch, German and US firms. These differences should be the result of differing opportunities presented to the particular companies in this study. However, if country selection is based on historic or geographical ties, then again sub-optimal use of resources may be occurring. Central and Eastern Europe is large geographically. Rational analysis of industry specific opportunities should be undertaken to select those locations that provide the greatest opportunity for the resources invested. Familiarity with target countries does not mean optimal choice.

Finally, we believe that US firms need to become more aggressive in CEE or they may find that Western European firms have gained dominant positions in most of these emerging markets. This more aggressive attitude needs to be manifested in the use of more integrated, higher investment entry modes by US firms to gain first-mover advantages, to achieve access to limited resources, and to provide needed managerial and financial support for the continued expansion of these newly emerging economies.

Notes

1. The authors would like to thank Q. van Dam and Bart Bakkum for their research assistance. The authors and publishers are gratified to The Regents of the University of California for permission to use information from A. Shama, 'Entry strategies of US firms to the former Soviet Bloc in the newly independent states, Baltic states and East European Countries', *California Management Review*, vol. 37, no. 3. Copyright © 1995 The Regents of the University of California.
2. Other explanations of differing entry mode selection have also been suggested in the literature. Firm motives and strategies have been shown to influence entry mode

selection (Hill *et al.*, 1990). Dunning (1988) suggests ownership and location advantages in addition to risk influence entry mode selection. However, because of the limited information available for the US firms risk and culture are the only measures available for this study.

References

Agarwal, S. (1994) 'Socio-cultural distance and the choice of joint ventures: a contingency perspective', *Journal of International Marketing*, 2(2), pp. 63–80.

Agarwal, S. and S.N. Ramaswami (1992) 'Choice of foreign market entry mode: impact of ownership, location, and internalization factors', *Journal of International Business Studies*, 23(1), pp. 1–27.

Brouthers, K.D. (1995) 'The influence of international risk on entry mode strategy in the computer software industry', *Management International Review*, 35(1), pp. 7–28.

Brouthers, K.D., L.E. Brouthers and S. Werner (1996) 'Dunning's eclectic theory and the smaller firm: the impact of ownership and locational advantages on the choice of entrymodes in the computer software industry', *International Business Review*, 5(4), pp. 377–94.

Buzzell, R.D. and B.T. Gale (1987) *The PIMS Principles: Linking Strategy to Performance* (New York: The Free Press).

Dunning, J.H. (1988) 'The eclectic paradigm of international production: a restatement and some possible extensions', *Journal of International Business Studies*, (Spring), pp. 1–31.

(EBRD) European Bank for Reconstruction and Development (1994) *Transition Report* (October).

Erramilli, M.K. (1996) 'Nationality and subsidiary ownership patterns in multinational corporations', *Journal of International Business Studies*, 27(2), pp. 225–48.

Hill, Charles W.L., P. Hwang and W.C. Kim (1990) 'An eclectic theory of the choice of international entry mode', *Strategic Management Journal*, vol. II, pp. 117–28.

Hofstede, G. (1980) *Culture's Consequences* (Beverly Hills, CA. Sage).

Hofstede, G. (1989) 'Organising for cultural diversity', *European Management Journal*, 7(4), pp. 390–7.

Kogut, B. and H. Singh (1988) 'The effect of national culture on the choice of entry mode', *Journal of International Business Studies*, 19(Fall), pp. 411–32.

KPMG (1994) *Investeren in Oost-Europa; cijfers, trends en verwachtingen*, (April).

Meyer, K.E. (1995) 'Foreign direct investment in the early years of economic transition: a survey', *Economics of Transition*, 3(3), pp. 301–20.

Pan, Y. (1996) 'Influences on foreign equity ownership level in joint ventures in China', *Journal of International Business Studies*, 27(1), pp. 1–26.

Rolfe, R.J. and T.S. Doupnik (1996) 'Going east: western companies invest in east/central Europe', *Multinational Business Review*, (Fall), pp. 1–12.

Schneider, S.C. (1989) 'Strategy formulation: the impact of national culture', *Organization Studies*, 10(2), pp. 149–68.

Shama, A. (1995) 'Entry strategies of US firms to the newly independent states, Baltic states and Eastern European countries', *California Management Review*, 37(3), pp. 90–109.

Shane, S. (1994) 'The effect of national culture on the choice between licensing and direct foreign investment', *Strategic Management Journal*, 15, pp. 627–42.

12 The Business Environment for IJV Formation in LDCs: A Case Study

Habte Selassie and Roy Hill

INTRODUCTION

Until the early 1980s, foreign capital was widely regarded as violation of sovereignty in many less developed countries (LDCs) in general and newly independent countries in particular. In many LDCs, including sub-Saharan African countries (SSACs), colonial administration appeared to have left an intense mistrust – a feeling that domestic resources would inevitably be exploited by foreign capital (Oman, 1989; Akinsanya, 1989). More recently, however, the policies and attitudes of governments of LDCs are said to have changed. The last two decades had seen a shift in government policies of LDCs in order to attract foreign direct investment. Generally, restrictive regulations have given way to reducing obstacles and restrictions, and to granting guarantees and incentives. Many governments of LDCs have adopted a policy of encouraging private foreign investment mainly in the form of joint ventures (JVs) to overcome their investment and technological problems, and ultimately to achieve their economic development goals.

Buckley and Casson (1996) point out that international joint ventures (IJVs) flourished worldwide in the 1980s spurred by the rapid globalization of markets, rapid innovation and new technologies. In many LDCs, JVs were given a boost by the policy reviews towards privatization during the later part of the decade. Though hesitant, withdrawal of the state from business activities has meant in some cases the creation of JVs between the state firms and private firms within the host country, and also with foreign firms. The establishment of a JV with a host partner increases the participating foreign firm's potential for purchasing raw materials and intermediate products and for servicing final markets from the host country. The multiplier effect of the JV on the economy, such as developing indigenous entrepreneurial skills and stimulating economic and service activities in the particular regions or country, are among the motivations (Artisien, 1985; Beamish, 1985; Cavusgil and Ghauri, 1990). JVs are also considered to be relatively better for ensuring the transfer and diffusion of technology (Sethia, 1988). The post-investment long-term benefits from the establishment of the JV is regarded highly by many host countries.

However, besides corporate intentions and strategies, many conditions in the host country affect the decisions of foreign firms in forming JVs, such as host government policies on foreign ownership of investment, availability of capable host partners, the socio-economic system, political stability, availability of local managerial talent and skilled manpower, etc. (Stoever, 1989). It is further pointed out that identifying and selecting an appropriate partner, particularly for the foreign partner, is not only the most important undertaking, but also a difficult and time-consuming affair (Beamish, 1988; Raveed and Renforth, 1983). Beamish (1988) stresses that in spite of its determining importance to success or failure, partner selection has not been given the time and attention that it deserves. A previous study (see Selassie and Hill, 1993) into the determinants of JV formation in SSACs also identified the 'lack of capable host partners' as a crucial problem the prospective foreign partner faced. This study investigates the JV formation environment, which has prevailed until very recently, in the agribusiness sector in an African country setting, and focuses specifically on government policies and the conditions of the prospective host partners.

LITERATURE REVIEW

Studies by Gullander (1976) and Davidson (1982) focused on what determines JV formation. Davidson's (1982) study draws from the experiences of US-based MNCs, while that of Gullander (1976) is an empirical research of companies in Europe. Both authors identify more or less the same three groups of factors that determine entry into a JV by companies. For instance, in Gullander's (1976) model, these are (a) 'country', (b) 'industry', and (c) 'company'. The country factors refer to the general environment, in the form of business climate of an entire country as it affects the firm; industry comprises of those factors that characterize a given industry; and company addresses the internal company characteristics that are decisive in launching a JV.

Though Gullander's (1976) model provides a useful framework for the study of JV entry determinants, some shortcomings are in evidence. The framework is constructed on the basis of experiences of ventures in European industrialized countries, and its application in a different setting is not tested. For instance, under the determinant 'country' only nationalism is discussed, which anyway is not so much of a problem between European firms but which can be critically important in many LDCs. In many LDCs, policies and regulations impacting upon foreign participation are exercised, which are more tangible and measurable than the concept of nationalism. Another point is that the discussion is based on experiences of manufacturing firms and does not include the non-manufacturing sectors. More important, there is reason to believe that the agribusiness sector may differ from the manufacturing sector in general, particularly when it involves LDCs. Agribusiness has unique characteristics, and it requires a different management approach from other economic sectors (Torok *et al.*, 1991; Glover and Kusterer, 1990). Gullander (1976) himself pointed out that the framework is tentative, and further refinements are necessary by looking into different industries, and by 'a formal testing procedure'.

For SSACs, the technology input of the foreign partners is to remain crucial, for the following reasons (UNCTC, 1988; Afriyie, 1988):

- Technology needs to get more sophisticated as the stage of processing (e.g. food or drink products) progresses.
- Many SSACs depend on export of agricultural products, and many aspire to diversify and upgrade to high standard manufactured agricultural products for earning foreign exchange.
- Competition in the international market place for food and drink products is highly competitive, requiring modern processing technology to meet the high standards.

Literature on the role and trend of JVs in countries of sub-Saharan Africa, and the determinants of their formation, operation, success or failure are relatively scarce. There is a lack of tangible information regarding IJVs in general, and the situation is worse in LDCs. The majority of the literature focuses on interfirm relations in the economically developed countries. The limited literature on JVs in developing countries is based on the experiences of the emerging markets of Asia, the Middle East, and Latin America. SSACs differ in many ways (politically, economically and socially), and the experiences of countries of other regions may not be relevant. Bennel (1990) pointed out that the paucity of research attention to Africa is not only in the case of JVs, but regarding foreign direct investment in general.

For this study, within the general framework of Gullander's (1976) model, one of the three determinants, that is, the host 'country' business environment for IJV formation in the agribusiness sector, is investigated through a case study of a particular African country, Zimbabwe. For the purpose of clarity and focus, 'country specific determinants' is defined to mean two most important factors: 'government policy, including attitudes of major actors in the JV formation process', and 'capabilities of host partners'.

Theoretical Propositions

The following theoretical propositions were generated in order to analyze and match the data, and arrive at conclusions. The propositions are stated as follows:

Government Policy
As a developing country, Zimbabwe lacks many critical resources for its development programmes, and depends on external sources to acquire these resources. As a balancing mechanism in meeting the objectives of acquiring these resources and control over its economy, Zimbabwe finds joint venturing an attractive option. It is proposed therefore that these objectives are expressed as policies, and that strategies to promote JVs in terms of incentives and other supports are made available to JVs and/or to the partners. JVs that are established have benefited from such incentives and supports, and companies that intend to form JVs are expecting these benefits.

Host Partners
One of the major determinants of IJV formation in LDCs is the availability of firms that are considered by foreign firms as capable partners. Prospective host partners are few, and have different existing or potential strengths and weaknesses in resource allocation. It is also expected that the limited availability of capable host partners has hampered the pace of IJV formation in the agribusiness sector of Zimbabwe.

METHODOLOGY

In circumstances where the nature of inquiry is basically exploratory, and where the researcher seeks to collect and examine as many data as possible regarding the subject of study, the case study approach is considered appropriate (Yin, 1989; Bennett, 1986). Therefore, the methodological approach adopted was the case study technique applied to Zimbabwe. During fieldwork in the period August to October 1991, a number of companies, and other national and international organizations that were in one way or other involved in JV formation and their promotion, were identified and interviewed. In total, 32 Zimbabwe-based organizations were contacted to gather data; of these organizations six were JVs, five were private and public companies, five were parastatals, and the sixteen others included government departments, associations, international organizations, trade missions, etc. Face-to-face interviews based on a case study protocol were conducted with executives of sixteen of these organizations. The other

sixteen organizations were visited with the purpose of obtaining information of a general nature, such as printed material, and views on the general
business environment.

Selecting the Case Study Design

Yin (1989) identifies four types of designs in the case study strategy: single-
case (holistic) designs, single-case (embedded) designs, multiple-case (holistic) designs, and multiple-case (embedded) designs. The primary
distinction in a design is between single case and multiple case designs. To
address the research questions of a study a single-case or multiple-cases
may be used. The next decision to be made is whether the study involves
more than one unit of analysis. If the study examines a single unit of
analysis, that is, only the global nature of the subject examined, then the
design is 'holistic'. But if the invetigation involves more than one unit of
analysis the design is 'embedded'.

For this study, the data were to be gathered in one country and the
ensuing generalization was to be made from these data; therefore a single
case design was appropriate. Data to be gathered were in the form of
opinions and attitudes of executives of various organizations, as well as
published and unpublished information on some variables explaining
the business environment. The several variables or issues lend to multiple
units of analysis. The main units of analysis are: government policy,
host partners, barriers to JV formation, and opportunities for JV formation.
Therefore, the design belongs to the 'single-case (embedded) design'
type.

Cognizant of the criticisms (for example, see Bennett, 1986) and following the recommendations of proponents (Yin, 1989; Smith, 1990; Miles and
Huberman, 1984) in the case study research literature, some tactics were
developed to enhance validity and reliability. Accordingly, therefore, theoretical propositions based on the literature were formulated and a case
study protocol has been prepared. Further, the procedure of data collection
and analysis undertaken for the study has been recorded and summarized
below.

Case Study Procedure and Validity

Using the case study questions as a guide, the major portion of data was
gathered through face-to-face interviews. The interviews were conducted in
a form of open discussion, rather than seeking specific answers to specific
questions. The discussion started with the researcher explaining the purpose of the visit, and asking the interviewee to share his or her views on the
subject from personal experience. Other available information from published and unpublished sources was also referred to, in the meantime check-

ing and comparing for clarity. When some interview items were vague or contradictory, clarification was sought by telephone or a second short interview. In most cases, there was no problem in following this procedure.

To make comparisons possible:

- Like organizations were grouped together. These are (a) operating JVs, (b) medium/small agribusiness firms forming JVs, (c) large agribusiness firms seeking JVs, (d) investment promotion organizations, and (e) foreign trade missions.
- Responses which were in phrases were transformed into standard codes. The codes were developed during the primary analysis in the field. The respondents were pressed to clarify each issue so that there would be no problem in coding the responses.
- From the data presented in the matrices, comparisons were made, similarities and differences noted; and the pattern explained based on the propositions prepared before the field study.

To enhance validity of findings, the following was undertaken:

- Theoretical propositions were prepared.
- The firms and organizations were selected to include various types, differentiated by business experience in joint venturing, and size (large and medium/small).
- Data were gathered from different sources: published and unpublished sources, from organizations of differing viewpoints on the same issues such as government institutions, executives of business firms, parent organizations of JVs, JV managers (where possible different executives of the same organization), trade missions of major investor countries.
- Some of the organizations selected were in different stages of the JV process. The fact that some firms selected were in different stages of the JV process made it possible to build a chain of evidence. For example, operating JVs could indicate 'what has been' the condition for starting JVs, firms in the process of forming JVs could indicate 'what is' the current condition, and those firms intending joint venturing could indicate 'what ought' to be the condition for joint venturing.
- A pattern matching approach of data analysis was applied.

SUMMARY OF MAJOR FINDINGS

Government Policy

Following independence in 1980, the government of Zimbabwe had as one of its objectives the reduction of the foreign domination of the economy.

Thus, 'the maximisation of local ownership of industry in order to reduce the disbenefits associated with preponderant foreign control of economic activity in the country' was reported as one of the objectives of the Ministry of Industry and Technology (Maya and Tongoona, 1989, p. i). Another related objective outlined was to effect a transition in the ownership structure towards a socialist structure; implying a desire for heavy state involvement in investment. 'State capitalism' was to be welcomed as a necessary transitory stage to a socialist ownership structure. The 'localization policy' applied during the late 1980s substantially influenced the ownership ratios of businesses.

Though there was little published information made available, and interviewees approached were not prepared to discuss the issue in detail, there is evidence indicating that there has been a shift of ownership from foreign to local, particularly augmenting the government's share. A compilation of ownership changes reported in the national press during 1987 and 1988 reveals that in all the nine companies studied the transfer of shares was such that they have changed from being 'foreign companies' to being 'local companies' (for details see Selassie, 1995). Further, in four of the companies (Mardon Printers, Astra Corporation Ltd, Delta Corporation Ltd, and Hunyani Holdings), the government or its nominees obtained controlling shares in the localization process.

The debate on the role of government in economic development and the level of its intervention in the market is likely to continue for a long time. Wade (1994), drawing from his extensive study of East Asian industrialization, suggests that LDCs (including SSACs) can learn a lot from their experiences in this respect. He argues that the question should not be whether governments of LDCs need to intervene in the market, but whether they had the 'right' policy and programme when intervening.

Since early 1991, the government has launched the 'Economic Structural Adjustment Programme' (ESAP) to be implemented in a 5-year period (1991–5). Some elements of the programme relate to JV promotion and formation, and include:

- setting up of the Zimbabwe Investment Centre (ZIC): a 'one-stop' investment approval body
- simplification and liberalization of exchange controls on dividends and profit remittance
- introduction and expansion of OGIL (Open General Import Licence)
- price de-control
- reduction of company basic tax rate
- rationalization of public enterprises (some to be sold in whole or in part, some to be reformed into JVs with foreign and/or domestic private investors).

ESAP has been a controversial programme, subject to a heated internal debate during the early 1990s. Proponents regarded it as the only strategy that would solve the economic problems of the country, and pointed out the support the programme enjoys from the developed countries and international financial institutions. The critics, particularly from the academic circles and some sectors of the political establishment (for example, see Moyo, 1991; Mashakada, 1991), argued that ESAP would aggravate the unemployment problem and worsen the social injustice (price de-control on essential products), that the economy would become export oriented neglecting the broad social development objectives, and that ESAP was foreign imposed (the World Bank), etc. When fully operational, ESAP is expected to create the right environment for attracting foreign investment, including IJVs in agribusiness.

There are a large number of organizations and agencies that have promotional activities to encourage both foreign and domestic investors.[1] While all contribute towards encouraging foreign investment in the form of wholly owned subsidiaries as well as JVs, there is little evidence of their success. Each organization is limited in its own way, but the most common limitations are lack of commitment, resource scarcity, selective rather than comprehensive approach, etc. (Mramba, 1990).

The apparent change in government policy has not really been believed by the foreign interests. International organizations, trade missions, banks and some foreign companies are of the opinion that the government though appearing to support liberalization and privatization, has in fact increased its involvement in controlling businesses, and that the policies introduced are often not clear, stable, or properly implemented. Though the Zimbabwean government provides guarantees of no nationalization and expropriations, these appear to be insufficient for many foreign parties. Separate Zimbabwean bilateral agreements are required with the governments of countries which have the highest number of prospective investors (for example, UK, USA and Germany) before such countries will fully commit themselves to encouraging investment by their companies.

Almost all companies and involved organizations contacted indicated strong interest and enthusiasm for JVs. However, no particular incentives or advantages provided for JVs are in evidence. All informants, established JVs, JVs under the process of formation, and even government organizations could not suggest any particular incentive or support provided. Whatever incentives or support exist are common to all investors, and not determined by the nature of the recipient organization. The proposition cited previously, that the government has devised special policies and strategies to promote JVs in the agribusiness sector, and that JVs or their partners enjoy special status, therefore, cannot be supported.

Capabilities of Host Partners

The capabilities of local companies as host partners vary substantially. The big firms in agribusiness in Zimbabwe are of the opinion that they are financially strong and have got ample technical base to undertake agricultural production and processing on their own. However, almost all the interviewed executives indicated the need for JV partnerships with foreign companies in some particular circumstances. The need for JV partnership are felt in such situations as the following:

- acquiring up-to-date technology
- undertaking new business activities which are out of the mainstream of the firm's activities
- to overcome difficulties in obtaining foreign exchange permits to finance plants and machinery
- to enter markets of the developed economies.

The big firms, with their large resources, experiences, marketing networks, and production bases, have wider opportunities to present themselves as capable partners to interested foreign investors. Such firms, however, are few in number. On the other hand, the situation of the medium/small firms was found to be different. They generally lack the resources to attract and convince the prospective foreign investor to go into partnerships. From this study of the situation of the host firms that may aspire to form IJVs, a pattern has emerged which groups them into three categories: (a) readily capable partners, (b) potentially capable partners, and (c) incapable partners.

Readily Capable Partners
These firms can typically be described as follows. They are companies with substantial capabilities, which can commit financial, technical and managerial resources. They are long established and have developed markets, channels of distributions, and a network of business relations. They are generally internationally orientated, through their activities such as export and import operations. They are well informed, and have mechanisms to identify business opportunities internationally, regionally, and within the country. They can influence the business and political systems (for example, financial institutions such as banks, government departments formulating policies, etc.) of the country. They are generally adequately staffed (management and experts are academically qualified and experienced) and their various operations are carried out by specialized departments/branches. They are capable of searching for and identifying their prospective foreign partners if they desire to form JVs, or, as such firms particularly in the

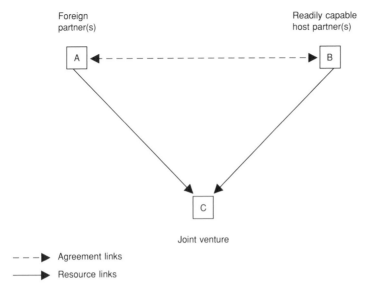

Foreign
partner(s)

Readily capable
host partner(s)

Joint venture

– – –▶ Agreement links

——▶ Resource links

Figure 12.1 IJV relationship model

agribusiness sector are relatively few, the foreign firm looking for a host partner can easily identify them. Thus, this group may not require any assistance in setting up JVs. Their IJV relationship can take the form of the typical model as shown in Figure 12.1.

Potentially Capable Partners
These were found to have the following major characteristics. They are generally well-established companies which are medium or small in size, often with enthusiastic and potential management, but short of resources to grow or to diversify. They have little international experience, but are aspiring to participate internationally, mostly by starting exports. Individually, unlike those firms described above, they find it difficult to influence the business and political systems to their advantage. Though most know how to go about collecting information and seeking support, they are generally dissatisfied with the information and support they get.

Typically, the management of such firms are rich with ideas, and generate several proposals but often fail to exploit the opportunities. For most of them, everything else appears to be in place except one or two elements they lack out of the numerous conditions one has to fulfil to grow or diversify. The situation of this group calls for a 'fourth link' in JV formation, that plays the role of strengthening the position of the host partner on the one hand, and on the other, enhancing the confidence of the prospective foreign partner. Thus, an IJV formation model can be suggested that would

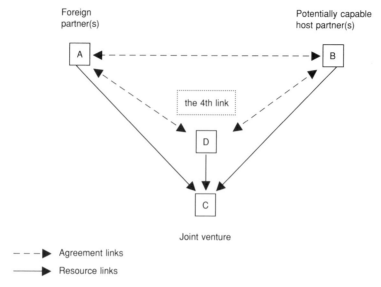

Figure 12.2   Proposed IJV formation model

be appropriate where there is a lack of readily capable host partners, but there are potentially capable host partners (Figure 12.2).

The model presents a general framework which can be adopted to specific needs of prospective partners, countries and donor organizations. Conceptually, the 4th link can be a non-profit-seeking organization sponsored by the governments of the developed economies, international donor organizations and/or private organizations. The basic assumption made in building the model is that such organizations are committed to playing a role in the development of SSACs by providing various aid programmes. This is nothing new, but there have been doubts as to the effectiveness of past aid programmes, the major portion of which were administered through government institutions of the LDC concerned. Recently there has been not only the need for more aid but also a rethinking of how aid is implemented and used. Among the options gaining more support is the use of aid to develop entrepreneurship and privatization by supporting the medium/small firms since they are widely spread in different regions of SSACs.

The salient characteristics of the 4th link can be described as follows:

- It participates in the JV by investing resources the host partner is unable to provide, particularly foreign currency.
- It provides guarantees for the acquisition of machinery and equipment, if the JV required importation of such machinery.
- It guarantees the profit repatriation of the foreign partner through its injection of foreign currency.

- It works along with local chambers of commerce and other trade associations which represent entrepreneurs and businesses, and which generally are more committed and less bureaucratic.
- Its role may be temporary, until the JV reaches maturity. Its share can be bought by the existing partners or by new local partners.

The nearest programme to this model being undertaken currently is the 'sister industry programme' in Tanzania and Zambia with Swedish assistance. Unlike other similar programmes, this one enjoys higher degree of commitment by both the respective national and Swedish 'participants', resources put forward are relatively generous, and the approach is comprehensive. (For details, see Carlsson, 1990; and Mramba, 1990.)

Incapable Partners
This category of firms may be described as follows. Though some medium-size firms may lie in this category, the vast majority are small in size. Such firms are relatively recent in their establishment, thus lacking in experience and specialization, and without a significant share of the home market. Some lack the managerial vision to identify their niche, or potential, and therefore their operations are unfocused. As a result their operations lack stability, and they generally tend to shift from one operation to another frequently. Their capacities to collect business information and seek assistance vary greatly. As in the case of group two, there is a general dissatisfaction with the type and extent of support available to them. They are more interested in short-term benefits and fail to develop a long-term perspective. Their management and staff is often built around the family. Individually, this group is the least capable of influencing their environment to their advantage.

However, it is also this group that recognized the advantage of forming associations. For instance in Zimbabwe, the Indigenous Business Development Centre (IBDC) is set up to advise and assist small businesses. Aware of the resources they lack to survive and grow, entrepreneurs in this group also seek various alternatives, among which is entering into JVs with possibly foreign firms. But obviously, there is little they can show to attract any potential foreign partner. For this group, the immediate needs appear to be establishing themselves in the domestic markets, and seeking various government assistance. Finding appropriate accommodation for their projects (including factory units), seeking concessionary loans, training, market and management development are called for.

The evidence, therefore, supports the proposition cited previously; that is, local firms differ in their capability as host partners, and firms with considerable resources and which can be considered readily capable partners are few in number. The findings also show that there is a strong need to promote and develop supporting measures for medium/small local firms to enhance their capability as host partners.

CONCLUDING REMARKS

To play a more effective role in the economy JVs have to be promoted through implementing clear and supportive policies. Given the general preference for wholly owned subsidiaries by foreign firms, they have to be wooed into JVs. Discriminative tax incentives and profit repatriation could stimulate them more towards joint venturing. The informational and promotional activities of LDCs such as Zimbabwe should be marketing oriented, putting forward the advantage the foreign investor could attain in a JV, and how government and other concerned bodies will handle the various problems and obstacles that the foreign firm may face.

Though the agricultural sector in Zimbabwe is relatively advanced, the case for IJVs and foreign investment was strong for the following major reasons:

- As in most SSACs, there is a high population growth rate and rapid urbanization in Zimbabwe, which calls for an expansion of high quality food production and processing capacities to help guarantee food security, and also to create employment opportunities.
- Machinery and plants in many agribusiness firms are obsolete and need renovation.
- Zimbabwe has launched an aggressive export programme which includes agribusiness products to developed country markets which will require up-to-date technology, skills and financial resources.

The general reluctance of foreign firms to take state-owned firms as partners on the one hand, and the paucity of capable private firms on the other, calls for a strong programme of support and promotion not only of the medium/small private firms, but also the informal sector and entreprenuership in general. In most SSACs, the informal sector plays a very crucial role. Some estimate that over 80 per cent of economic activity in almost all SSACs is accounted for by the informal sector (Adesina, 1996). The entrepreneurial potential and the innovativeness of people in this sector is rarely duly appreciated. Such support can come from the national government, international organizations, and donor agencies. By developing more capable host firms, LDCs can give foreign firms more choice and confidence in forming IJVs.

Among recent initiatives to enhance increased international trade and industrialization are the 'the USA–African trade and economic cooperation forum', and 'the Alliance for Africa's Industrialization'. The former initiative appears to be rather long range; envisaging the establishment of 'a US–sub-Saharan Africa Free Trade Area ... and the development of a plan for entering into one or more trade agreements with sub-Saharan African countries ... by 2020' (*West Africa*, 1997, p. 53).

While these and some other initiatives show some glimmer of hope for economic development of SSACs, the old concern still lingers on: that the national and international programmes existing and projected are 'too little too late'. Some see the danger of increased marginalization of SSACs as a result of the excessively high debt burden, continuous reduction in development aid, and limited direct private investment (Adesina, 1996). The increased marginalization of SSACs appears already evident in this decade which is characterized by rapid globalization, integration, and liberalization of international trade (see Buckley, 1996).

Due to the shortage of foreign exchange that restricts repatriation of profit and capital, and the smallness of national markets, many foreign firms from Europe and North America have been reluctant to enter into JVs in SSACs. Governments and local firms in SSACs may be tempted, therefore, to look for partners from the newly industrialising countries (NICs), particularly from those in Asia. There is evidence to suggest that, as IJV partners, companies from NICs are likely to be more forthcoming and accommodating to business conditions in LDCs. For instance, Lee and Beamish (1995), based on their study of Korean IJVs in LDCs, concluded that, compared with developed country JVs, Korean JVs were more stable, and resulted in more satisfactory performances. Further, in most cases, Korean partners had the minority share in the JVs. Within Africa, the Republic of South Africa, which has resources comparable to developed countries, may play a crucial role in the continent in promoting economic cooperative initiatives including IJVs.

This study has attempted to draw a general picture of the business environment for IJV formation in SSACs from a case study of Zimbabwe. It is important to point out here that, though there are similarities in business environments across SSACs, it would be erroneous to overlook individual country and regional characteristics. Therefore, similar studies across countries and regions of sub-Saharan Africa that examine the theoretical propositions posited for this case study are recommended.

Note

1. These include: Zimbabwe Investment Centre (ZIC), Confederation of Zimbabwe Industries (CZI), Zimbabwe Development Bank (ZDB), Indigenous Business Development Centre (IBDC), African Project Development Facility (APDF), UNIDO, developed countries' representatives such as the CDC (Commonwealth Development Corporation), JODC (Japan Overseas Development Corporation), FMO (Netherlands Development Finance Company Ltd), SWEDFUND (Swedish Fund for Industrial Cooperation with DCs), SBI (Belgian Corporation for International Development), DEG (German Investment and Development Bank), FINNFUND (Finnish Fund for Industrial Development Corporation Ltd), and IFU (Danish Industrialization Fund for DCs). (Kunjeku, 1991).

References

Adesina, K. (1996) 'Alliance for industrialisation', *West Africa* (4 November), pp. 1720–1.

Afriyie, K. (1988) 'Factor choice characteristics and industrial impact of joint ventures: lessons from a developing economy', *Columbia Journal of World Business*, 23(2), pp. 51–61.

Akinsanya, A.A. (1989) 'Economic nationalism in Africa: illusion and reality', *TransAfrica Forum*, 6(2), pp. 49–60.

Artisien, P.R. (1985) *Joint Ventures in Yugoslav Industry* (Aldershot, Hants: Gower Publishing).

Beamish, P.W. (1985) 'The characteristics of joint ventures in developed and developing countries', *Columbia Journal of World Business*, 20(3), pp. 13–19.

Beamish, P.W. (1988) *Multinational Joint Ventures in Developing Countries* (London: Routledge).

Bennel, P. (1990) 'British industrial investment in sub-Saharan Africa: corporate responses to economic crisis in 1980's', *Development Policy Review*, 8(2), pp. 155–77.

Bennett, R. (1986) 'Meaning and method in management research', *Graduate Management Research*, 3(3), pp. 4–56.

Buckley, P.J. (1996) 'Regional and global issues in international business', in F. Burton, M. Yamin and S. Young (eds), *International Business and Europe in Transition* (Basingstoke, Hants: Macmillan).

Buckley, P.J. and M. Casson (1996) 'An economic model of international joint venture strategy', *Journal of International Business Studies*, 27(5), pp. 849–76.

Carlsson, J. (1990) 'The sister-industry programme in Tanzania and the Zambian Alternative', *Small Enterprise Development*, 1(2), pp. 34–40.

Cavusgil, S.T. and P.N. Ghauri (1990) *Doing Business in Developing Countries: Entry and Negotiation Strategies* (London: Routledge).

Davidson, W.H. (1982) *Global Strategic Management* (New York: John Wiley).

Glover, D. and K. Kusterer (1990) *Small Farmers, Big Business* (Basingstoke, Hants: Macmillan).

Gullander, S. (1976) 'Joint ventures in Europe: determinants of entry', *International Studies of Management and Organizations*, 1–2(6), pp. 85–111.

Kunjeku, P.F. (1991) *Project Finance and Technical Support Available Zimbabwe* (Harare: Confederation of Zimbabwe Industries).

Lee, C. and P.W. Beamish (1995) 'The characteristics and performance of Korean joint ventures in LDCs', *Journal of International Business Studies*, 26(3), pp. 637–54.

Mashakada, T. (1991) 'What unique attributes do we have to perform wonders with ESAP', *The Financial Gazette* (Harare, 22 August).

Maya, S. and H. Tongoona (1989) *Ownership Structure of the Manufacturing Sector: Consultancy Report No. 9* (Harare: Zimbabwe Institute of Development Studies).

Miles, M.B. and A.M. Huberman (1984) *Qualitative Data Analysis* (Beverly Hills: Sage).

Moyo, J. (1991) 'Economic reform programme is a foreign product', *The Financial Gazette* (Harare, 5 September).

Mramba, B.P. (1990) 'Technology transfer through the sister industry programme in Tanzania – an alternative view', *Small Enterprise Development*, 1(2), pp. 41–7.

Oman, C. (1989) *New Forms of Investment in Developing Country Industries* (Paris: OECD).

Raveed, S.R. and W. Renforth (1983) 'State enterprise–multinational corporation joint ventures: how well do they meet both partners' needs?', *Management International Review*, 1(1), pp. 47–57.

Selassie, H.G. (1995) *International Joint Venture Formation in the Agribusiness Sector* (Aldershot, Hants: Avebury).

Selassie, H.G. and R.W. Hill (1993) 'Factors determining joint venture formation in the agribusiness sector between UK based firms and firms in SSACs', *Journal of International Food and Agribusiness Marketing*, 5(1), pp. 73–93.

Sethia, N. (1988) 'From regulation to innovation: emerging trends in India', *New Management*, 6(2), pp. 32–6.

Smith, N.C. (1990) 'The case study: a vital yet misunderstood research method for management', *Graduate Management Research*, 4(4), pp. 4–26.

Stoever, W.A. (1989) 'Why state corporations in developing countries have failed to attract foreign investment', *International Marketing Review*, 6(3), pp. 62–78.

Torok, S.J. *et al.* (1991) 'Management assistance needs of small food and kindred products processors', *Agribusiness*, 7(5), pp. 447–61.

UNCTC (1988) *Transnational Corporations in World Development: Trends and Prospects* (New York: United Nations).

Wade, R. (1994) *Governing the Market: Economic Theory and the Role of Government in East Asian Industrialisation* (Princeton: Princeton University Press).

West Africa (1997) 'Rooting for Africa' (13 January), p. 53.

Yin, R.K. (1989) *Case Study Research: Design and Methods* (Newbury Park: Sage Publications).

13 Networking in the Baltic: The 'Kieler Modell'[1]

Godfrey Carr

GERMANY AND THE BALTIC REGION

Before the Second World War the German province of East Prussia extended beyond present day Kaliningrad to the borders of Russia. After the First World War some land in the east had been lost to the newly created state of Lithuania and the province was cut off from the rest of Prussia and Germany by a strip of Polish territory known as the Danzig corridor. The Baltic States had been conquered and converted by the German monastic military orders of the Knights of the Sword and the Teutonic Knights from the thirteenth century to the fifteenth century. The Old Prussians from whom the German state derived its name were in fact eradicated during this process of forcible conversion. The result was first a German domination of Baltic trade in the mediaeval period through the Hanseatic cities and later the emergence of the militarily and economically advanced Prussian state along the shores of the Baltic. Before the Second World War, Königsberg, the capital of Prussia, was a flourishing university city with a population of over a quarter of a million. During the war over 90 per cent of the city was destroyed by bombing and shelling, and in 1945 its population was driven out and replaced by Russians. Königsberg's fate is typical of that of the whole of East Prussia which disappeared from the post-war map. The territory was divided between Poland and Russia.

After the First World War the Baltic states Estonia, Lithuania, and Latvia were granted independence. On the eve of the Second World War Hitler abandoned them and their German-speaking citizens to the Soviet Union, and most of the Germans were forced in 1940 to leave their homes and to resettle in the newly conquered Polish territories further west. Some came back to their homelands in the ranks of the invading German army one year later, but had to leave again in 1945 as the Soviet Army once again took over the Baltic states. At the end of the war those who had settled in the former Polish territories were once again forced to move further west and many then emigrated to America or Canada. The five-hundred-year German presence in these countries has now ended, but memories of the Germans remain and so, of course, do their buildings and cities, but now occupied by a different population.

The Situation After the Second World War

For fifty years after the war the territories to the east of the former German Federal Republic, the German Democratic Republic, Poland, Lithuania, Latvia and Estonia, remained firmly under the control of the Soviet Union. They were run by loyal communist party officials whose gaze was focused on Moscow, with the result that their countries had little contact with each other. Lines of communication and trade were for the most part with Russia, and their economies were distorted to meet the needs of Russia with the emphasis on heavy industry rather than commerce. The infrastructure and in particular the road and rail links with the West were neglected. Agriculture degenerated badly under collectivization and a great deal of damage was done to the environment. Both the German and Jewish minorities in these countries had disappeared and there was little scope for the cultivation of national culture and identity. In any case, there had been massive shifts of population so that many of the people now living in a particular area had no roots there whatsoever. Of all the Baltic states only Estonia, thanks to its close proximity to Finland, had any access to Western culture.

The Situation After 1989

After the unification of Germany and within a year or so of the collapse of the Soviet empire it now became possible to think again of the Baltic as an area that had once been united by a common maritime culture, where Germans had once played a dominant role. It was even possible to dream of rebuilding that unified culture, but there still remained a strong danger of fragmentation arising from the petty national rivalries between the newly liberated former communist states. Certainly the German government was aware quickly both of the dangers and the opportunities presented by the new situation in the Baltic. The trading potential is huge. Approximately 50 million people inhabit the area and the majority live in cities with a population of at least 50000. There are 49 cities with populations of over 100000, and 76 significant sea ports. On the other hand the Baltic area contains sharp divisions between haves and have-nots. There are huge differences in GDP between the former soviet states and the Western countries. Denmark, Sweden, Finland and Germany are all in the 20000 USD per capita bracket, in contrast to Poland, Russia, and the three Baltic republics which have GDP per capita of 5000 to 6000 USD. Lithuanian workers have monthly wages of around 30 USD, whereas Estonian and Latvians receive 60–65 USD and Russian levels are around 100 USD. Polish workers earn 170 USD, but in Sweden, Denmark and Germany wages are often over 3000 USD a month. Environmental problems such as the pollution of the major rivers and the disposal of radioactive waste remain a major issue, as does the need to build up a transport and communications infrastructure. A still unresolved but potentially dangerous issue is the situation of the Russian minorities in Estonia, Latvia and Lithuania and the status of the Russian majority in the enclave of Kaliningrad. Relations with a suspicious and unstable Russia are bound to remain difficult especially as the Baltic states appeal ever more insistently for Western aid and integration into both the EU and NATO.

The German response to the new and difficult situation has been extremely cautious and low key. The preferred option has been to channel help and advice through the many former or newly created super-regional Baltic organizations such as:

- The Baltic Tourism Corporation
- The Union of Baltic Cities
- The Nordic Council
- The North-European Club
- The Pro-Baltica Forum
- The Baltic Council
- The Baltic Ports Organization
- The Helsinki Commission
- The Nordic Council of Ministers

The overriding problem in the area is, however, the collapse of trade between the Baltic states and the remaining parts of the former Soviet Union. Before the Second World War about 70 per cent of the total exports of these countries had been with the West with approximately the same percentage of trade in imports. After the war the situation was reversed with 70 per cent of the total trade going to the Soviet Union. With the almost complete disappearance of these markets the economies of these countries sagged disastrously, and unemployment has risen to between 30 per cent and 40 per cent. In order to survive they must once again penetrate Western markets, for they have hardly any service industry and agriculture is still in decline. Privatization is proceeding at varying rates, but Western investment is slow because of the lack of information, financial guarantees and acceptable banking practices. There is still a lack of legal clarity as to who owns what in the new situation, and border practices and customs regulations are constantly changing. Clearly, there is a major role in these countries for business start-ups of every type, and there is a particular need for small and medium size enterprises, but the Germans, who are best placed to make this sort of investment, will not risk it until they feel they are operating in a familiar business framework. In Germany this framework is provided by the Chambers of Industry and Commerce, and it is for this reason that the initiatives of the German Chambers in Schleswig-Holstein, and the Kiel Chamber in particular, are likely to be so important in the long term. To understand their particular significance it is important first to understand the role of the German Chambers.

GERMAN CHAMBERS OF COMMERCE

The functions of the German Chambers are broadly similar to those of their English counterparts: that is, to aid exports, to encourage training, and to promote commerce in their own area. But there are major differences with regard to the basis on which they perform these tasks. German Chambers are institutions established by public law which defines their membership and their structure and functions. Membership is compulsory, and contributions take account of the size and turnover of the companies. As a result, the Chambers have at their disposal far greater funds and are required to perform a much greater range of duties than would be the case in the United Kingdom. Some of their responsibilities would, for instance, in the UK be carried out by local authorities. Furthermore, there are two key but interrelated differences between the German and British groups of Chambers which are not always well understood. First of all, a German Chamber of Commerce has very close connections to its regional government and regional banks, and, secondly, through these connections it is linked to the national government and national financial institutions. What is more, through its access to Bonn and to representatives of the Chambers in Brussels, it has very good communications with the EU and with those who control special EU funds. German Chambers of Commerce are thus very good at networking both with each other and with governmental bodies. A recent example of this form of networking in practice is the presentation in Bonn of a ten-point programme designed to increase the competitiveness of industry in the north-east of Germany.[2] The programme is the result of collaboration between nine Chambers, including Kiel and Flensburg, and is designed to earn for the area the maximum benefits from any possible augmentation of the EU through the membership of the Baltic states and Poland.

THE KIEL CHAMBER OF INDUSTRY AND COMMERCE

The Kiel Chamber has a membership of 44 000 firms, and 2300 persons are entitled to attend its full assembly. There is a parliament of 44 seats for which every member firm can vote. It is financially independent, obtaining its income from a mixture of membership levies (assessed on a sliding scale according to the size of the firm) and fees which it charges for legal and commercial advice and for the supervision of training. The Chamber is a partner in the Wirtschaftsakademie Schleswig-Holstein and the Uberbetriebliche Ausbildungszentrum in Elmshorn (UAZ) where each year 3400 students are trained or retrained for careers in industry and commerce.

The Chamber can call on a body of 150 experts to provide expert advice on a huge range of over 50 specialist fields, and with the help of a database this advice can be extended to 200 specialisms. In conjunction with the Chamber in Flensburg the Kiel Chamber publishes a monthly magazine *WNO* ('*Wirtschaft zwischen Nord und Ostsee*' or '*Business between the North Sea and the Baltic*'). It acts as a link between the region of Schleswig-Holstein and the Federal Government, both giving and receiving advice and information. There is also a subsidiary body, the Technologie-Transfer-Zentrale or ttz, which provides expert advice on the latest advances in technology with the help of university and research institutes in the area. The Chamber also takes the economic temperature of the local area through a series of regular questionnaires carried out among local industrialists and traders.

It is at first sight perhaps surprising that Kiel rather than the much older hanseatic city of Lübeck should have taken such a leading role in promoting the business affairs both of Schleswig-Holstein and of the whole Baltic region. But Kiel is the focal point of the many ferry lines which crisscross the Baltic and its connections with the surrounding countries are excellent. In addition Kiel is the seat of the regional government and the Chamber of Commerce collaborates closely with this body. For these two reasons the Kiel Chamber has been able to respond quickly to changes in atmosphere around the Baltic. Shortly after the signing of the Warsaw Treaties between the Federal Republic and Poland in the 1970s an economic delegation from the Kiel Chamber went to the Gdansk region at the invitation of the Poles. At the time the visit was felt to be a momentous occasion in German–Polish relations.

As a result of already good lines of communication with the peoples of the Baltic and with its regional government the Kiel Chamber of Commerce was already very much aware of a marked improvement in the political atmosphere in the late 1980s. In particular it would have noted the desire of the former premier of Schleswig-Holstein, Björn Engholm, to create a new sense of Baltic unity and to diminish the isolation of Poland and the Baltic states. In 1988 on the occasion of an exhibition of avant-garde Latvian art in Kiel, Engholm called for the foundation of a new body to promote a Baltic cultural identity, and indeed Ars Baltica came into being a year later. It is not therefore surprising that immediately after the collapse of the Soviet Union the Chamber of Commerce was also prepared to take similar unifying initiatives.

INITIATIVES BY THE KIEL CHAMBER

The Link with Gdansk and the 'Kieler Modell'

After the collapse of communism it was immediately made clear to both the Kiel Chamber and the regional government of Schleswig-Holstein that the newly emergent states in the Baltic (Estonia, Latvia, Lithuania and Poland) had a desperate need for contacts and know-how from the West. Numerous visitors from these countries to Kiel in 1989/90 emphasized that only if such help were forthcoming would stability and progress in the area be possible. What differentiated the representatives of the Baltic states from those of the former GDR was their awareness of Western business methods and their remarkable self-assurance. Even under Russian domination those charged with the running of industry had always had a sharp awareness of the latest developments in business and commerce in the West through their contacts with the Scandinavian countries. As soon as liberation came they had to hand a shopping list of the goods and services needed to modernize their economies. For years they had successfully paid lip-service to communist orthodoxy whilst trying to smuggle into their economic systems as many Western ideas as possible. In this they differed from the East Germans who had accepted the communist system far more whole-heartedly, and who were initially stunned and disoriented by its sudden disappearance.

In responding to these new demands the Kiel Chamber could build on its previous commercial contacts with Gdansk dating back to the late 1970s. A number of personal contacts had developed from the initial meetings and particularly strong links had been established with the Chamber of Foreign Trade in Gdingen. In 1990/91 a partnership was established between the Chamber in Kiel and GIG, the economic association representing the three towns Gdansk, Zoppot and Gdingen. On 5 February 1992 the partnership treaty between the Kiel Chamber and GIG was signed and with financial support from the Federal Government a bilateral partnership later to be known as the 'Kieler Modell' was formed. The purpose of the GIG link was to mediate between state and public bodies on the one hand and private economy on the other and to encourage the decentralization and independence of the commercial sphere. Those involved also set themselves the task of articulating the overall interests of the business economy in the regions. The main aims of the project can summarized as follows:

- To strengthen the institutional structure of the Gdansk Chamber of Trade
- To build up a practical range of services
- To improve the internal organization of the Polish Chamber. In practice this has meant setting up a database with details of firms in the area and

the provision of advice on trade fairs and new markets. In addition practical help is to be offered with further training and the acquisition of technological data.

The Kiel Chamber provided help in actually setting up the office and a seminar room, but was particularly useful in facilitating the transfer of business know-how. One worker from Kiel was seconded to Gdansk on an indefinite basis and experts in particular fields were brought in for brief periods. All foreign delegations visiting the Polish area are now looked after and advised by the Chamber.

In addition to the obvious commercial benefits the link had political consequences leading to a partnership agreement between the cities of Kiel and Gdingen. To this was added in 1992 a partnership between the Schleswig-Holstein and the Gdansk regions. A concrete expression of this new link is the joint support of the two regions for a new further education institution to meet the needs of business (Wirtschaftsakademie) in the Gdansk area. The success of the initiative has been made possible because of the good personal contacts which have been established over a long period, and the concentration on practical measures in a limited region. Because the benefits are focused directly on one small area of Poland there could be potential here for friction with the government in Warsaw, but so far any such tensions seem to have been avoided.

The Link with Tallinn

The second example of the 'Kieler Modell' is the link between the Kiel Chamber and the leading Chamber of Commerce in Estonia. With considerable financial help and advice from Kiel the Tallinn EKTK (Eesti Kaubandun Töötuskoda) has recruited over 800 members and is the leading economic agent in Estonia. Once again, Kiel seconded a member of staff for the length of the project and brought in experts where necessary. Rapid progress has been made in the following areas:

- Hardware and software (with federal help)
- Establishing a database
- Advice in the use of trade fairs
- Advice on the setting up of firms
- Preparation of trade documentation
- Providing training seminars for managers through the agency of the newly founded Estonian Baltic Academy – a further education institution offering courses for managers and the training of experts
- Informative publications
- Invitations to members of EKTK to visit Kiel for training and to observe the working of the Kiel Chamber of Commerce.

The ongoing strength of both of these forms of the 'Kieler Modell' is revealed in a number of recent developments described in the October edition of the Kiel Chamber's house magazine *WNO*. An office has now been opened in Tallinn to be used jointly by a group of six firms from Schleswig-Holstein in order to further their business in Estonia. The project was initiated and supported by the Chamber of Commerce, but the running costs are paid by the firms. In addition, in a new joint venture by the state government and the Kiel Chamber of Commerce a Schleswig-Holstein office has been opened in Tallinn. Significantly, the office is located in the same building as the recently opened offices of the Schleswig-Holstein Landesbank – the first German bank to have a branch in Estonia since its liberation. In his address on the opening of the office Dr Fritz Süverkrüp, the President of the Kiel Chamber, pointed to the crucial need for political and economic forces to work together in harmony in order to secure the competitiveness of Schleswig-Holstein in international trade.

In contrast to these practical commercial initiatives there are also reports of a visit to Gdansk by Heidi Simonis the Prime Minister of Schleswig-Holstein in order to commemorate the attack on Poland in 1939 and the beginning of the Second World War. In her speech, the Minister, who was accompanied by Wolf-Rüdiger Janzen from the Kiel Chamber, described the links between the Kiel Chamber and those in the Gdansk area as providing a locomotive to boost foreign trade generally in the region. During this visit talks also took place about the involvement of Schleswig-Holstein in the celebrations in 1997 to mark 1000 years of Gdansk's history and the mounting of a Schleswig-Holstein week.

As a result of the successful development of these two examples of the 'Kieler Modell', discussions are now taking place about the introduction of further bilateral links of the same kind. Underlying such developments is the discrete help and encouragement of the government of Federal Republic and other federal bodies. Although itself able to find the resources for very basic needs such as rooms and some hardware and software, the Chamber in Kiel can also draw on the financial expertise and resources of such bodies as the Bundesministerium für Wirtschaftliche Zusammenarbeit und Entwicklung (BMZ) and the Stiftung für wirtschaftliche Entwicklung und berufliche Qualifizierung. GmbH (SEQUA).[3]

THE BALTIC SEA CHAMBERS OF COMMERCE ASSOCIATION

Shortly after the successful establishment of these two bilateral links in the Baltic the Kiel Chamber of Commerce played a leading role in the foundation of an organization linking Chambers across the whole Baltic region. Known as the Baltic Sea Chambers of Commerce Association or BCCA it was founded in Rostock-Warnemunde in July 1992 with originally 23 members and is made up today of over 40 Chambers of Commerce from ten countries. It represents 350 000 firms from all sectors of the economy, but mainly small and medium-sized businesses. A deliberate decision has been taken not to establish new independent offices and the BCCA does not have its own separate staff. Instead, facilities and some staff are provided by the Kiel Chamber within its own offices. The aims are to consolidate existing links and to seek to achieve virtual parity in economic performance among the Baltic nations. In pursuit of these goals the BCCA has so far campaigned for more straightforward legal trade regulations, the removal of trading obstacles, the achievement of greater uniformity in training systems, the exchange of know-how in research and technology and for improvements in both in the telecommunications and transport infrastructure.

The BCCA is a network based on the individual commitment of the chambers involved and for larger projects it depends on third-party financing. Its programme is decided every year at an AGM. From the beginning the Secretariat has also been provided by the Kiel Chamber, and its responsibility is to see that the agreed programme is carried out. It has an Executive Committee made up of the President, Wolf-Rüdiger Janzen, the General Manager of the Kiel Chamber, the Vice-President, Sten Bengtsson, President of the Southern Swedish Chamber of Commerce, Ryszard Ferworn, Vice-President of the Chamber of Commerce in Gdansk, and Peeter Tammoja, President of the Estonian Chamber of Industry and Commerce. The successful working links forged by the earlier forms of the Kieler Modell are thus at the heart of the BCCA.

Hansa Days

In 1994 the BCCA became a co-sponsor of the annual hanseatic business conventions – or Hansa Days. The idea for these came from the Chamber of Commerce of Southern Sweden in Malmö, and the fifth was held in Kiel from 15 to 17 March 1994. It was organized and run by the Kiel Chamber, but the BCCA network was also important in diffusing information. There were more than 500 guests from the Baltic area and from England, France and Netherlands. A new feature at this meeting was the introduction of a 'marketplace' for firms, and for this the BCCA received EC money from the INTERPRISE programme. The market place focused on key areas such as the food industry, and food technology, construction industry, and environmental and energy technology. In 1994 there were 260 applications from interested firms; 148 of these appeared in the catalogue and 10 000 copies of the catalogue were circulated. Over 1000 contact meetings took place. Most of the BCCA's member Chambers were there and were represented by experts. A number of major banks too were present and the Euro Info section of the Kiel branch of the Investititionsbank had an information stand. The sixth of the Hansa Days took place in Karlskrona in March 1995 with a similar format.

In addition to the Hansa Days the BCCA is committed to a number of other projects. Plans have been made for a Baltic information network, and a trial electronic communications link between Kiel and Tallinn has already been established, so that the first network will eventually operate between Riga, Tallinn, Vaasa, Malmö and Gdansk. Some EU money from the PHARE scheme has been obtained for this venture. The BCCA is also helping to run the Baltic Summer University, which brings together ten students from each of the Baltic states for a period of two weeks in the summer at a different site each year. Recently this project has been augmented by a summer university for professors. The idea is that each of the ten states involved will send two participants who, over a period of two weeks, will write papers on selected subjects, such as: regional policy, energy supply, interlinking traffic and transport systems, environmental policy measures, developing post-graduate colleges, employment policy in the Baltic region, technology transfer and other research projects.

Publications

The BCCA has been involved in the production of a range of publications on the Baltic. In 1994 it supported a brochure on the region commissioned by The Nordic Council of Ministers. It also produces annual reports, regular information bulletins and three calendars a year listing business events in the area. An information chart for use at international trade fairs which emphasizes the Baltic as an economic unit was also been produced. With support from the European Commission a guide was also produced in 1994 for firms establishing business relations in the St. Petersburg and Kaliningrad region of the Russian Federation as well as Lithuania, Latvia and Estonia (Koopmann 1994). The actual application for EU money for this project was prepared by the Kiel Chamber, whereas the BCCA was responsible for its implementation. Finally, the BCCA has published a number of memoranda including one in September 1993 on the lifting of trade barriers in the Baltic Sea area and one in July 1994 on the structural and institutional deficiencies of the region from a business perspective.

Research Funding

In addition to its publications the Association has also recruited a team of international researchers to carry out a quantitative analysis of the future development of the region reflecting the likely impact of a number of alternative trade policies and international techniques. The study has focused on:

- Communications innovation and transport infrastructure
- Future trade and capital flows and associated horizontal mobility.
- The deregulation of institutional arrangements including the removal of institutional barriers.

The research is being carried out by the Institute for Regional Research in Kiel, the Institute for Future Studies in Stockholm and the Department of Economic Policy at the University of Gdansk.

Lobbying

A further important role for the BCCA has been as a lobbyist in Brussels. In October 1994 a working group on the economy, led by Wolf-Rüdiger Janzen, ascertained the special needs of small and medium-sized businesses, and, in November 1994, a fifteen-strong BCCA delegation pressed for accelerated clearance at national borders and further progress in improving the technical infrastructure in the area. The members of the BCCA are keenly aware of the so-called 'Green Banana' effect in the Mediterranean core area and are convinced that the northern region, given similar help, could achieve equally spectacular results. They know that projects and bids emerging from a large regional organization are more likely to be taken seriously in Brussels than are national or even bilateral initiatives.

An important result of the lobbying activity of the BCCA was the decision in 1994 to hold a EUROPARTENARIAT in the Baltic. It was the first time that such an event had take place outside the EU. This twice yearly major trade fair is intended to provide a boost to regions within Europe which are suffering from structural crises, and it receives considerable funding from Brussels. In 1994 the fair was held in the three cities of Gdansk, Gdingen and Zopot and some 2000 firms from all over Europe attended. After the success of this venture the BCCA is drawing up plans for a travelling trade fair and contact centre to be known as the BALT-PARTENARIAT which will move around the Baltic. The aims of this contact trade fair will be:

- To give firms greater access to foreign buyers and markets
- To highlight the potential of the Baltic region
- To encourage cooperation round the Baltic
- To strengthen the sector of small and medium-sized businesses. Talks have gone on with the world trade centre in Gdynia and attempts are being made to secure EU support.

An example of a concerted intervention by the BCCA to protect development in the region is its recent protest against a demand by the environment ministers of Northern Europe that the number of flights in the Baltic area should be limited. The BCCA pointed out that given the desperately inadequate rail infrastructure of the area and the time required for rail and ferry journeys there was no alternative at present to air transport if the momentum of economic expansions was not to flag.

A further and perhaps slightly unexpected side-effect of Kiel's involvement in the BCCA has been the impact on at least one of its partner cities. Kiel has many such links and one of the oldest is with the city of Coventry in England. The Kiel Chamber decided to brief the business community of Coventry on developments in the Baltic, and sponsored a seminar and workshop for the Coventry and Warwickshire Chambers of Commerce on trading opportunities in the Baltic states and Russia in the spring of 1995. The result has been a marked revival of interest in the link with Kiel and a plan by the two English Chambers of Commerce to send a DTI-sponsored trade mission to Latvia and Estonia during 1996 to assist the growth of exports to these markets.

CONCLUSION: THE LONG-TERM SIGNIFICANCE OF NETWORKING

The Kiel Chamber's response to the urgent needs of the Baltic states after 1989 is significant in three ways. Firstly it shows a recognition of the innate cautiousness of German industry which was unwilling to move into a new and potentially risky area without detailed information, and without some reliable regulatory and financial systems in place. Secondly it shows what remarkable results in the way of effective networking can be achieved in a very short time by using modern communication techniques. Thirdly it shows the innovatory potential inherent in Chambers of Commerce when, as in the German case, they have the resources and freedom to take independent initiatives in the cause of international trade.

Networking is very effective in overcoming excessive caution and potential misunderstandings. Much networking in the commercial sphere takes place between groups of firms, usually with a multinational company at the core and occasionally including non-business organizations such as universities. Linked together through relational contracting they compete globally with other networks. What has been put together in the Baltic, however, is something different: a networking infrastructure which links a large number of companies in many countries and is meant to serve wider, longer-term ends than the competitive needs of a group of firms or a particular industry. What has been attempted is extremely ambitious, namely, to create a new sense of regional identity and interdependence, a feeling of membership in a community with a rich tradition (however tenuously relevant this might be to the present situation!). The involvement of a range of cultural institutions and initiatives such as the Baltic Summer University has further added to a pyschological framework which is designed to provide reassurance, hope and something of a vision for the future. This is a remarkable achievement and one which certainly could not have been achieved so quickly by the efforts of governments. Either they would have had no money for such initiatives, or, as in the case of the Federal Republic, their very wealth and economic power would have induced fear and resentment and been counterproductive.

Future research may wish to consider the degree to which this ambitious framework has been able to grow in strength and provide an effective instrument for the revitalization of the area, or whether international trade has expanded independently of it through the activities of individual entrepreneurs, multinationals and regional governments. The outcome will be significant because the Kiel-led initiatives in the Baltic very much reflect the German view of international trade, in which competition takes place within an ordered framework presupposing a degree of cooperation and incorporating long-term goals. Significantly, the framework in this case has been established by business itself through the agency of the Chambers of Commerce. Whether this form of self-regulating and self-sustaining capitalism is the most appropriate vehicle for the development of international trade should become clear in the Baltic over the next decade. What is clear, however, is that the approach to international trade behind the 'Kieler Modell' is very much a reflection of the 'German Modell'.

Notes

1. The material for this chapter is taken from the publications of the Kiel Chamber of Industry and Commerce and from the Baltic Sea Chambers of Commerce Association. In addition the author visited the Kiel Chamber and interviewed Werner Koopman, Assistant to the Secretary General, with particular responsibilities for links with the BCCA, and Rainer Wiechert, Foreign Affairs Adviser in the Economics Ministry of Schleswig-Holstein. The author also interviewed Malcolm Vaughan, Deputy Director of the Coventry Chamber of Commerce.
2. Outlined in the October 1995 issue of *WNO* (*Wirtschaft zwischen Nord- und Ostsee*) (*Business between the North Sea and the Baltic*), the house magazine of the Kiel Chamber of Commerce.
3. SEQUA is defined as 'eine Gemeinschaftseinrichtung des Deutschen Industrie- und Handelstags, des Zentralverbands des Deutschen Handwerks und der Bundesvereinigung der Deutschen Arbeitgeberverbände' – that is, a body set up jointly by the national body of German Chambers of Commerce, the Central Committee of the German Craft Organizations, and the Federal Association of German Employers Organizations.

References

Bennett, R.J., G. Krebs and H. Zimmermann (1993) *Chambers of Commerce in Britain and Germany and the Single European Market* (London: Anglo-German Foundation).

von Flotow, L., B. Halford and A. Höfer (eds) (1994) *The Baltic Sea Region: A Presentation* (Pfaffenweiler: Hagbarth).

Koopman, W. (ed.) (1994) *Guide for Establishing Business Relations in the St. Petersburg and Kaliningrad Region of the Russian Federation as well as in Lithuania, Latvia and Estonia* (Kiel: BCCA).

Randlesome, Collin (1994) *The Business Culture in Germany* (Oxford: Heinemann Professional).

Index